RISE OF NATIONS™

Michael Rymaszewski

SYBEX

San Francisco • London

ASSOCIATE PUBLISHER: DAN BRODNITZ

ACQUISITIONS AND DEVELOPMENTAL EDITOR: WILLEM KNIBBE

PRODUCTION EDITOR: KELLY WINQUIST

COPYEDITOR: LAURA RYAN

COMPOSITOR: DIANA VAN WINKLE, VAN WINKLE DESIGN GROUP

PROOFREADER: TRICIA TONEY

BOOK DESIGNER: OWEN WOLFSON

COVER DESIGNER: VICTOR ARRE, RGRAPHICS

ACKNOWLEDGMENTS

The book you're holding in your hands is a collective effort. It was put together by Willem Knibbe and Kelly Winquist at Sybex, it reads the way it does thanks to both Willem and Laura Ryan, and it looks the way it does thanks to Owen Wolfson (responsible for design) and Diana Van Winkle (responsible for production). Its contents include a chapter authored by Paul Stephanouk at Big Huge Games, and all of it has been read, corrected, and commented on by the big people at Microsoft and Big Huge Games: Danan Davis (*RoN*'s program manager), Doug Kaufman, Rick Lockyear, and Brian Noonan; a separate thank you is due to Graham Somers for help with the book's art, and to Paul Stephanouk and Doug Kaufman for setting the record straight on many things.

CONTENTS

1 RULES OF THE GAME   1

2 PLAYING THE GAME YOU WANT TO PLAY   11

3   RAGS TO RICHES: THE GAME ECONOMY   31

4   WHY RESEARCH IS POWER   53

5   THE WONDERS OF WONDER   75

6   THE ARMY   85

7 THE NAVY AND THE AIR FORCE   105

11 ADVANCED TACTICS 163

12 MASTERING MULTIPLAYER 181

C APPENDIX C: UNIQUE NATIONAL UNITS   221

FOREWORD

So, the plan went like this, see: We had all quit our perfectly good jobs, and now all we had to do was talk a publisher into spending a staggering amount of money funding the development of a new real-time strategy game we planned to make. Then it would just be a matter of finding 30+ people eager to work 80-hour weeks for the next two-and-a-half years to bring the game to life. After that we could just sit back and wait for the royalty checks, because everyone knows that what the world really, really needs is another real time strategy game, right?

Well, OK, maybe the world didn't need another *classic* real time strategy game. Not that there's anything wrong with classic RTS, mind you—we were and are some of the genre's biggest fans. But it seemed like the existing games in the genre were already mining the tried and true formula for all it was worth. And we had all these...ideas. We knew that switching genres from the turn-based games we'd been making would be a lot of work, but we thought it might give us some advantages, as well.

As we played the great RTS games of the day, we realized that there was a lot that *hadn't* been tried yet. For instance, what if there were a concept of national territory that would limit what many considered the silly tactic of constructing "defensive" buildings in the middle of (or behind) the opponent's town? Wouldn't that also give the players a new and interesting dimension in which to compete? And then we could enhance the value of adding territory to your nation with concepts like taxation, attrition, and rare resources.

And how about that economy thing? Sure, chopping down every tree/crystal/whatever in the county and then moving on to some new area was fun the first 2,000 times we did it, but wouldn't it be fun to zoom out to a "continental scale" where the resources weren't all depleting over the course of the game? Then the map might start to look more like a growing and prosperous nation and less like a series of strip-mined ghost towns. We could limit the rate at which you could extract resources from any one bit of territory (not an unreasonable position, historically, either) so that you'd still have to keep expanding your nation in order to get the resources you need.

We knew that ultimately, at its heart, we wanted *Rise of Nations* to be, clearly, a real-time strategy game. We wanted the amazing graphics. We wanted the epic battles. We wanted the pulse-pounding multiplayer matches. But other than that, we questioned everything. We brought our newcomer and turn-based design perspectives to bear on every RTS issue we could think of. Why do so many RTS players eschew "sea" maps? Do free-for-alls always have to favor the guy who hides in the corner and does nothing? Since 40% of games created in online lobbies seem to be titled "No Rushing!" can we offer anything to help with that?

We also had some diabolically difficult choices to make on the art and technology side. For instance, we apparently missed the meeting where they said that after 2001 it's okay to allow only 100 units per team. A highly respected RTS designer (of one of the first-rate families of games I'm now so rudely taking potshots at) once told me that when you're entering a crowded genre, you have to look at the leading competition: Their weaknesses are your opportunities, and their strengths are your "min spec" (minimum specification). We figured "huge, epic battles" was our min spec, and we wanted to show three figures per foot unit to boot, so our programmers sweated and cursed and pulled their hair out—and danged if they didn't make it work.

In the art department, we had to deal with questions like: Are we willing to give up the ability to change the camera angle to triple (or more) the amount of detail we can put into the art for the buildings? We switched back and forth several times before finally deciding that—yeah—we wanted the detailed buildings. We also spent quite a lot of time figuring out how to make cities look like cities. The *Rise of Nations* "city" is central to the nation-building game, but it was the devil to figure out how to make it look good. We went through a whole series of sizes—from four times the size of the current city (!) down to the current size of a Barracks—and we tried many wild ideas like having Libraries, Markets, and so forth be integral "subsections" of a city. Finally, we arrived at the current size combined with the "automatic roads," which made it work visually.

For many reasons, we decided that we weren't going to go down the traditional "scenario-and-cinematic" path for our solo campaign game. First of all, it didn't fit very well with our theme and scope —it's hard to find authentic historical narratives that thread their way through many historical eras, and it would be downright silly to look for individual heroes that could be present in a story spanning thousands of years. Second, although some RTS games have done an exceptionally good job with these, it didn't seem to be an intrinsic strong point of the genre overall—for that kind of story-based content, role-playing games and first-person shooters were already delivering really high quality fare that was frankly better than anything one could hope to achieve with an RTS engine. And third, it didn't really play to our strengths, such as strategic depth and replayability.

So we instead turned to an idea that did play to our strengths, and added (surprise!) a strategic turn-based game on top of our real-time game. Rather than have the solo campaign narrow your scope by putting you into a limited "scenario," we allowed Conquer the World to widen your scope by giving you a world-wide perspective on history and allowing events to develop across a detailed strategic map.

And now here we are! At the end of two-and-a-half years of work, *Rise of Nations* is a real-time strategy game that we trust will play like none you've ever seen. None of this would have been possible without the extreme dedication of the staff of Big Huge Games—the designers, programmers, artists, producers, testers, and admin staff who worked many, many, *many* long hours to bring this game to life. Huge thanks are also owed to the absolutely awesome people at Microsoft Games Studios who not only believed in us enough to provide the aforementioned funding, but also contributed invaluably to the design, polish, and overall quality level of the game.

If you've just bought this book, be glad you did. With help from some of the expert players and testers at Big Huge Games and Microsoft, author Michael Rymaszewski and Sybex have filled this book with all kinds of behind-the-scenes secrets and hardcore strategies that will help you maximize your enjoyment of the game and crank up the effect of your "Roman Rush," your "Bantu Border-push," and your "Egyptian Wonderfest." Have fun!

—Brian Reynolds

INTRODUCTION

This book should help you win at *Rise of Nations*. It builds upon the game manual and the in-game help, which of course you should read, so by definition it isn't a comprehensive compendium of everything there is to know about the game. *Rise of Nations* is a big game, and thousands of people are going to write millions of words about it in the coming years. To partake of their wisdom, be sure to visit *Rise of Nations* discussion boards regularly; you can get an updated list of these by typing the name of the game into your Web search engine.

In the meantime, use this book. The advice it contains is the result of hundreds of hours of game-play at the three higher difficulty levels: Tough, Tougher, and Toughest. Because of that, it may seem overcautious if you're playing the game at a lower difficulty level (as you should if you're new to games). However, stuff that works when playing Survival of the Fittest against seven opponents on the Toughest level also works in easier games.

Chapter 1 explores general and *RoN*-specific observations about playing real-time strategy games. Chapter 2 discusses setting up good games; it should be particularly helpful to new gamers who find *RoN*'s array of pre-game options staggeringly big. The game's economy is reviewed in Chapter 3, and the game's research is covered in Chapter 4. Chapter 5 deals with Wonders of the World: semi-mythical structures with semi-magical benefits, while Chapters 6 and 7 review the game's armies, navies, and aerial forces. Chapter 8 provides a rough template that should get you off to a good start in most games, and Chapter 9 discusses game war and offers advice on military leadership. Finally, Chapter 10 takes a look at what it takes to win the campaign game ("Conquer the World"); Chapter 11, written by Big Huge Games producer Paul Stephanouk, offers another take on what's important to win; and Chapter 12 focuses on the differences between winning play in solo and multiplayer games.

The book concludes with three Appendices (Buildings, Units, Unique Units) that contain statistics and extra information about game units and buildings in a format suitable for reference purposes.

RULES OF THE GAME

1

Rise of Nations has the two most important characteristics of a great game: it's very easy to learn how to play, but it isn't easy to win.

The purpose of this book is to maximize your enjoyment of Rise of Nations. For the vast majority of players, this means winning. And winning is possible only once you understand the game, which is a step beyond knowing the mechanics of how to play.

This chapter will help you understand how Rise of Nations works. In addition, this chapter compares RoN to other real-time strategy games, highlighting its unique features. General gameplay, technical, and other miscellaneous issues are also discussed here. First, a piece of good advice: read the game's readme document (you'll find it in the RoN folder). It contains late-breaking information that's neither in the game manual nor in this book!

HOW IT ALL WORKS

The game's premise is simple: you gather and use resources to build new structures and units, and to conduct research that will let your chosen nation advance through the ages. Your priorities will be determined by the victory conditions and other pre-game options (all of which are discussed in Chapter 2). Simple, isn't it? So, what's the problem?

The problem is that your opponent(s) will be doing all that, too. To win, you'll have to excel in the following areas:

- Efficient gathering of resources. In *Rise of Nations*, this is a task that requires quite a lot of foresight. Your nation's economy will undergo many changes as it advances through the ages, and it will also be affected by game events such as someone's declaration of war on your peace-loving nation. You just have to gather stuff as fast or faster than everybody else. *Rise of Nations* offers many options and approaches in this area. You'll find all this discussed in detail in Chapters 3, 4, and 8.

- Efficient use of resources. The way you spend resources is just as important as their accumulation. Being ultra-efficient at gathering won't do you any good if you don't set the right spending priorities. You cannot hope to use resources effectively without doing quite a bit of planning. Chapters 3, 4, and 8 discuss the subject; also, Chapters 6 and 7 offer pointers on military spending.

- Good unit management. This refers primarily to creating and managing military units and unit formations in a war—a task of great importance in the vast majority of *RoN* games. However, it also includes civilian units, especially since citizens can be used in a military role right from the start of the game (see Chapter 9). You'll find plenty of advice on unit management in Chapters 6 through 8.

- Decisiveness. You have to think fast—fast, d'ya hear? A not-so-good move executed quickly can be better than a brilliant move put into motion after a lengthy deliberation. This applies to everything: gathering resources, building, moving units, you name it.

The Real Meaning of Time

Time is a dimension, not a resource. Yet in importance it can outdo all the game resources put together. This is because *Rise of Nations* is a real-time strategy game. All the players play simultaneously, without taking turns, so naturally the player who moves fastest often moves best.

There are significant differences in the way time works in solo and multiplayer games. The sections below sum them up.

Time in Solo Games

In solo games, you're up against the computer, and the computer doesn't have to click the mouse, scroll the screen, and so on. You do, so theoretically you've lost the battle for speed even before it's begun. However, in practice your swiftness matters little:

FIGURE 1.1: *Caught on the wrong foot during a solo game? Hit Pause to sort things out in peace.*

- You can pause the game and issue unit/building commands during the pause after giving them the appropriate amount of thought. You can take as much time as you want while your computer opponents are literally frozen (see Figure 1.1). This automatically hands you the initiative. If you're a new gamer, you'd be wise to use this feature very often; before long you'll see that it enables you to play the computer opponents as if they were puppets—they cannot act, they can only react to what you do. It's definitely possible to win a Survival of the Fittest game (constant war) against seven computer opponents on the Toughest difficulty setting using the Pause feature.

- You can play at Very Slow or Slow speed, thus minimizing the computer's no-hands advantage. Very Slow is the recommended speed once your nation has grown to include several cities and over a hundred units. This gives you enough time to admire the view on the screen and still micromanage your nation as necessary. *Rise of Nations* is a very good-looking game, and there are no ideal empires—timely little tweaks here and there can, in fact, hand you the winning edge.

Tip

When playing against the computer, you can slow down the game to the point where your speed hardly matters. You don't have to make fast decisions as much as you have to make the right decisions. Time is on your side.

Multiplayer Time

In multiplayer games, you'll be playing against other mouse-clicking, screen-scrolling humans. Good news, no? Well, not really:

- You cannot pause the game. Instead, each player is allotted a pre-set amount of "cannon time": periods of super-slow motion. These are very precious and are best saved for emergencies. New players should note that multiplayer games are very rich in emergencies.

- Everyone plays at the same game speed, so your own personal speed truly matters. What's more, being faster can give you an important psychological edge.

    Multiplayer gaming is discussed in more detail in Chapters 11 and 12; for now, let's just say that new gamers are strongly advised to, er, get up to speed playing against the computer before venturing into multiplay. There are hundreds of quick-on-the-draw gamers out there. Hundreds? Thousands. Playing online against them before you're ready can be very frustrating.

> ## Warning
>
> *Multiplayer games require you to be much swifter than solo games. Time is **not** on your side, and a faster player can defeat a better but slower player.*

Getting Up to Speed

The quick way to get fast is very simple: you play with both hands, not one. One hand operates the mouse while the other plays the keyboard hotkeys. Yes, you'll have to forget about drinks and snacks while playing if you want to be fast.

The Options and Profiles button opens a menu that lets you customize game features to your liking. I won't discuss all this here—it's described in loving detail in the game manual. Instead, I'll focus on just two tabs on the Options and Profiles menu panel. This panel opens by default on the Game tab. Here are selected Game tab recommendations for new (and maybe also not-so-new) gamers:

- Autocitizen. After a couple of introductory games, set this to Idle for a while to see if you can manage your workforce better than the computer after a few games. When the game gets too busy for you to oversee all the details, change this setting back to the default Gather.

- Building Stances. Initially, choose Defensive. All the soldiers featured in *RoN* are very eager to get into a brawl, and this will make sure they won't stray far from their assigned positions. You'll be using other Building Stances too, setting them within the appropriate military building; this is discussed in Chapter 9.

- Game Speed. Set it to Slow or Very Slow, and regulate the speed from within the game (the minus and equals default hotkeys slow it down and speed it up, respectively).

- Difficulty. New players should choose Easiest. Almost everyone else should set the Difficulty slider at Moderate, and adjust it up or down after playing a single Quick Battle game on a Small map against a single opponent. Veterans should set the slider to Tough at the very least—come on, guys. You wanna win right away?

- Once you know the game well enough to absorb more info, set Help Message Detail to High, and Message Duration to Long. The texts displayed whenever you move your cursor over something are best read with the game paused (see Figure 1.2). Make a point of reading them carefully and you'll be able to switch them off entirely fairly quickly.

 Recommended checkbox options: there are two groups of checkboxes—one at the top of the Quick Battle panel and one in the lower right corner of that panel. New gamers should select Start Game Paused in the top group. Once you're somewhat familiar with the game, go to the top group on the Quick Battle panel and select Show Advanced Options.

The Hotkeys tab is right next to the Game tab. The number of game hotkey filters, let alone hotkeys (several hundred of these!), can be a bit overwhelming if you're a new gamer. Relax; to start with, you just need to learn two: Pause (defaults "P," Pause/Break), and Game Options (default Shift+F10). This lets you access the Hotkeys panel for reference and tweaks. Every single featured command can be customized to your liking; if you're a new gamer, it's wise to leave everything as is and play a few games first to discover your hotkey preferences. Be sure to check out the hotkey card that came with the game.

FIGURE 1.2: *The game's pop-up help texts merit careful reading.*

Finally, note that your hotkey preferences might change as you gain experience. For new players, the right hotkey for a specific command is always the one they'll remember. For seasoned players, the right hotkey is the one that's most conveniently situated on the keyboard. Related time-sensitive commands (for example, different military unit formations) are grouped together on the keyboard, allowing the player to issue orders without looking.

RoN and Other RTS Games

Although *Rise of Nations* belongs firmly to the numerous and beautiful family of real-time strategy (RTS) games, it also has many unique features. Discovering these is great fun, so here are just the most important ones:

> **Tip**
>
> *Assigning your own custom hotkeys to game commands helps you acquire the habit of using the keyboard while playing. You'll become a better player, more quickly.*

 The game's campaign mode (Conquer the World) that marries real-time action with turn-based strategic play. Players of *Risk* will find the concept somewhat familiar; however, in *RoN* each turn/move on the strategic map is subsequently played out in real time on the standard game map, which plays the role of a tactical battlefield. Chapter 10 discusses the campaign game in detail.

- There is an incredible amount of game options, which allows you to set up any type game you can possibly imagine. These are reviewed in Chapter 2.

- *RoN* handles resources differently than other RTS games. Players of *Warcraft* and *Age of Empires* should note that natural resources, such as wood and metal, do not deplete. Also, resources can be exploited/produced only following construction of appropriate structures (for example, a lumber camp is required to gather wood). Other structures (for example, a lumber mill) exist solely to boost the gathering/production of a specific resource within city limits. Note that citizens are assigned to gathering/producing a specific resource by clicking on the appropriate building (lumber camp/mill for wood).

- The game features a time span that stretches from the beginning of civilization to modern times. As a result, every unit and structure in the game undergoes numerous transformations as your nation advances through the ages.

- You can build Wonders, a concept familiar from the venerable turn-based *Civilization* as well as the real-time *Age of Empires* series. However, these Wonders are markedly more wonderful and grant you some excellent powers. It is even possible that they can win you the game outright under Standard victory conditions (see Chapter 5), but unless Wonders are the main victory condition, think of them more as power granters than game enders.

- There's a terrific amount of research to be done, and a lot of it takes place out of the Library—check there often for new technologies. The game manual and Chapter 4 in this book have the details; just note that non-Library research can be just as important as the mainstream Library stuff. For example, upgrading your infantry to a newer type necessitates prior research conducted in your Barracks.

These are just the highlights of the differences between *RoN* and other RTS games intended to make you aware that such differences do indeed exist, and have a profound effect on the gameplay. For a comprehensive list of all the game features, please refer to the game manual.

STARTING RIGHT

If you're a new gamer, you should know there are two ways to approach a new game. Most gamers prefer to jump into the game right away, learning it while they play. *Rise of Nations* is very accommodating in this respect. It features a comprehensive set of tutorials, including a "Quick Learn" scenario, accessed through the Learn To Play button on the main game menu. The tutorials are reviewed at the end of this chapter.

Warning

The jump-right-in approach has its drawbacks. Playing the game is exciting and doesn't exactly encourage you to focus on larger, strategic game issues.

The second approach to learning a new game consists of actually reading the manual, cover to cover, before and while playing the game. Not surprisingly, it's practiced by a tiny minority of gamers. If you adopt this brave approach, don't stop halfway through the manual because you think you've got the hang of things (you don't, and won't until you've put in some serious gaming time). Read the manual to the very end, including the credits—don't you want to know who created the game? Yes, it's a little tedious, takes up time that could be spent beating up on your unlucky opponents, but ultimately will *save* you lots of time. You'll begin winning more quickly. More: if you persist with this approach, then one day you might find you're the lucky person *writing* the game manual for *Rise of Nations 4*, or maybe even the strategy guide. Whoopee!

Installation Notes

You really should read what the game manual has to say about installing the game, even if you absolutely hate reading game manuals. As mentioned earlier, at least skim through the readme document. Here are a few extra steps you might consider to ensure a trouble-free gaming experience:

1. Check the amount of space you've got free on your hard drive (right-click the My Computer icon on your Windows desktop, select System Properties, and click the Drive tab on the System Properties panel). When installing the game, you should choose Full Install for optimum game performance, and that will take up around 630 megabytes on your hard drive. Also, remember that you should keep 10% to 20% of your hard drive free at all times (more is better); this helps ensure smooth running of complex applications.

2. Defragment your hard drive and run Scandisk prior to installing the game.

3. Reboot the computer after installing and before playing the game for the first time.

FIGURE 1.3: *And this ain't nothing yet.* Rise of Nations *can feature a game world populated by a couple of thousand units.*

Your first few games of *Rise of Nations* will most likely involve relatively small populations and few opponents. However, sooner or later you'll find yourself at the helm of a huge nation competing against several big huge opponents (see Figure 1.3).

Making RoN Run Well

Rise of Nations is big in scope in yet another sense: it allows huge game world populations. If you set the population cap at its maximum in a "peaceful" (no war allowed) game, you might see well over 2,000 units when playing against seven opponents! Games that allow war (the vast majority) rarely see game world population reach such high numbers, as a nation growing in size invariably swallows competitors. However, the special effects and animations accompanying combat place an extra burden on the computer.

RoN offers the choice of several screen resolutions: 800×600, 1024×768, 1280×1024, and 1600×1200. The lower resolution results in better game performance at the expense of both image quality and viewable game world area; higher resolution lets you see more. This last quality is absolutely invaluable, but unfortunately places bigger demands on your computer. If your box happens to meet or barely exceed the minimum system requirements, it might start to hiccup and stutter as soon as the game population surpasses half a thousand units. However, there's something you should check before you begin fiddling with the graphic settings or before you start lowering the population cap.

What you should do is make sure your computer's in optimum running condition. This means a clean system that's serviced regularly. At the very least, you should periodically defragment the hard drive, run Scandisk and/or any other diagnostic programs you have, and update as appropriate your hardware drivers plus possibly your computer's operating system. The majority of problems encountered while running an application aren't caused by the application, but by the system that's running it.

Note

When faced with a difficult problem, remember you're not alone! The gaming community is always eager to help out newcomers; it's one of the most altruistic communities on this planet. Connecting to the **Rise of Nations** *home page lets you link up with other* **RoN** *players via message boards; you can also use a search engine such as google.com to scan the Web for* **RoN**-*related sites. And failing everything else, there's always Technical Support.*

Naturally, *RoN* runs best when it runs alone, that is, when all other applications are closed. In solo games, you might see a performance boost if you deactivate your machine's network card. If nothing helps and the game still doesn't run the way you want it to, consider adding more RAM (random access memory) before splurging on a new video card or processor. It's much less expensive, and can help considerably.

Obviously, game performance can be strongly affected by the pre-game choices you make. Bigger maps featuring more players make much bigger demands on your system. The difficulty level can have an effect, too: at high difficulty, the A.I. is much more active and builds more units quickly.

FIRST GAMES

You should begin with the tutorials (Learn to Play button on the main game menu) and select Quick Learn even if you're a relatively experienced player. The tutorials do not have to be played from start to finish; players confident of their abilities can choose to play just one or two. The learning experience should be rounded off with a few Quick Battle games, starting with a Survival of the Fittest game against a single opponent. You'll know you've mastered the basics once you've been victorious a couple of times. From then on you can confidently experiment with the game's myriad gameplay choices; Chapter 2 has relevant advice.

The Learn to Play Tutorials

The tutorials are largely self-explanatory. While learning to play, take the time to observe larger issues: balancing spending against output of resources, speed of armies depending on unit composition, choosing city sites, selecting research priorities, and so on. The tutorials run on Normal speed by default; slow them down a notch. Watch what's happening and commit it to memory.

Note that all tutorials will have you leading the British, which means you'll enjoy a higher commerce cap (20% bonus). It's quite an advantage! Your opponents belong to several different nationalities, which change from game to game.

Tutorial 1: Quick Learn

This tutorial is an Easiest-difficulty Quick Battle game in which you'll be leading the British against the Barbarians (represented here by the Bantu). It will help you evaluate your gaming skills, but if you're a very new gamer, you should skip it and play Tutorials 2 and 3 first. Midway through this tutorial, you'll be given the following options: to continue it (recommended for new players), restart it (good move for very new players who are too impatient to play the other tutorials first), or abandon it and begin a regular Quick Battle game (good choice for experienced players who find an Easiest level game not challenging enough). The Bantus aren't a pushover by any means, so it might be wise to play this tutorial through to the end even though you're familiar with RTS games. It will help you quickly grasp the game's unique features.

In the unlikely event that you find the in-game hints inadequate, turn to Chapter 8; it contains advice on building an empire that is relevant to this tutorial. You do not need to advance to the Classical Age to win; in fact you can practice a classic RTS strategy called the Rush. It consists of churning out military units at the expense of economic development and research, and immediately throwing them into action against an enemy that hopefully hasn't even started to think about creating an army. The initial advantage thus gained can be turned into final victory.

Tutorial 2: Boadicea

This tutorial deals with game basics and is simplicity itself. You'll be fighting very feeble Romans. They're so weak you can try experimenting a little and form two groups of troops instead of one as recommended in the tutorial. Put Boadicea and the light cavalry unit in one group, and the remaining infantry in the other. You'll see a big difference in the speed of the two formations; if you group all the units together, the resulting army marches at the speed of the slowest unit (heavy infantry). Grouping slower and faster units separately is very useful when fighting full-fledged battles later on in the game (see Figure 1.4).

FIGURE 1.4: *Way to go, Boadicea! The fleet-footed queen begins demolishing the enemy barracks while her soldiers tie down enemy infantry.*

Tutorial 3: Alfred the Great

This tutorial is slightly more difficult; you'll be building structures and units. Use all three citizens to build everything from the start. When you've built your army and are ready to liberate Ethandum from Germans masquerading as the Vikings, stop your troops just short of the flashing marker. The defending Viking troops will be forced to march to close in with your men, and you'll thus learn another useful tactic: making the enemy come to you through a hail of your missiles.

Tutorial 4: The 100 Years War

This tutorial introduces gathering resources and researching advances, and also has you fighting the French, who are equipped with firearms. When attacking Compiegne, consider reconnoitering with a couple of Knights instead of advancing with the whole army right away. This will let you position your army out of range of French arquebuses while allowing your trebuchets to pummel the enemy into dust. If your army engages in hand-to-hand combat, you'll suffer avoidable losses. When the French counterattack with a detachment of pikemen, pull your cavalry (knights) back, and let the archers do all the work! In *RoN*, military units are finely balanced; each type of unit is good at fighting a certain type of enemy unit and bad at fighting others. Knights fare badly against pikemen, but archers slaughter them. Remember that wars are often won not by the player that produces the most units but by the player that loses the fewest.

Tutorial 5: Henry VIII

This tutorial drives home the importance of researching military advances and upgrading your military. Your opponent: the French masquerading as Scots. In addition, you're given a lesson in planning the expansion of your empire by building new cities so that you can take advantage of additional natural resources. Note the role played by the narrow pass between mountains north of Winchester; it's easy to block, and Scottish attacks are beaten back without much effort. Strategic placing of new cities is of utmost importance in all games of *Rise of Nations*; you should always aim to include plentiful resources within city radius as well as expand your territory as much as possible. City sites protected by impassable mountains and/or forests are also much easier to defend.

Tutorial 6: Battle of Britain

This tutorial introduces diplomacy along with a new resource (oil), modern military units, generals and their special abilities, setting patrolling waypoints for fighter aircraft, and more. When entrenching troops, note that in full-fledged games you have to rest the flanks of your line on natural obstacles, otherwise it can be bypassed. Real opponents, especially human ones, won't line up obligingly in front of your guns! Do pay special attention to the general and his abilities; they're very valuable. Note also that patrolling aircraft automatically return to base for refueling; this "travel time" has to figure in all your future aerial-defense planning.

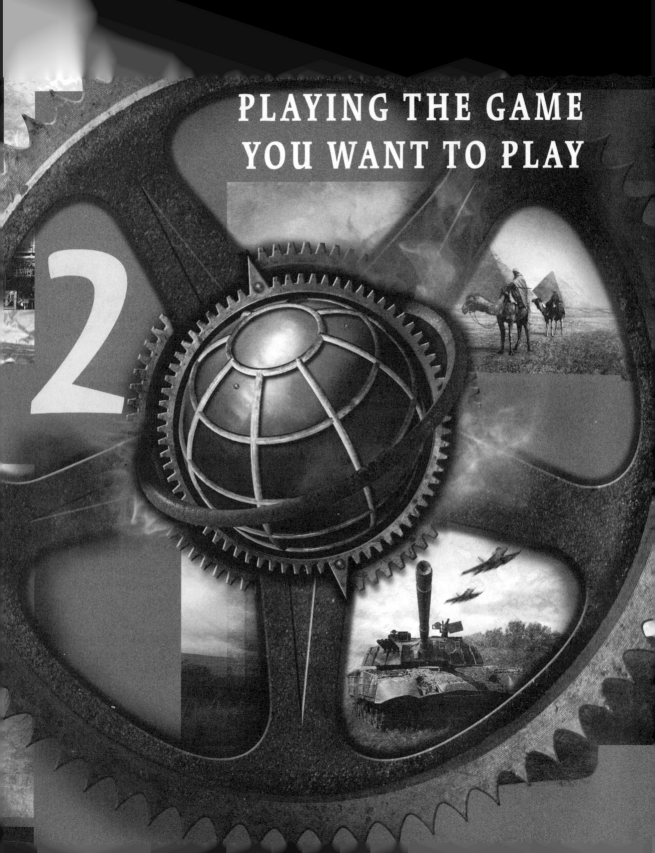

PLAYING THE GAME
YOU WANT TO PLAY

2

After you've completed the tutorials, the second step to mastering *Rise of Nations* involves playing a number of solo games. It's best to begin with Quick Battle; it's less complex than the Conquer the World campaign game (discussed in Chapter 10). Don't feel you'll somehow be shortchanged on the gaming experience, because you won't. A Quick Battle game can be over in a few minutes, or it can stretch over several days. It all depends on the pre-game choices you make.

The Quick Battle panel features a staggering amount of options; you could spend a couple of years trying out every combination possible. This chapter reviews these options, and comments on the consequences of each pre-game choice. New gamers should find it particularly helpful. All gamers should make maximum use of the game's tooltip help: holding the mouse cursor over an option brings up a panel that describes it.

GETTING INTO QUICK BATTLE

Begin by deciding how long you want to play. A game against seven opponents on a huge map can take a very long time, particularly if you're eliminating enemies through conquest, which involves capturing every enemy city on the map.

So, decide on the number of opponents first. You can even play alone; this is done by selecting None from the Other Nations pull-down menu on the Quick Battle screen. However, I don't recommend this "sandbox" mode. The game is both more exciting and more instructive when there's a computer player present. This doesn't necessarily have to mean war. You can set up a game in which no fighting is allowed. Watching the computer-controlled nation pays off in a big way for new players, and if you're absolutely determined to go it alone, maxing out the difficulty level and letting the computer share control of your empire might be a wise move! It allows you to simply sit back and watch how the computer goes about things when at its most evil, that is, the Toughest difficulty setting. It's actually a good move to do this even if you're an experienced player; knowing your opponent is very helpful when devising your own strategy.

Note

The number of opponents you may play at any one time might also be limited by your computer. A relatively slow system might restrict you to just a couple of competitors if you don't lower the population cap.

The following sections discuss all the Quick Battle panel choices in some detail. They are described in their order of appearance on the panel for ease-of-reference reasons only. Most new players will instinctively move to select their nation and its colors on the sub-panel in the upper left of the Quick Battle screen (see Figure 2.1). This is a mistake; in fact, making any hasty choice when setting up a solo game is a mistake.

This is because almost every pre-game choice influences other pre-game choices. A nation that enjoys a distinct advantage on one type of map might be at a big disadvantage in another—and that's just one of many factors that come into play. The overall character of the game (set in the Teams & Allies pull-down menu), map style and size, number and individual nationalities of the opponents, even your starting location on the map—they all play a role. Choosing the best nation to play on a particular map provides an advantage—why not take it?

Finally, a little "secret": the sub-menu where you set your own and your opponents' nationalities has a feature that can be of immense help to all players. It is accessed through the Name pull-down menu, and it lets you *completely* transfer the leadership of your nation to the computer. The options available there even let you choose between two computer player strategies (Rush, which broadly means attacking from the start of the game; and Boom, which roughly means attacking after developing a strong economic base). Set up a Survival of the Fittest game with a revealed map, and watch the computer play against itself at the Toughest difficulty setting. If you're new to games, it gives you a very good idea of what the game priorities are; if you're an experienced player, it will let you know what to expect before you begin your own experimentation.

FIGURE 2.1: *All nations might be created equal, but sometimes certain nations are better than others.*

National Choices

Rise of Nations offers 18 nationality choices, and each nation has a sharply defined unique character by being able to do some things a lot better than any other nation. Note that no nation is penalized in any way; whichever nationality you choose, your people will be competent in all areas and pursuits. A really skilled player should find it possible to win with any nation in any game.

Warning

Sticking to one nation in all your games is good only while learning the game basics; later on, it quickly becomes a handicap. Don't fall into this rather popular trap.

Things are always more exciting when they're unexpected, and so *Rise of Nations* lets you lead a nation randomly picked by the computer. You may also ask it to pick a nation with strong offensive, defensive, or economic potential. Here's who belongs to which group:

- Offensive: Aztecs, Bantu, French, Germans, Japanese, Mongols, Romans, Turks
- Defensive: Chinese, Koreans, Maya, Russians
- Economic: British, Chinese, Egyptians, Germans, Greeks, Inca, Koreans, Nubians, Spanish

Note that three nations—Chinese, Germans, and Koreans—belong to two groups; this means, for example, you might get the Chinese as both Random Economic and Random Defensive options. Also, the fact that a nation belongs to a particular group shouldn't dictate your strategy when leading that nation. Several nations are strong in all three areas: offense, defense, and economy. The Germans are a perfect example (see Figure 2.2). Quite a few other nations are doubly talented: for example, the Romans are equally well suited to offensive and defensive play (and also have a nice economic bonus).

The sections below review the nationalities in *Rise of Nations*. They do not purport to be comprehensive—the size of this guide doesn't allow for that. But they will help you make an informed national choice, and possibly uncover hidden implications. The remaining chapters of this guide contain plenty of nation-specific information and advice; Chapter 6 in particular discusses unique national units along with standard units.

FIGURE 2.2: *The Germans assembling to make mischief*

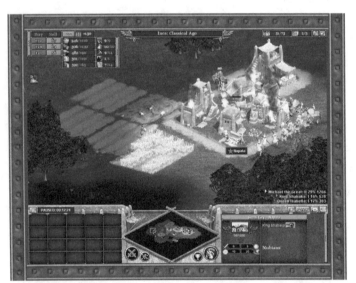

FIGURE 2.3: *Special bonuses don't commit a nation to following a single strategy. Here, the peace- and gold-loving Inca attack the Nubian capital.*

If you read all the descriptions carefully, you'll notice a certain pattern: every nation has its own special moment in the sun. The importance of national bonuses varies with time; for example, the Bantu +1 city bonus and fast foot units are most valuable in the early stages of the game. Time your victory grab accordingly, remembering also that things work differently in solo and multi-player games. In a solo game, earlier is always better; in a multiplayer game involving more than two human players, that's not necessarily so (see Chapter 11).

Finally, the entries recommend a workable approach or strategy for each nation (the strategies are explained in detail in Chapters 3 and 9) as well as to which maps the nation is particularly suited. They also state which Random category a nation belongs to: Economic, Defensive, Offensive. Remember that these entries are meant to guide new players and aren't set in stone; in fact, a skilled player can win with any strategy, and any nation, by using the right strategy on the right map against the right opponents at the right time.

Recommendations notwithstanding, experiment with the game (see Figure 2.3). Who knows, maybe *you* will be the next one to come up with a brilliantly original approach that will shake the gaming world to its foundations. Why not?

Aztecs

- 15 bonus resources per Age whenever a unit created at your barracks, stable, or docks destroys an enemy unit

- +100% plunder from destroyed enemy buildings. Free light infantry with each barracks (1 from start, 2 with Classical Age and Military level 1, 3 with Gunpowder Age and Military level 3)

- Military lineup features 5 unique light infantry units: 3 appear in the Classical/Medieval Age time frame, 2 in Modern and Information Ages.

- Random category: Offensive

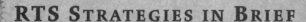

RTS STRATEGIES IN BRIEF

RTS games have been around for a while, and during that time gamers have come up with several distinct ways to play a winning game. These are discussed in more detail in Chapters 3, 4, and 9, but here's a brief overview:

Rush: Player focuses on producing military units as early in the game as possible. These are immediately thrown into action against a hopefully unprepared enemy. This approach sacrifices economic development and research on the military altar, and it's more or less a one-shot deal. If you're successful, you win; if not, you might have great difficulty in catching up with development and research.

Boom: This strategy consists of developing the economy and conducting a respectable amount of research before building an offensive army and attacking. For example, you might want to build a fort plus siege factory, then create a general and build some artillery before setting out to conquer an enemy.

Border Push: This approach is a take on static, positional warfare. The player focuses on defense, building defensive structures that steadily and mercilessly push your border forward and the enemy back; armies are created solely for the purpose of mobile defense, and used to invade enemy territory only to secure space for extra cities and forts. It's not hard to win a defensive action when supported by a network of cities, forts, towers, and other military buildings. Eventually the enemy runs out of both resources and living space, signaling the time for a coup de grace.

Needle and Hammer: This is a versatile strategy that works especially well in multiplayer games; it's also a good choice for the underdog. It consists of turning out military units parallel to your development and research effort, thus involving a clever balancing act. Newly created fast units (cavalry, light infantry, vehicles) are immediately sent into enemy territory on Aggressive or Raid setting (these are the "needles"). Slower units (heavy infantry, artillery) are assembled into small battle groups ("hammers") and sent to attack buildings for which the loss will hurt the enemy most (choices vary depending on the game circumstances). This strategy calls for good micromanagement skills; making a good effort is rewarded by weakening the enemy to the point where you can throw a big heavy anvil at his head (big siege army) to wrap up the game.

Comments: The Aztecs might be the right choice for you if you like to play a fast, aggressive game. Aztec bonuses reward offensive war, and Aztec unique units are particularly suited to the Rush approach. The bonus resources you receive when you destroy an enemy unit are always the kind of which you have least: if you're low on food, you get food, and so on. A peaceful game erases *all* of the Aztec special advantages; keep that in mind when setting victory conditions. Your best bet: small to medium land-only maps with adequate resources.

Bantu

- +1 city limit with Civics level 1
- Cities 75% cheaper to build. Double (+100%) population limit at every level; +75% to maximum population limit
- Citizens and barracks units move 25% faster.
- Unit upgrades do not require Military research.
- Five unique military units: 3 light infantry (Ancient through Medieval Ages) and 2 fighter aircraft (Modern/Information Age)
- Random categories: Offensive

Comments: The Bantu are perfect for players who like to expand quickly and relatively peacefully. Their national bonuses give the Bantu a pronounced economic edge that makes winning peaceful games easier. In games that allow war, you should exploit the national characteristics by focusing on expanding your territory through building cities as fast as you can; the unique Bantu light infantry is helpful in dealing with anyone limiting your living space. Like the Aztecs, Bantu are a nation that enjoys a particularly strong advantage in the early stages of the game. Smaller maps allow you to literally crowd the enemy into the corner, implementing a Border Push strategy (see Chapters 3 and 9). Your best bet: medium-sized land-only maps.

British

- +25% Commerce cap
- Double income from Taxation. Foot archer upgrades for free
- Forts and towers have +2 range.
- Anti-aircraft units and buildings 25% cheaper and created 33% faster
- Ships created 33% faster
- Random categories: Economic

Comments: The British are the proverbial safe bet. They enjoy powerful economic bonuses that let them perform well in all kinds of games on all kinds of maps; the defensive bonuses let the British shine on maps featuring numerous obstacles to unit movement. The British are very versatile if not particularly gifted in any one area: Rush, Boom, Border Push, and Needle and Hammer strategies are equally viable options (see Chapters 3 and 6). British unique units include five of ranged infantry

(Classical through Industrial Ages) and a Modern Age bomber. Your best bet: sea and land maps with plenty of resources, any size.

Chinese

- Science research 20% cheaper
- All cities are Large from start.
- Citizens, caravans, merchants created instantly
- Free granary technologies (upon reaching prerequisites): Herbal Lore, Medicine, Pharmaceuticals
- Random categories: Economic, Defensive

Comments: The Chinese are at their best in peaceful games, where their economic bonuses can be applied to research and development without worries about war. The Science research bonus has far-reaching implications, as each Science level reduces by 10% the cost of all other research. Instant creation of civilian units greatly speeds up early development, and lower research costs can give your military a modern edge. The five unique infantry units at your disposal (Medieval through Enlightenment, then Industrial/Modern Age) aren't a great help. Free granary technologies and large cities boost defense; Boom, Border Push, and Needle and Hammer approaches work well. Your best bet: maps that are relatively scarce in resources, with many obstacles to unit movement.

Egyptians

- Start with granary; free granary upgrades upon reaching prerequisites
- Food Commerce cap +10%, and can build 7 farms per city
- Each farm generates +2 wealth
- Wonder advantages: can build 2 per city, can build Wonder an age early, all Wonders cost 25% less.
- Random category: Economic

Comments: Obviously, the Egyptians are prime candidates for playing a winning peaceful game—especially if the game victory conditions allow you to win by building Wonders. The extra food production strongly stimulates fast economic development provided there's enough timber to meet fast-rising construction costs—as you remember, in *RoN*, each extra farm costs more timber. Unique Egyptian units include no less than eight models of light and ranged attack cavalry (Classical through Gunpowder Age). This gives the Egyptian army especially good offensive qualities during the time indicated; Boom and Needle and Hammer work well. Your best bet: land-only maps with forests and other obstacles to unit movement.

French

- Free general with every new fort and free supply wagon with each new siege factory; supply wagons heal troops.
- Start with lumber mill, and receive free lumber mill upgrades once prerequisites are met.
- Timber commerce cap +10%, +2 citizens per woodcutter's camp
- Siege factories and artillery are built 50% faster, and cost 25% less. Artillery moves 25% faster.
- Random category: Offensive

Comments: The French are an ideal choice for gamers to fight with finesse; you need some playing experience to take full advantage of the French military bonuses. These give the French army an excellent offensive capability that is further boosted by economic bonuses helpful in the production of new units. Boom, Border Push, and Needle and Hammer are all workable strategies. The unique units consist of four models of heavy cavalry (Classical through Enlightenment Age), which provide the already formidable French with extra offensive punch. Your best bet: medium to large land maps with few forests.

Germans

- Cities gather +10 food, timber, and metal.
- Building completion bonuses 50% bigger
- Granary, lumber mill, and smelter upgrades cost 50% less, and are available earlier.
- 2 free fighters with each airbase, and air units created 33% faster
- Fireships and submarines cost 25% less and are created 33% faster.
- Random categories: Offensive, Economic

FIGURE 2.4: *A Gunpowder Age army assembling prior to attack*

Comments: Germans are the *wunderkind* of the game (see Figure 2.4). They enjoy terrific economic bonuses, and a lineup of eight unique military units: six infantry models (Ancient through Gunpowder Age, then Modern Age) and two tanks (Modern/Information Age). Boom and Rush strategies both work well, and usually you'll be tough enough not to need Needle and Hammer. The Germans are strong candidates for victory on any kind of map and under any victory conditions, and are absolutely lethal if allowed to develop relatively undisturbed. Your best bet when leading the Germans: medium to large maps (sea or land) that are relatively scarce in resources.

Greeks

- Library research costs 10% less resources (knowledge excepted).
- Libraries and universities cost 50% less.
- Scholars created 100% faster
- Random category: Economic

Comments: The Greek advantage lies strictly in cheaper, quicker research; there are no others. The four unique Greek military units (Classical through Enlightenment Ages) consist of heavy cavalry without ranged attack capability, and you won't find much comfort there. This puts the Greeks at their best in peaceful games; in games that allow war, you have to stay a technological step ahead of adversaries. A Needle and Hammer strategy works well. Your best bet: large sea or land maps with plenty of obstacles to unit movement.

Inca

- Wealth commerce cap +33%
- 25% unit cost refund for each unit lost to enemy
- Each miner produces 10 wealth in addition to 10 metal.
- Random category: Economic

Comments: The Inca are the ideal choice for players who think money can buy happiness—or victory. However, this nation's bonuses work best in a peaceful setting; games that allow war are tricky. The 25% refund you receive upon losing a unit to the enemy is less meaningful than it appears. What matters most in any fight are the units you have on the spot, not the extra ones you can produce in the future. The four unique military units aren't outstanding, consisting of two models of light infantry (Classical/ Medieval Age) and two of artillery (Enlightenment/Industrial Age). Safe strategy: Needle and Hammer. Your best bet: maps with plenty of obstacles to unit movement, and scarce resources.

Japanese

- Farms cost 50% less.
- Farms and fishermen produce 25% more food.
- Each Age *and* Military level advance reduces cost of barracks units by 7%, speeds unit recruitment by 10%, and increases barracks unit effectiveness against buildings by 5%.
- Ships cost 10% less and aircraft carriers are built 33% faster.
- Random category: Offensive

Comments: Players who like to attack, attack, attack should make a point of leading the Japanese. It's one of the best choices available for a Rush strategy: *banzai* all the way. However, both Boom and Needle and Hammer also work well. This lets the Japanese show well in peace and war alike, although of course they're most fun when fighting an offensive war. The Japanese infantry is a deadly weapon in the early to middle stages of the game: unique unit lineup consists of five heavy infantry models (Classical through Enlightenment Ages). Best bet: sea maps featuring large islands/continents.

Koreans

- Start with a temple and receive temple-researched technologies for free.
- Start with extra 3 citizens and get 5 free citizens with each new city.
- Receive Militia, Minuteman, and Partisan upgrades for free.
- Towers cost 25% less.
- Citizens repair buildings 50% faster and can do so under fire without penalty.
- Random Category: Economic, Defensive

FIGURE 2.5: *The Korean capital basking in the peaceful prosperity ensured by frantic military research*

Comments: You don't have to be particularly religious to appreciate the benefits of starting with a temple (see Chapter 3). Getting all those free citizens gives a tremendous boost to development, and is nicely rounded out with several defensive bonuses. The Koreans play well in all types of games and on all types of maps (see Figure 2.5). Unique units include four ranged infantry (Ancient through Gunpowder Ages) and two models of artillery (Classical/Medieval Age). If you want to wage offensive wars, it's better to do so relatively early; Boom, Border Push, and Needle and Hammer are all viable strategy choices, depending on the map. Your best bet: medium and large maps that have enough resources to keep all those civilians busy.

Maya

- Buildings cost 33% less timber, have 50% more hit points, and are built 50% more quickly.
- Cities, forts, and towers have power (firing rate) increased by 2.
- Cities without garrison can fire at enemies.
- Random category: Defensive

Comments: There's more to the Maya than meets the eye. Their national bonuses appear primarily defensive in character; however, the ability to build numerous, extra-powerful forts and towers cheaply and quickly lets you expand mercilessly, Border Push-style, bulldozing your adversaries off the map. Unique military units aren't especially exciting: you'll get three models of light infantry (Ancient through Medieval Ages) and two of heavy infantry (Modern/Information Ages). Your best bet: small to medium land-only maps.

Mongols

- 3 free ranged-attack cavalry/tanks with each stable/auto plant
- Mounted units/vehicles 10% cheaper, and created 20% faster
- Receive 1 food for each 1% landmass under control.
- Unit attrition halved
- Receive free Forage, Supply, and Logistics technologies upon reaching prerequisites.
- Random category: Offensive

Comments: Obviously, the Mongols are an excellent choice for aggressive players. Unfortunately, their national abilities don't help much in a peaceful game. Also, leading the Mongol means it's best to use an early Boom approach; it's simply a race to build plenty of stables as quickly as possible. If you unexpectedly find yourself on the defensive, Needle and Hammer works well. A game played with the Mongols is always extra exciting because of the numerous cavalry/vehicles involved. The four Mongol unique units consist of ranged-attack cavalry that can fire on the move (Classical through Enlightenment Ages). Your best bet: medium to large land-only maps that afford easy movement.

Nubians

- Start with a market, and trade resources from the start receiving a 20% bonus to market prices (buy for less, sell for more).
- All rare resources within national borders visible, and yield 50% more.
- Merchants, caravans, and markets cost 50% less and have 50% more hit points.
- +1 caravan limit
- Random category: Economic

Comments: The Nubians are an excellent choice in peaceful games. However, they're also a viable choice in games that allow war: Their unique unit lineup includes three ranged attack infantry (Classical through Gunpowder Ages) and four models of ranged attack cavalry (Classical through Enlightenment). The big boost received right at the start with the free market considerably speeds the process of assembling an army. Border Push and Needle and Hammer are workable strategies. Note that the Nubian special advantages tend to wane in the later stages of the game. Your best bet: medium to large maps, preferably land-only and relatively poor in timber and metal. If the map also has a lot of rare resources, you're on your way!

Romans

- Forts extend national borders +2.
- Free heavy infantry with each new barracks (1 from start, 2 with Gunpowder/Military level 3, 3 with Industrial/Military level 5)
- Each city generates 10 wealth.
- Random categories: Offensive

Comments: The Romans are the right choice for you if you want war. They don't exactly shine in peaceful games; constantly readjusting your national border by building new forts isn't cost-effective. The Romans' national advantages are suited for both defensive and offensive warfare, and both Boom and Border Push strategies work well. The extra wealth received from cities plays a role only in the early stages of a game; consider it a hint to start expanding early. Unique units include three types of heavy infantry (Classical through Gunpowder Ages). Your best bet: small to medium land-only maps with plentiful resources.

Russians

▷ National borders +1 at start, and +1 per Civic technology level (in addition to standard Civic border bonus).

▷ Attrition damage to enemy units doubled; attrition upgrades free

▷ Spies cost 50% less and stay hidden after using special ability.

▷ Cavalry units 50% more effective against enemy supply and artillery units

▷ Oil production boosted 20%

▷ Random category: Defensive

FIGURE 2.6: *Da is good place to set up logging cooperative.*

Comments: The Russians are a good choice for players who like war in general, and new players who like war in particular. Their excellent defensive qualities mean even total newbies stand a chance against somewhat experienced players. Do not be misled by Russian national abilities and assume they're good only at defense. Their unique units include three models of light cavalry (Medieval through Enlightenment Ages); this is complemented by two types of Modern Age infantry plus a unique artillery unit (Modern Age) and battle tank (Information Age). A delayed Boom strategy works particularly well. Your best bet: large land-only maps with plenty of resources (see Figure 2.6).

Spanish

▷ Map revealed from the start (including rare resource locations!)

▷ Start game with an extra scout (except when in Nomad mode); bonus scout for a total of 2 in games with revealed map

▷ All units in scout line are upgraded for free, have line of sight increased by +3, and take less time when using special abilities.

↠ Free heavy ship with every new dock (until Industrial Age only)

↠ +35 resources from ruins, and another +35 resources per Science level

↠ Random category: Defensive

Comments: The Spanish enjoy exploration bonuses that make them an outstanding choice in all multi-player games; in solo games, new players will be reassured by the semi-revealed map (with Fog of War in Place if selected on the Quick Battle panel). Truly experienced players can turn this bonus into victory almost every time they play, and thus might find the Spanish a little bland. This isn't much helped by the Spanish unique units: four models of good but somewhat unexciting heavy infantry (Classical through Enlightenment Ages). Needle and Hammer and Rush (on smaller maps) work well. Note that the Spanish don't perform as well in peaceful games. Your best bet: large sea maps with average resources.

Turks

↠ Citizens cost 33% less.

↠ 2 free artillery units with every new siege factory or factory

↠ All siege, artillery, and bombardment units are upgraded for free, and have a +3 bonus to line of sight and firing range.

↠ Military research at library costs 33% less.

↠ Conquered cities assimilated 200% faster

↠ Random category: Offensive

Comments: The Turks are yet another attractive choice for players who like to go on the offensive. Their national bonuses predestine the Turks to wars of conquest; Boom is a strategy that fits them especially well, with cheap citizens (so to speak) helping in quick initial economic development. The Turkish unique unit lineup includes two types of gunpowder infantry and two types of artillery (all Gunpowder/Enlightenment Age). Your best bet: large land-only maps with plenty of resources.

Choosing Map Style and Size

Map size has a profound influence on the length and complexity of the game, and map size is to a certain extent determined by map style. This is because a sea map requires a bigger map size to play well. There's less land, and so there's less space for the players to build. The pull-down menu on which you set map size carries a number-of-players recommendation: for instance, a Large map is recommended for a game involving six players. If you're also selecting a sea map such as East Indies, go one size up from the game's recommendation.

Keep in mind that breaking the rules can be entertaining and instructive, too. A game involving two players on a big map will help you learn how to develop your nation's empire along with a host of minor things such as the significance of setting assembly points well. And a quick game involving eight players starting with Nomad on a Small land map provides a lot of laughs in addition to frenzied gameplay (particularly in multiplayer).

Map Styles

The first three choices in the Map Style pull-down menu are Random, Random Land Map, and Random Sea Map. These random maps are selected from the choices described in this section. While reading the descriptions, keep the obvious in mind: nations with naval bonuses enjoy an advantage on sea maps, availability of metal and timber effectively defines speed of economic development, and the best defense always includes offensive action. Remember that each map is generated from scratch when you start a new game; don't expect the same distribution and amount of resources every time. All descriptions feature a recommendation you might want to heed when choosing to play a Random Economic, Defensive, or Offensive nation.

- **African Watering Hole.** This map favors aggressive players and nations with good offensive potential. Plenty of wide-open (though uneven) space allows Rush tactics, which you'll probably need if you want to grab your share of the special resources gathered round the map's center lake. Once you've got hold of a strip of lake coast, building a navy will help you bid for control of the entire shore and adjacent resources. Your starting location plays an important role. Metal and timber might be scarce. Advantageous Random national choice: Offensive, Economic.

- **Amazon Rainforest.** As you would expect, this map features plenty of trees and big rivers. Mountains tend to be few and far between, so metal production might need to be boosted by market purchases financed with a timber surplus. The abundance of timber promotes quick development, but numerous forests and rivers restrict unit movement and can cause city planning headaches (see Figure 2.7). Advantageous Random national choice. Defensive: Capturing the big mountain that is featured in the middle of this map can be a winning move.

FIGURE 2.7: *It's not easy to find a nice meadow like this in the middle of the Amazon jungle.*

- **Atlantic Sea Power.** Players start on separate continents separated by an ocean. Building a strong navy is definitely necessary to win, but a good army is equally important on larger maps. Aerial forces and missile weapons acquire special significance in the late game. Timber is relatively abundant, but metal less so. Advantageous Random national choice: Economic, Defensive.

- **Australian Outback.** A very interesting map that features a big continent surrounded by water. Adequate timber and good metal supply allows fast development. The map features include mesas and plateaus, offering a defensive bonus to whoever's in control, but little in the way of other obstacles to unit movement. A navy will enable you to execute flanking maneuvers on a strategic scale, bypassing elaborate land-defense systems. Advantageous Random national choice depends on map size: big maps favor Offensive, small maps favor Economic, Defensive.

- British Isles. As in Atlantic Sea Power each player starts on a separate continent/large island, but players are separated by narrow straits instead of an ocean. Resources are usually in good supply, allowing fast development. Aerial units can assume special importance later in the game; navies are helpful but not absolutely necessary. Advantageous Random national choice: Offensive, Defensive.
- Colonial Powers. This is a very interesting map featuring two continents separated by a sea, with all players beginning the game squeezed together on only one. Especially recommended for Diplomacy games. On land, there are few obstacles to unit movement; timber and metal might be scarce. Advantageous Random national choice: Economic, Defensive.
- East Indies. This map features a number of small to medium islands separated by relatively narrow channels and straits, but you'll also see something that qualifies as a sea here and there. Adequate timber and metal, but distribution of resources might be uneven. Advantageous Random national choices: Economic, Defensive.
- East Meets West. This map is best played in multi-player Team mode, which places each team on a separate continent. Otherwise it is very much like to British Isles, and plays similarly. Advantageous Random national choice: the one that complements your team.

- Great Lakes. This map features a number of medium to large lakes evenly distributed around the center. The lakes are big enough to serve as natural barriers and warrant a navy when part of an endangered border. Their presence might fuel a race to build "impregnable" defense systems; it pays to remember they don't exist, especially since resources are too scarce to allow a concurrent expansion of the army for much of the early game. Advantageous Random national choice: Defensive, Economic.
- Great Sahara. A land-only map without *any* water. Rich in oil, but that particular resource doesn't appear until late in a game. Metal and timber (especially) are scarce; you might be going to war simply to control a couple of groups of rather tired-looking palms. The terrain affords speed and ease of movement, while low timber availability puts strong brakes on development. Advantageous Random national choice: Economic, Offensive.
- Himalayas. A very enjoyable land-only map with plentiful metal and timber. Numerous mountains and forests result in a jigsaw that restricts troop movement and creates plenty of choke points. Advantageous Random national choice: Defensive.
- Mediterranean. This map features an inland sea in the center, and a big island in the center of the sea. Players start on a relatively narrow strip of land encircling the sea. Whoever controls the island controls the sea, and whoever controls the sea controls the map. Timber and metal are generally adequate, occasionally scarce. Advantageous Random national choice: Economic, Offensive.

- New World. Each player begins on one of the medium-sized islands surrounding an uninhabited continent. Generally there is more than enough timber, but metal might be scarce. An interesting map with plenty of potential for surprises! Advantageous Random national choice: Economic, Offensive.

- Nile Delta. Barring differences in landscape, this map is similar to the British Isles: players begin on continents separated by straits, not rivers. Good supply of both metal and timber. Advantageous Random national choices: Offensive, Defensive (according to your playing preference).

- Old World. This is a land-only map; no water except for the occasional river. Metal and timber are adequate but unevenly distributed. This puts special importance on placing your cities just right. Unit movement is somewhat restricted by natural obstacles. Advantageous Random national choice: Economic.

- Southwest Mesa. This land-only map is rich in mesas and plateaus elevated on a ring of cliffs with access from one side only. Plenty of metal (see Figure 2.8), but although timber is generally adequate, it might be scarce in some areas of the map. It's easy to link the forests, cliffs, and mountains with a system of defenses. Advantageous Random national choice: Defensive.

- Warring States. In a way, this map is a reversal of the New World: Players begin on an elongated continent surrounded by uninhabited islands. Resources can be scarce, and living space is tight. Advantageous Random national choice: Economic, Defensive.

If you're a new gamer, you'll likely find things a little easier if you start with land-only maps. You should be able to raise the difficulty level a notch, maybe even two, after a few games. This will let you lower it again when tackling a map that involves naval complications for the first time. Aggressive players will find things are easier if they begin with games on smaller maps, which will let them find and attack the enemy quickly. Other players might prefer larger maps with fewer opponents that allow breathing space before the fighting starts.

FIGURE 2.8: *Some maps, including Southwest Mesa, feature metal-bearing cliffs in addition to mountains.*

War or Peace: Setting Teams & Allies

The Teams & Allies setting determines the character of the game. Here is an overview of the available choices and their implications (discussed in more detail as applicable throughout this book):

◆ Diplomacy. Every nation starts the game in diplomatic isolation (no treaties or alliances) and at peace with everyone. On the easiest difficulty setting, you can play an entirely peaceful game; war is up to you. Things change when you go up in difficulty, but you'll still get time for initial development. All the game's diplomatic options are open: you can make and break alliances, declare war and subsequently grovel for peace or demand tribute, and so on, all as listed in the game manual. Basically, choosing Diplomacy means betting on your ability to conduct a victorious war at a time of your own choosing. Note that you can have only one ally, so a game involving eight players will have four competing alliances. Ground held by the ally counts toward a Territory victory.

◆ Survival of the Fittest. This means you'll be fighting everyone else all the time, whether you like it or not. It's an option for players who feel confident in their abilities. Even Easiest level opponents aren't a complete pushover, and winning against seven opponents on the Toughest level is the ultimate test of your skill at playing *Rise of Nations* (unless you fix the victory conditions in your favor— see below). Starting location can play a huge role: It's better to begin tucked away in the corner of the map.

◆ Assassin! This is a unique variation on the Survival of the Fittest theme. You still have to wipe the floor with all your opponents, but you deal with just two opponents at a time; as the game's tooltip help explains, one opponent will be given the task of eliminating you while you're attacking another. Assassin! games require at least three players to make any sense, and can get enormously complex when playing against seven opponents—more so than Survival of the Fittest, where you are free to attack anyone at any time. Starting location plays a role; it's best to begin in the *center* of the map.

◆ Barbarians at the Gates. Another twist on the Survival of the Fittest theme, only this time everyone is attacking *you*. Your eventual demise is taken for granted; you win as long as you've managed to survive for as long as you chose to on the Game Rules panel (Time Limit pull-down menu). It's excellent training for new players before tackling a Survival of the Fittest game.

◆ Teams of two to four players. This means a game featuring war between two alliances that are set in stone. This setting has limited value in solo games; it's primarily useful in multiplayer. If you're a new gamer, you might want to play a solo Teams game between computer players on a revealed map to see how the A.I. handles things (Computer Control All setting in the Nation Choice pull-down menu).

◆ Custom Open. This setting allows you to set up the starting alliances of a game in which players are given complete diplomatic freedom. It's interesting as a tool when you want to find out what makes a computer player declare war; overall this setting's most useful in multiplayer games, although in that instance there's little to distinguish it from Diplomacy.

◆ Custom Closed. The game's initial alliance setup cannot be changed. Of little value in solo games, but quite often useful in multiplayer games, when it can be used to neutralize any inequalities between players' skills.

The Teams & Allies setting doesn't really influence your choice of nation; Barbarians at the Gates are the only strong exception (naturally, nations with good defensive potential are at an advantage). However, it might have a bearing on your choice of map: A game of Assassin! played on a large map with elimination through conquest is going to take a long, long time.

Defining Game Rules

The choices on the Game Rules pull-down menu boil down to two options:

▷ You can choose one of the sets of rules put together by the designers; the consequences are clearly explained in the tooltip help. The rules were defined by professionals, and they work well in practice.

▷ You can put together your own set of game rules by choosing Custom. This is how mistakes can happen; a poorly chosen victory condition can result in hours of bland gameplay.

To help you avoid this dire fate, here are a few comments on the individual game rule settings:

▷ Start with. Large City means quickest development, Nomad means slowest, and also might result in the loss of certain national bonuses (no free buildings, scouts, extra citizens). However, choosing Nomad tends to give you an edge over the computer and adds a lot of spice to multiplayer games. City Center Only is a safe option that evenly distributes player capitals around the map.

▷ Resources. The more resources players receive at the start, the quicker the gameplay. New players should make a point of playing a couple of games with starting resources set to Low; it really drives home a few lessons in resource management.

▷ Technology. The cost of researching new technologies greatly affects the speed of events. Map size plays a role here; a small map combined with very high technology cost will slow things down to a crawl. Your choice of starting Age is another consideration.

▷ Reveal Map. New players should play a couple of games with the Reveal All setting. Otherwise, this works best set to the default Normal.

▷ Population. The number of players in the game and the speed of your system will define this setting more often than most players would like. Naturally, games with high population limits and many players demand most both from man and machine; they're both long and busy.

▷ Rush Rules. The very existence of this setting is grim testimony to how much people like beating up on each other. It is used to postpone the bloodbath to a mutually acceptable date. Starting Age is a consideration. Of course games with no Rush limitations are the most exciting. There's also a Non-Violent game option that's helpful for very new players.

- **Start Age.** This is the Age in which the game begins. Ancient Age is definitely most fun.

- **End Age.** Age after which no further research is possible. If you don't like messing around with oil, or simply feel an irresistible fancy for medieval warfare, go ahead. However, keep in mind that the outcome of most games is decided long before you research all eight Ages anyway; the smaller the map, the more quickly this happens. Naturally cost of technology, starting resources, and so on also play a consideration.

- **Elimination.** Sudden Death is the cruelest choice; Conquest is the most lenient, affording the losing side the most opportunities to make good. However, this makes for extra-long games.

- **Victory.** There is a range of attractive options here that are self-explanatory. One option, however, deserves special attention: Musical Chairs. Having the weakest players drop out of the game at pre-set time intervals makes for a very exciting game that also lets owners of slower computers experience the joy of playing against a full set of seven opponents. It's also very helpful in teaching new players efficiency, and results in fast and exciting multiplayer games with many players on a large map—settings that otherwise always produce a long and drawn-out game. Note that setting Victory to Standard lets you further define victory conditions (Territory needed for Territorial victory, and Wonder points needed for a Wonder victory). Now that's all sorted out, let's turn to the gameplay. The next chapter examines the *Rise of Nations* economy.

> ## Tip
>
> *Your best bet when playing on the Tougher or Toughest difficulty setting: relatively small land-only maps with Resources set to Low. Start with: Nomad, and Technology cost/research speed set to Very Expensive/ Slow.*

CHAPTER 2 PLAYING THE GAME YOU WANT TO PLAY

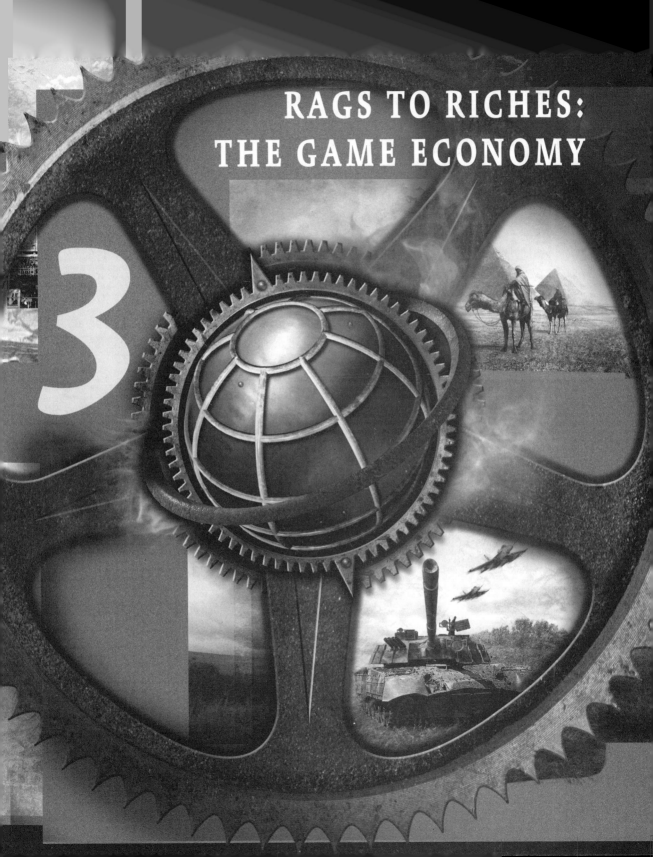

RAGS TO RICHES:
THE GAME ECONOMY

3

Rise of Nations features a deceptively simple economic model. The game has just six resources (counting knowledge, which functions as a resource in game terms only). In order of in-game appearance, these are food, timber, wealth, knowledge, metal, and oil. Doing anything—be it research or building a new unit— never involves more than two resources. For instance, you need timber and wealth to create archers, build a university, and research Science (level 1).

Experienced gamers will instantly spot a potential problem (shortages of timber and wealth), but if you're new to gaming, the intuitively simple economy in RoN might lull you into thinking it's a piece of cake. It isn't, because the game's designers have woven all economic factors into an intricate web. Game industries (food, timber, metal, and the like) need to be developed concurrently, and this chapter tells you why. It examines the significance of each game industry, and details ways and means to increase production of game resources. A separate section reviews rare resources such as diamonds or dye and their place in your economy. The chapter concludes with specific national advice and a couple of rules that can make you rich.

Note that the economy in the Conquer the World campaign game has special character: It introduces the notion of strategic resources, and lets you play bonus cards that can have profound effect on your economy. You'll find all the relevant comments in Chapter 10.

SOURCES OF PROSPERITY

First of all, let's define prosperity: It's the blessed state in which you can afford to do whatever you want. This might not occur even once you've researched Global Prosperity (a "future" Commerce advance—see Chapter 4). Nevertheless, you must be striving toward that elusive goal throughout the game, and a lot of the gameplay consists of working to improve your nation's economy. You cannot build an empire without solid economical foundations.

New players should note that economic progress is much easier in peacetime. The military units in *Rise of Nations* are expensive; a single unit can cost as much as an important advance in research or a new building. This is not to say that wars always bring economic loss. Most wars are fought for economic gain, after all, and they can be very profitable when fought at the right time and in the right manner.

> **Note**
>
> *In Diplomacy games, you may extract tribute from defeated rivals. In solo Diplomacy games, you frequently don't even need to ask: Computer opponents awed by your military successes are quick to offer enticements in exchange for peace.*

To sum up: There is no lack of sources of prosperity in *Rise of Nations*. Some maps might be poor in a given resource (timber, metal, oil), but the game features numerous ways and means of getting around these problems (production-enhancing buildings, specialized research, market trade, and so on). These are described in the sections that follow. We'll begin by taking a look at the game's central notion, the game feature that lets all the other features function: the city.

City Laws and Limits

All of the game's economic (and political) concepts center on the city. The city is the basic game structure that lets your nation come into existence as a state—a fact that is fully appreciated only once you try starting a new game in Nomad mode. Here are the main city attributes (note that all production values refer to number of units per 30 seconds of game time, irrespective of game speed):

▶ Production. Each city produces 10 food and 10 timber absolutely free of charge (no citizen worker required). Some nations enjoy special benefits: Roman cities also produce 10 wealth. German cities are all boomtowns: They produce an extra 10 food, 10 timber, *and* 10 metal (upon advancing to Classical Age).

▶ Construction. Almost all of the game's non-military buildings can be constructed only within city radius. What's more, in most cases you can construct only one building of a kind; if you want to build extra markets, universities, and so on, you'll have to found new cities first. Note that all resource-gathering buildings except farms can be built outside city limits.

▶ Expansion. Each city gives you control over extra territory. This means a boost in resources even if you don't build a single new farm or mine because more territory means higher tax income (after researching Taxation at the temple).

The number of cities you can build is determined by your Civic research level: You can build one city prior to any research, and one extra city for each new Civic advance. Some nations enjoy city-building bonuses: The Bantu have a +1 city limit (upon researching Civic level 1), and spend 75% less when building a new city. The Chinese start with a Large city, which confers such benefits as longer sighting range, bigger influence on national border, more hit points, and a bigger city building radius (city limits). See Appendix A for all city stats.

Founding new cities is a very important part of the gameplay (see Figure 3.1); it's discussed in detail in Chapter 8. In economic terms, every new city is an investment that pays terrific returns. Cities are very reasonably priced, so to speak, although costs rise steeply: Your very first city (your capital) costs only 10 food and 10 wood (20 of each for a Chinese Large city), however, every new city costs an extra 50 food and 50 timber. It's not that much, but can really hurt: building up your empire carries heavy costs in general, and every 10 food or timber counts.

FIGURE 3.1: *This city is destined to become a major lumber production center.*

> **Note**
>
> *You need both food and timber to repair damaged cities.*

RoN RESOURCES

There are six resources in *RoN*; five (food, timber, wealth, metal, and oil) are discussed here. The sixth, knowledge, is discussed in depth in Chapter 4, however, it is referred to in this chapter when it has bearing on your economic efforts.

The comments on the game resources also discuss their relative importance. Do not let this lead you into thinking that one resource is more important than the others. It might be so at times, depending on your current goals and game conditions, but keep in mind that the game's five economic resources are closely interlinked. It's impossible to increase production of one resource without an ample supply of others; building farms costs timber, wood-cutting camps cost food, and the like. Creating any military unit always requires two resources (for example, food and timber, metal and wealth), and building an effective army depletes all resources across the board.

Note

Chapter 8 features a grand economic strategy that contains numerous tips on resource management.

For ease of reference, the game resources are discussed in the same order in which they appear in the game. Note that all production figures use the game scale: number of units gathered in 30 seconds of game time, irrespective of game speed.

Food

In *RoN*, food truly is the stuff of life. It plays a particularly important role in the game's early stages, especially so if you begin playing in the Ancient Age. Here's a summary of food uses:

Warning

You'll need all the food you can get to advance through the final couple of ages in the game. You'll also need plenty of food when a war turns for the worse: Replacing lost civilians on top of creating large numbers of new military units can instantly drain food reserves.

◆ Creating new units. The basic cost for a citizen is 20 food, increasing by one food for every citizen you already have. Caravans cost a minuscule amount of food; much more importantly, you'll be spending many thousand units of food on new military units.

◆ Research. There's a research-induced food crisis in every game that starts in Ancient Age (mostly Quick Battle scenarios; the campaign game is different—see Chapter 10). Knowledge isn't available as a game resource until Classical Age; prior to that, Ancient Age research consumes more food than any other economic activity. Civic and Age advances always carry food costs. Age advances are particularly expensive, progressing well into four-digit numbers in the later stages of the game. Quite a lot of ancillary research conducted outside the library requires food, too.

◆ Building Wonders. Building a Wonder can carry heavy food costs; the Statue of Liberty, for example, consumes 600 units. Exact stats for each Wonder are available in game.

Occasionally, food is also required for new buildings (such as a lumber mill). In most games, food demand follows a pattern: It hits the roof right away and then gently plateaus in the middle game. Don't make the mistake of neglecting the food industry when demand slackens briefly!

The next sections describe buildings and other means of increasing food production. Note that food can also be produced by fishermen—the waterborne equivalent of merchants.

Farm

Each farm produces 10 food, and there's a limit of five farms per city (Egyptians can build seven). Thus, base food production of a single city equals 60 units.

Your first farm will cost you 40 timber; each subsequent farm costs four timber more. Building a full set of five farms around your first city costs 240 timber, and jumps by 100 timber for each subsequent city. Building the maximum number of farms in a rather modest empire consisting of three cities costs 1,020 units of timber! This timber investment translates into a base food output of 180 units (more for nations with food bonuses). On top of that you have to consider the cost of creating citizens to work on 15 farms: 420 food for 15 new citizens. Fortunately, there's also a +20 food farm completion bonus that helps offset the citizen cost.

It's good to build farms right next to the city, even though it might not please you aesthetically (see Figure 3.2) This will let you defend them more easily in case of an enemy raid. Losing a couple of farms right at the outset of a game greatly harms your chances of victory; at the two highest difficulty levels, you might as well start over again.

FIGURE 3.2: *What, pigs next to my palace?*

Granary

You can build one granary per city once you've researched Science level 2 and advanced to Classical Age. It will cost you 60 timber and 10 wealth to begin with, and 40 timber for every subsequent granary. Benefits: A granary in a city boosts *farm* food output of that city by 20% (a full set of five farms translates to 10 food). A granary also lets you research three types of techs: Herbal Lore, Medicine, and Pharmaceuticals, which are principally useful in war and exploration. Agriculture, Crop Rotation, and Food Industry boost a city's farm food output by 50%, 100%, and 200% respectively. See Chapter 4 for more research-related details.

Wonders and Other Means

Some of the game's Wonders benefit food production. The Pyramids increase your food gather rate by 20% while raising the food Commerce limit (production cap) by 50. The Pyramids are available as early as the Classical Age and relatively inexpensive, so they make a very attractive Wonder. The Industrial Age Kremlin Wonder increases your food production cap by 200! See Chapter 5 for more Wonder details.

Sending merchants to exploit rare resources such as Whales, Spice, and Citrus also boosts food production. The rare resource bonus can then be increased by researching the Taxation line of techs at the temple—see Chapter 4 for more research details.

Note

In Diplomacy games, food (or any other economic resource) can be sent or received as tribute. You may also obtain food as plunder from enemy buildings/cities.

Final Thoughts on Food

A system of farms and granaries is the mainstay of any developed food industry. Exploiting rare resources for their food bonuses is especially helpful in the opening stages in the game, but don't count on those heavily, especially since trading posts are easily destroyed (they have only 90 hit points—exactly the same as a merchant, and less than most military units, let alone buildings).

Food is especially important in the early stages of any game. Experienced players know that early stages of a game are often also decisive: Yes, you might ultimately win the game just because you put in an extra farm or two before your opponent did. If you want objective proof, include Egyptians among your next set of opponents. You'll see that the A.I. puts the big national food bonus to good use, and that Egypt almost invariably emerges as a strong contender. However, even the Egyptians cannot build farms out of thin air. To win at *RoN*, you need a strong timber industry to build a strong food industry. The next section discusses everything to do with wood.

Timber

The foundations of your empire are built of timber. Just look at the many roles timber plays in the game:

- Building and repairing structures. The vast majority of game buildings are made of timber. All of them get more expensive with each subsequent building. Roughly half the Wonders that can be built in the game require large amounts of timber, too. This should be quite enough to convince you to put a priority on developing a timber industry. You already know you'll need plenty of timber to build a food industry. Well, you'll also need plenty of timber for building just about anything else; just look at the stats available in game.

Tip

Build granaries! You do need only one granary to conduct granary research, but you should build one in every city with a full set of farms. Remember that a new farm needs a citizen to work it; a granary doesn't. Building granaries lets you create more military units within your current population limit.

- **Research.** Players that begin in the Ancient Age are due for a particularly heavy timber hit: You need a lot to research Science level 1 just at the time when it's desperately needed for everything else. Later, you'll need timber for mainstream Commerce and scholar productivity techs.

- **New units.** From Ancient through Enlightenment Age, the health of your military depends on timber. It's needed for all ranged attack units (light infantry, too). Juggling military and construction timber needs is so difficult that if you opt for the military route, it's better to follow through fully and capture cities rather than build them from scratch. Both caravans and merchants require timber; merchants can be a problem because you'll be sending them out while concurrently expanding in all other areas, and the cost (30 timber and 10 gold for the first merchant, 10 more of each for every subsequent merchant) can hurt. Caravans aren't really cheaper (10 food and 30 timber for the first, 10 food and 5 timber more for each subsequent), but they're easier to accommodate because you'll be creating more merchants than caravans in the early game.

Building a strong timber industry is much easier than building a strong food industry. A single farm can accommodate just one citizen worker who produces 10 food (national bonuses excepted). A single wood-cutter's camp can accommodate, in practice, up to 12 workers (see Figure 3.3; once in a blue moon you'll get 13 or 14). Your first camp costs 50 food, every subsequent camp 20 food more. In most games you'll be hitting the timber production cap (just 70 units at the starting Commerce level) with the very first camp you build. Unlike farms, camps can be built outside city limits, but still must be built within your national borders. It's easy to achieve a gather rate of 200–250 timber with just three camps, which costs 210 food.

It all adds up to this: You won't regret developing the timber biz first. This doesn't mean ignoring the food industry; that whole strategy is fully explained in Chapter 8. It does mean hitting the timber Commerce cap the moment you research at least the first three Commerce levels. Failure to do so might mean losing the game on anything but the Easiest or Easier difficulty levels, and leaves you without no chance at the three higher difficulty levels (Tough, Tougher, Toughest).

FIGURE 3.3: *This is a good spot for a woodcutter's camp.*

The next sections discuss the means and ways of increasing timber production. Note that rare resources are a fairly reliable source; many provide 10 base timber, as listed in the "Rare Resources" section further on in this chapter.

Woodcutter's Camp

This should be the very first structure you build in all games starting with Nomad or City Center Only. If you start in Nomad mode, your first priority is to find a city site that allows at least one very productive woodcutter's camp within city radius, or two to three less productive ones. Remember that hitting the timber Commerce cap is priority number one! Occasionally, you might have to settle for building a camp outside of city limits, but next to a particularly lush forest. Unfortunately, camps outside city limits aren't included in the timber production bonuses granted by a lumber mill, which can boost city timber production by up to 200%.

Make sure you can protect your camps in times of war! Remember that timber is essential for repairing buildings as well as replacing the ones that get destroyed. In most games, it really pays to locate a couple of camps well away from possible enemy approaches, and shift production there when danger threatens. Unfortunately, placing them within city firing range means the city has to be built close to a forest in the first place, which limits city space available for remaining buildings. See Chapter 8 for more city planning details.

Lumber Mill

A lumber mill increases the timber production of all woodcutter's camps within city radius by 20%; researching appropriate lumber mill technologies will further raise the gather rate by 50%, 100%, and eventually 200%. The other lumber mill research option consists of researching three levels of construction technology, which reduces construction times, increasing the buildings' hit points; see Chapter 4 for research details.

Given the importance of timber, a lumber mill will often be your first production-enhancing building. It's an inexpensive investment, costing just 50 food and 20 metal to start with. Each subsequent lumber mill costs 40 metal extra, however, you'll never need to build more than two if you take the trouble to designate a city or two as timber production centers.

Wonders and Other Means

The Temple of Tikal increases your timber gather rate by 50%, and your timber Commerce cap by 100. Unfortunately it isn't available until Gunpowder Age, which generally makes it an unexciting production-boosting option. The Kremlin raises your timber Commerce limit by 200. Most importantly, numerous rare resources supply timber; the majority provide a 10 timber bonus, but some yield more; see the "Rare Resources" section later on in this chapter.

> **Tip**
>
> *Make sure at least one of your cities, preferably your capital, is a major timber-producing center.*

Final Thoughts on Wood

The timber biz is pretty straightforward. Concentrate on developing it to the point where you can work on two new cities concurrently while creating military units.

Note that quite a few maps are scarce in timber (see Figure 3.4). It's not easy to become a timber potentate in Great Sahara, for example. If you find yourself playing a map like that, put a priority on founding (or capturing) new cities.

Wealth

Wealth is the last of the three economic resources that appear when you begin playing in Ancient Age. Generating wealth is a fascinating mini-game within the game; it

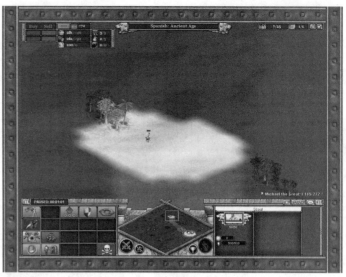

FIGURE 3.4: *Lucky I brought my own toothpicks.*

can be done in an amazing variety of ways, all of which are reviewed here. You need wealth to:

- Create new units. You need wealth to create merchants and many military units. Wealth is partly replaced by oil as a military unit requirement once you advance into the Industrial Age. But life is cruel, and you'll most likely be spending all that extra wealth on oil. Some of the most useful military units (including generals and airplanes) in the game require wealth—lots of wealth. See Chapter 6 for details.

- Build new structures. Not many buildings require wealth, but those that do are indispensable: universities and forts, for example. Wealth is also a requirement for a couple of Wonders (Porcelain Tower, Supercollider). Exact stats can be found in game.

- Conduct research. Again, wealth is not a particularly common requirement in that area, but the advances that require it are very important. Science (mainstream library research) and attrition "technologies" researched at the tower (Allegiance, Oath of Fealty, and the like) are very good examples. See Chapter 4 for more research details.

- Buy needed resources. Researching Commerce level 2 lets you buy and sell resources at the market (see next section). The ability to do so gives you great flexibility and can go a long way toward relieving shortages; for example, the sudden metal shortages that plague most Quick Battle games can be largely alleviated through judicious buying. You have to have the coin, of course; tips here and in Chapter 8 will help you there.

Wealth can assume decisive importance in a game, because wealthy players can weather almost any crisis by buying their way out. The next few sections tell you how to become one of these lucky players.

Secrets of Wealth

Wealth production isn't limited to particular game units or buildings. It's all around you. Literally. All you have to do is pick it up. Just count the ways, friend:

▷ **Markets.** You have to reach Commerce level 1 to build markets. Each market pumps 10 wealth into your coffers and carries a nice building bonus of 35 wealth (building bonuses and their place in empire development strategy are discussed in Chapter 8). Most importantly, owning a market lets you build merchants and caravans, and later also trade in resources (Commerce level 2). The cost of the first market is 80 timber, each subsequent market 30 timber more. It often gets expensive, because you want a market in every city.

▷ **Caravan routes.** Naturally, first you need to either own two cities or have an alliance with a nearby foreign city. Income from caravan routes is influenced by the size of the connected cities and the dis-

tance between them, number of buildings in the connected cities, and whether the route is national or international. Caravans to allied nations' cities are worth more money, but their income is split between you and your allied trading partner. You'll be getting your share from *their* caravans to your cities, too—the A.I. is quick to set them up. The main rule you should remember is that caravan income always increases with time: You can usually count on a 300% increase within 2–3 Ages, provided you don't retard city development (see

FIGURE 3.5: *Build a second city fast just so you can start a caravan route.*

Figure 3.5). Thus a caravan that begins by bringing in 11 wealth contributes 30 or 40 wealth by the time Age advances turn it into a truck.

▷ **Temples.** The temple is your second most important moneymaking building, and that doesn't mean just the 25 wealth building bonus. A temple lets you research increasingly effective ways of collecting a sort of real estate tax, plus new means of increasing your territory, which brings in still more tax (see Chapter 4 for research details). It's a beautiful little scheme but shouldn't be jumped into too early; researching Taxation isn't inexpensive, and commonly yields just 8–10 wealth with your initial pair of cities (capital plus brand new city; exact income can vary according to map, proximity of other nations, and so on). Your first temple costs 80 timber, each subsequent temple 30 timber more. It gets very expensive because enemy cities are easier to capture if you destroy the city temple first, and once they become yours, you want a temple in there too, for obvious reasons.

- Merchants and fishermen. Many rare resources exploited by merchants and fishermen contribute 10 or even 20 wealth (which can be boosted further by researching the three levels of taxation—see Chapter 4). As explained earlier, merchant costs, although not high, often have to be incurred at a particularly expensive time, and can be a bother. Fishermen are even more expensive if you consider you need to build a dock first, however, they receive a terrific production boost once you research the agriculture line of techs at the granary: up to 200%.

- Industry buildings. Any building that produces or boosts production of resources is automatically a moneymaker once you can trade it, which is early (Commerce level 2).

- Any buildings/structures within city limits. Every single thing you build inside the city radius increases the income from caravan routes to that city by one wealth per building. Farm, mine, temple, market, barracks, tower, lumber mill—they all count.

- City size. This ties in with the number of buildings within city limits. As you know from the in-game city panel, a certain number of buildings plus Age advance brings about an increase in city size (for instance, five buildings plus Medieval Age turns a Small city into a Large one). Each increase in city size increases the value of caravan routes to that city over the income provided by the buildings within city limits. Your territory increases in size along with your cities; the larger the city, the stronger its effect on your national borders (+2 for each increase).

FIGURE 3.6: *Forts are worth every penny spent.*

- Territory size. More territory means more tax income and longer caravan routes; longer routes make more money. Don't try to save on building forts (see Figure 3.6)! They cost a lot of metal plus wealth, but increase your national territory and thus tax income. They also significantly cut military casualties, which saves plenty.

- Research. This doesn't just mean just Commerce; it means practically all research. That might seem far-fetched, but consider: Civic advances enlarge your territory and let you research increasingly efficient forms of taxation; Science research cuts research costs in general, lets you build production-boosting buildings, and subsequently research production-boosting techs; Military lets you build better military units, which means fewer losses and more captured cities plus adjoining territory.

- Plunder. If you're a good military leader, this can mean periodical bonanzas of all game resources except knowledge (knowledge cannot be seized, bought, or sold, which makes *RoN* a highly idealistic game and should silence anyone critical of the large number of corpses that tend to appear).

Wonders and other means. The Colossus, Porcelain Tower, and Taj Mahal affect your wealth very directly and drastically, however, practically all Wonders bring potential wealth benefits. The same applies to rare resources; they're worth money even if they don't produce wealth as such. Yet other means include forcing other players to pay you tribute.

The one other thing you need to become wealthy is patience. You cannot expect three small cities with caravan routes to satisfy your needs right away. You have to make the cities grow along with your industries.

Final Thoughts on Wealth

Becoming wealthy requires logical, consistent development of your whole empire. Look to that, and the money thing will work out all by itself. Do not be afraid to trade through the market; just watch how much you sell! Consistently selling a single resource in large amounts depresses its market price quickly and fairly permanently.

Market prices rise and fall within limits defined by other factors: commodity selling patterns, stock levels, production, and finally a random factor. Becoming the Wheat or Timber King isn't a solution: It will drive the price of the oversold commodity very low. There's no limit to how high or low prices can go, but it's far easier to drive the selling price down to one wealth (per 100 units) than to raise it to more than 100. In consolation, buying prices rarely rise over 200 wealth per 100 units.

To get good money for your stuff, sell excess units in small batches, varying commodities: a couple hundred timber, then a couple hundred food is often the pattern in the later stages of the game. Similarly, space out purchases over a period if you can. Don't wait for the actual emergency to strike! Emergencies tend to come in pairs, sometimes even groups.

Metal

Metal makes an appearance in Classical Age and gradually grows in importance for the rest of the game. Its value rises especially sharply when you enter Industrial Age; however, note that in non-violent games, metal is of marginal importance. As the list here shows, almost all its practical applications are military. You need metal to:

- Create new military units. At first, metal-consuming units consist of just heavy infantry, heavy cavalry, and artillery. The bubble grows and bursts with Industrial Age: all of a sudden, you'll need tons of metal to control land, sea, and air. See Chapters 7 and 9 for more details.
- Research. Metal is a factor in all military-related research after Ancient Age: both in the library and out of it (for example, attrition techs at the tower). See Chapter 4 for research details.
- Build structures. Structures that require metal fall into a few distinct classes. All military buildings that don't produce new military units, such as towers and forts, require metal. The second group is oil industry buildings (oil well, oil platform, refinery). Lumber mills also require metal, and several later-Age Wonders require *substantial* amounts of metal.

Metal is a relatively scarce resource. Even maps that abound in metal-bearing mountains and/or cliffs yield less metal than timber as a rule. It's fortunate that for much of the game you need less metal than timber. Things change radically in the last three Ages; plan ahead!

Mine

There can be only one mine per mountain/cliff, and you'll occasionally go to war because of that. Mine productivity depends on the size on the mountain/cliff it adjoins *and* whether it falls within your national borders (that will lead to a couple of wars, too). Mines aren't expensive: 50 timber for the first, 20 more timber for each subsequent; however, a mine site that will accommodate many workers is much harder to find than a comparable site for a woodcutter's camp. Mines that produce 50–70 metal are the norm; occasionally you'll be able to cross 100.

Smelter

The smelter is a very valuable building: In addition to boosting the metal production of all mines within city limits by 20%, it lets you research advances that reduce your army's vulnerability to attrition. Like with other production-boosting buildings, you can also research boosting metal production by 50%, 100%, and 200%. Making a point of being ahead with metal production can win a

game! Unfortunately, prior to building a smelter you have to research Science level 3 (one level higher than required for a granary or a lumber mill). Your first smelter will cost 70 timber and 50 wealth; each subsequent smelter costs 40 timber more. Most games will see you building just a couple of smelters, so this won't break your back.

Wonders and Other Means

The Angkor Wat is the designated metal Wonder (+50 metal to production, +100 to metal commerce cap). It has other wonderful benefits fully described in Chapter 5; what you should note for now is that it arrives on the scene with perfect timing: Enlightenment Age, right before the big metal hunger begins. The Kremlin increases your metal Commerce cap by 200. Other Wonders (Statue of Liberty, Space Program) have an indirect effect.

You can also obtain metal by sending a merchant or a fisherman to exploit an appropriate rare resource. This is especially helpful in the earlier stages of the game. Naturally, you can also blackmail a weaker nation into a metal tribute (Diplomacy games). Plunder can be a surprisingly good source.

Final Thoughts on Metal

A game that begins in the Ancient/Classical Age can be over before Industrial Age comes along. If it isn't, metal suddenly becomes almost as important as oil. You might have had enough metal all along to build strong armies and multiple forts; once tanks and airplanes appear on the scene, you'll get a chance to replenish metal reserves only if you run short of oil and/or the wealth to buy oil.

Oil

Oil is the stuff that nearly turns everything onto its head when it appears in Industrial Age. What's more, on many land-only maps, oil is available in meager quantities: Not every rocky patch is an oil field! This is probably why every refinery boosts the production of *all* the oil wells and platforms in your territory. Oil is needed for three purposes:

- Creating new military units. A modern military drinks up oil as if there were no tomorrow. It results in a major drain on all your resources: You'll be selling plenty of food and timber at rock-bottom prices just to buy a little more oil.
- Building new military structures. There are only a couple that require oil, but both are important (air base, missile silo).
- Research. Specifically, oil is needed to advance to Modern and then Information Age. As you might guess, both of these Age advances are crucial.

This list might be short, but the needs are long. The oil field situation is often better on sea maps, but owning oil platforms necessitates owning a powerful navy as well as air force (which soaks up all the extra oil, and often more). If you must see what a big oil surplus looks like, play a solo sandbox game.

Tip

Some land maps such as the Old World have little oil; others (Great Sahara, Australian Outback) have plenty. You can check out each and every map type's potential by setting the game to start in Information Age with All Revealed (Quick Battle Options screen).

Oil Well/Platform

Oil wells come in land and sea varieties (platforms). They both cost 100 timber and 50 metal to begin with, and both produce 40 oil; however, the cost of the oil wells grows in increments of 15 timber and 15 metal for each extra well, while platforms grow in increments of 20. Platforms are also much easier to destroy than oil wells (because of the big difference in hit points as well as difficulties inherent in a sea defense). They're expensive, they're invaluable, and they can be a source of both oil and constant worries.

Refinery

You need to research Science level 6 to build a refinery. You can build one per city, and you should as long as you can afford it. Every new refinery increases the output of all your oil wells/platforms by 10 oil each (25%). Four refineries mean doubled output. If you're still fighting for victory in modern times, be aware that refineries make prime strategic targets for missile and air strikes.

Final Thoughts on Oil

There's never enough oil, unless you play an oil-rich map (Great Sahara, Australian Outback) against inferior opponents. In other words, you'll have enough oil only when you don't need it. You'd be wise to build up a cash reserve before advancing to Industrial Age; instantly buying 1,000 units of oil is mandatory in serious games. Oil is truly a strategic industry in the game: Protecting yours and damaging or destroying the enemy's always belongs among your top strategic priorities.

Rare Resources

One of the nicer features of *RoN* is that it features rare resources: little treasure troves scattered around the countryside. Most rare resources yield 20 units of basic game resources: 10 food and 10 timber, for example, or 10 wealth and 10 knowledge. In addition to these 20 units, a rare resource usually confers a special benefit: It might be cheaper military units, a bonus to your national border, ships that heal at sea, and so on. All rare resources and their benefits are listed here and accompanied by short comments. These are meant to help you make decisions concerning exploiting a rare resource yourself and destroying the enemy's (see Figure 3.7).

Not all rare resources are present in the game from Ancient Age. Some appear later; the entries here note that where applicable. These latecomers usually carry bigger resource bonuses.

FIGURE 3.7: *In the late game, helicopters are great weapons for hitting enemy merchants.*

- Aluminum. +20 metal, +20 oil. Appears in Industrial Age. Special bonus: Aircraft are 25% faster, and cost 15% less. An extremely valuable resource in the end game—provided the game's outcome hasn't been decided yet.

- Amber. +10 timber, +10 wealth. Special haggling bonus: Market prices (buy and sell) are adjusted 10% in your favor. A very handy resource, particularly once you've researched Commerce level 2 (which you'll do quickly).

- Bison. +20 food. Special bonus: Granary-based research costs 33% less. Not exactly a showstopper, but good value once you've got a few farms and building more gets expensive.

- Citrus. +10 food, +10 timber. Special bonus: Ships at sea heal automatically (usually they must be docked to do so). This is a very nice rare resource with a value that skyrockets on every sea map. Might be worth fighting over!

- Coal. +15 metal, +15 knowledge. Appears in Industrial Age. Special timber bonus: all timber costs (buildings, units, research, etc) are reduced by a whopping 25%. Very, very useful.

- Copper. +20 metal. Special bonus: Factory and dock-made units (later artillery, ships throughout the game) have +20% hit points. Another very useful rare resource that you should grab the moment you've advanced to Classical Age. Especially important on sea maps; grows in value when you enter the end game.

- Cotton. +20 timber. Special bonus: Barracks, stable, and dock units are created 25% faster. The timber bonus is very handy in the earlier stages of the game, less important later. The ability to make units slightly faster might be helpful now and then, but doesn't exactly make or break your empire unless special circumstances occur.

- Diamonds. +20 wealth. Very special bonus: Commerce cap is raised 10%. Predictably, a very valuable rare resource that should be exploited as soon as it's discovered. It's especially helpful in the early game!

- Dye. +10 wealth, +10 knowledge. Special research bonus: Civic research costs 25% less. This one's very helpful in the early to middle game, less so later. It's a very nice resource that facilitates Science research, too (it costs wealth and knowledge later on in the game).

- Fish. +10 food, +10 wealth. No special bonus. This rare resource's value is comparable to that of cotton even though it does not have a special bonus. Particularly helpful early on in the game, but requires sending a fisherman instead of a merchant. This in turn requires building a dock first.

- Furs. +10 food, +10 metal. Special military bonus: Mainstream (library) military research costs 25% less. This is a nice resource that becomes more valuable as military research grows more expensive (it's not that expensive to start with).

- Gems. +10 wealth, +10 knowledge. Special border bonus: national borders +2. This is one of the best rare resources in the game and is definitely worth fighting over!

- Horses. +10 food, +10 metal. Special military bonus: All units created at the stable cost 15% less. This is very valuable in the early to middle game, somewhat less so later.

- Marble. +10 timber, +10 metal. Special Wonder bonus: Constructing any Wonder costs 10% less. An extremely valuable rare resource that, unfortunately, doesn't show up very often.

- Obsidian. +10 metal, +10 knowledge. Superior bonus: Ranged attack infantry (bowmen unit line), cities, forts, and towers gain one attack. It's extremely valuable in the early stages of the game, very valuable throughout the game. Grab it!

- Papyrus. +10 timber, +10 knowledge. Special science bonus: Science research costs 25% less. This is very valuable from Classical Age onward.

- Peacocks. +10 metal. Special bonus: Population limit is increased by 10%. Initially somewhat unexciting, the value of this rare resource rises greatly as the game goes on.

- Salt. +10 timber, +10 metal. Special military bonus: All barracks units (infantry) cost 15% less. A very nice, solid rare resource that will suit warmongers especially well.

- Relics. +20 knowledge. Special research bonus: All research, mainstream or not, takes 33% less time. A uniquely valuable rare resource that is quite common on all maps. Worth fighting a whole war in some circumstances, and grabbing as soon as you see it even though the knowledge bonus is worthless in Ancient Age.

- Rubber. +20 timber, +20 oil. Appears in Industrial Age. Special military bonus: All auto plant units cost 15% less. It's very valuable in the end game because it lets you assemble an armored corps fast.

- Silk. +10 timber, +10 wealth. Special research bonus: Commerce research costs 25% less. An extremely valuable resource in the early/middle game, and only slightly less so in the end game.

- Silver. +10 metal, +10 wealth. Special research bonus: All Age advances cost 15% less. An extremely valuable rare resource throughout the game.

- Sugar. +10 food, +10 timber. Special food bonus: All food costs (units, research, Wonders, and the like) are reduced by 10%. This is extremely valuable until the end game, when its value decreases quite sharply.

- Sulphur. +15 metal, +15 wealth. Appears in Gunpowder Age. Special military bonus: Artillery costs 20% less. This is a very nice rare resource to own as soon as it appears in the middle game.
- Tobacco. +10 wealth, +10 knowledge. Special construction bonus: Citizens build new buildings 10% faster. This is extremely useful in the early to middle game, slightly less so later on.
- Titanium. +20 food, +20 oil. Appears in Industrial Age. Special military bonus: Attrition in enemy territory is reduced by 50%. Useful when it appears, mainly thanks to the oil bonus; the attrition bonus might matter little in the end game, when smelter-based anti-attrition techs have been fully researched.
- Uranium. +20 metal, +20 oil. Appears in Industrial Age. Special bonus: Nuclear missiles are 33% faster and cost 20% less. This is extremely valuable and deadly in the end game.
- Whales. +10 food, +10 metal. Special bonus: Ships are 20% faster. A very important rare resource— if you're going to build a navy. Somewhat less valuable otherwise. Requires sending a fisherman.
- Wine. +10 food, +10 knowledge. Special military bonus: Unit upgrade research costs 20% less. It's a valuable asset throughout the early and middle game; less important in the end game.
- Wool. +10 timber, +10 knowledge. Special economic bonus: Citizens are created 33% faster and cost 15% less. It's a very useful rare resource in the early to middle game; its importance decreases later.

There are no useless rare resources; all are useful. If you don't need it, you can sell it: An unneeded +10 timber brings in 4–5 wealth on the average (provided you keep an eye on market prices and sell prudently, as explained earlier).

The downside is that both merchants and fishermen are very fragile, and make ideal targets for the enemy. They're easily destroyed by infantry and cavalry (even light cavalry); it's often a good idea to erect a tower nearby. Naturally, you should attack enemy merchants whenever you get the chance, too.

> **Note**
>
> Merchants and fishermen are very efficient workers; on the average, one merchant or fisherman is worth three working citizens. This lets you save resources and build more military units within your population limit.

Two Rules for Getting Rich

Happily, getting rich in *RoN* is easier than in real life. You can achieve it through the following means:

- Increased production. *RoN* lets you boost production of resources in several ways. You can build new resource-gathering structures (farms, woodcutters' camps, mines, oil wells, and the like), which gets increasingly expensive with each structure built. You can send out merchants to exploit special resources (such as wine, spice, gems), which yield one or more needed commodities plus special bonuses (see the "Rare Resources" section earlier in this chapter for details). After conducting relevant research, you can build special buildings that provide a resource production bonus (granary, lumber mill, smelter, refinery). Specialized research conducted in these buildings provides yet more production benefits. You might also enjoy higher production through selecting one of the many *RoN* nations that have special economic bonuses, such as the Nubians, Germans, Egyptians, and Japanese.

Wise spending. It is always much easier to squander resources than to produce them. Squandering resources occurs very frequently, even among the best players, because it's easy to get carried away by the excitement of the game. Wise spending is absolutely necessary to win solo games at the Toughest level, where the computer player(s) enjoys greatly boosted resource gather rates.

You may also choose to stack the deck a little by playing a nation that enjoys economic advantages.

National Economies

As you know from the game and from Chapter 1, practically all nations have unique economic bonuses. The next sections review these briefly, providing basic advice on national economies. For entertainment as well as practical purposes, each nation is assigned its "birthstone" rare resource.

FIGURE 3.8: *Fast Bantu progress even faster with wool.*

Aztecs. The Aztec economic bonuses derive from war; peace isn't a good option. The earlier you step on the warpath, the better; and that's why the ideal Aztec rare resource is cotton. The extra timber makes it easier to build your economy while creating new military units, and the increased unit creation speed is most helpful when you've got only a couple of military-unit-producing structures.

Bantu. You enjoy a strong economic bonus with the Bantu thanks to the ease with which you can found new cities. It's best to enjoy a moment of peace to start with, so that you actually get to build a few cities before beginning to capture them. The Bantu optimum rare resource: wool (see Figure 3.8). It will help you speed the development of your empire still more!

British. The British enjoy one of the strongest national economic bonuses in the game: a higher Commerce cap and doubled income from taxation. The British economy easily thrives in both peace and war; economic matters aside, British forts and towers have extra range, while the bowmen line of ranged infantry is upgraded free of charge. Reinforcing these bonuses with obsidian will make your forts, towers, and ranged infantry the most lethal in the game, which might give you an unbeatable advantage.

Chinese. On the surface, the Chinese economic advantages consist solely of Large cities from the beginning of the game, but you've been advised of the wealth angle, and so you know that the Chinese bonus to Science research can have profound economic consequences. Dye is an ideal rare resource that complements the Chinese national bonuses: It makes Science advances even easier, and throws in cheaper Civics research as well. The Chinese economy works best in times of peace.

- **Egyptians.** The Egyptians have the best farms in the game: They can build seven per city, and each farm produces 2 wealth over any contribution to caravan route value. The "national" rare resource of marble lets you really put to use the Egyptian bonus of two allowable Wonders per city. The Egyptian economy rivals the British in terms of potential, but performs slightly better in peace than in war.

- **French.** The French lumber bonus helps you wage war without neglecting the economic development of your empire. The French economy is thus particularly suited for warmongers, although it doesn't fare badly in peacetime, either. The "national" rare resource is silver. Silver's metal bonus contributes to creating plenty of military units, and its unique research bonus lets you stay ahead in research in spite of all the costly fighting.

- **Germans.** The German economic bonus is particularly advantageous in the early game thanks to their +50% building completion bonus, and early acquisition of production-enhancing buildings and techs. Also, their extra city production means production that's lost only when you lose the city, not the moment a couple of workers get hacked down by raiding enemy cavalry. This puts the robust German economy at its best advantage in wartime. Diamonds are the ideal rare resource: The higher Commerce cap lets you take better advantage of extra city production, while the strong wealth bonus is especially helpful in early wars.

- **Greeks.** The Greek national bonuses all pertain to Science and research. In economic terms, this means you'll be able to save resources in these areas while modernizing your industry, hopefully a step ahead of the others. It's always easier to pursue this course in peacetime than during a war. The Greek national bonuses are ideally complemented by relics +20 knowledge and +33% to research speed. It makes acquiring new technologies really easy.

FIGURE 3.9: *This boy is worth his weight in gold.*

- **Inca.** Here, we enter El Dorado: Every metal miner produces 10 wealth (see Figure 3.9), plus you enjoy a higher wealth Commerce cap (33%). You'll have quite a lot of wealth, and as you know the biggest asset of wealth is the flexibility it gives you. Avoid war; it's easy to lose all these Midas miners to marauding enemy raiders. Best rare resource: amber. It will let you take advantage of better market prices.

- **Japanese.** The Japanese enjoy a food bonus that rivals the Egyptians': a 25% productivity boost for every farmer and fisherman. Salt complements the Japanese food bonus with metal and timber, and makes the already cheap Japanese infantry still less expensive. Naturally, you should exploit all these advantages by fighting.

- **Koreans.** What good are extra, free citizens if you're already pushing the population limit? Peacocks are the Korean rare resource of choice, also kicking in some metal toward the attrition research line in the free temple. The Korean economy decidedly prefers peace to war.

- **Maya.** The Maya build stronger buildings with less timber, which gives them a nice head start in economic development, however, they aren't especially strong militarily and have to compensate with a more modern army; furs will help. The Maya economy prefers peace.

- **Mongols.** This is another nation whose bonuses favor warmongers. Mongols enjoy a unique economic bonus that depends on the number of competing nations and the percentage of game world territory under Mongol control; at the start of a new game, it can amount to anything between five (poor starting location, one opponent) and 40 (excellent starting location, seven opponents). Best rare resource: horses. Creating hordes of cavalry has never been easier!

- **Nubians.** This nation has super-strong economic advantages that function best in times of peace. Amber increases the Nubian market price bonus to 30%, meaning you can actually swap one resource for another (for example, food for timber) without losing money. Yes, amber again! It can be worth more than silver.

- **Romans.** The modest Roman economic bonus (10 wealth per city) works best when priming early flames of war. Best rare resource: gems, reinforcing the national border bonus conferred by Roman forts.

- **Russians.** The big Russian economic bonus kicks in only in the Industrial Age, but it's very nice: +20% to oil gather rate! Best rare resource: titanium, just because then no one else gets to exploit it. Best economic time: peace.

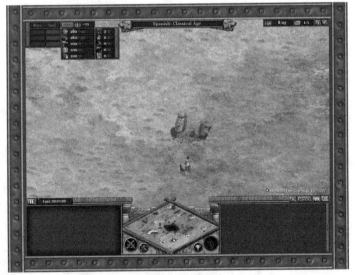

FIGURE 3.10: *I'd be clever, too, with a head like that.*

- **Spanish**. The Spanish are predestined to favor Dye (see Figure 3.10), just like the Chinese! Dye complements Spanish exploration bonuses (revealed map, 35 knowledge from Ruins, extra 35 knowledge with each new Science level) by supplying extra wealth and knowledge, which are both needed for Science research. Cheaper Civic research means it will be easier to put your knowledge of the game world to practical use by building new cities in just the right spots.. The Spanish economy is indifferent—in peace, in war, and in general.

- **Turks.** Cheap citizens and Military research (costs for both reduced by 33%) are the main Turkish economic assets. Free artillery upgrades plus other national bonuses predestine this nation for war. The rare resource of choice is sulphur, which makes the lethal Turkish artillery less expensive.

Keep in mind that these descriptions are done with a tongue in cheek; although the advice certainly works, specific game circumstances wield great influence over the respective importance of all rare resources. A couple of obvious examples: Citrus is of mediocre value on land-only maps, but blooms on sea maps. Cotton won't matter much on an Amazon Rainforest map, but will be more valuable than diamonds on the Great Sahara.

As far as national choices go, be guided by your own gaming experience in addition to the national bonuses. A new player might have problems developing the Spanish into a victorious power, but the experienced player will find them an excellent choice. You have to know how to trade to take full advantage of the Nubian bonuses; you have to know how to assemble armies and organize sieges when you play the Turks; the Maya bonuses won't mean much to many experienced gamers, but newcomers might find them very helpful. Chapter 8 contains comprehensive strategies, while the next, Chapter 4, explains research.

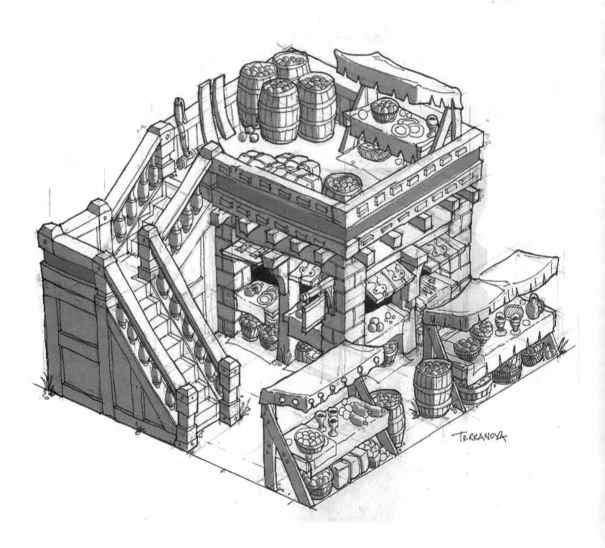

CHAPTER 3 Rags to Riches: The Game Economy

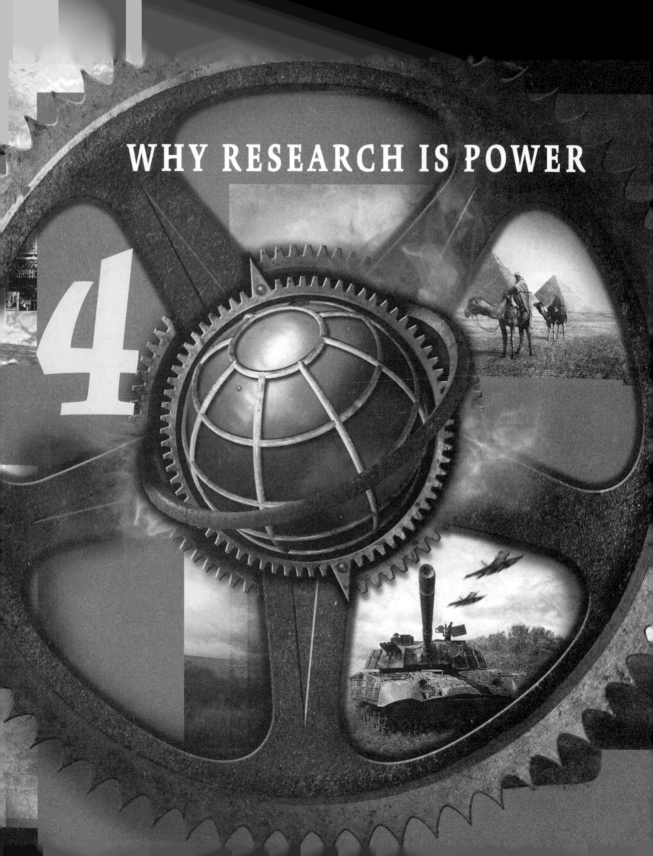

WHY RESEARCH IS POWER

4

Acquiring new advances, technologies, and upgrades is one of the most important and interesting activities in Rise of Nations. It's vital for victory, and adds great depth to the game. This chapter examines research in RoN, discussing in detail the meaning and consequences of every advance. You'll also find some general do's and don'ts that should be useful, but bear in mind the first and foremost factor determining your research strategy is your situation. For example, playing the Romans with their city wealth bonus means less emphasis on researching Commerce and building a market.

The special character of research in campaign games is discussed in Chapter 10.

RESEARCH ABCs

There are many types of research possible in *Rise of Nations*, but they all belong to one of two categories:

- Mainstream (library) research. This includes five research lines, from top to bottom: Age advances (orange icon), followed by four areas of research: Military (red icon), Civic (blue), Commerce (green), and Science (yellow). Age advances carry the most significance, but don't let this lead you into thinking the ordering of the four research types (Military to Science) reflects their order of importance.

- Non-library research. This generic moniker embraces the specialized research conducted in buildings such as the granary, barracks, temple, or fort. One of the secrets of winning consistently is learning that some of this seemingly less important research plays a vital role, and all of it is important.

All non-library research requires prior mainstream research. At the same time, the non-library techs and upgrades often assume such importance that you'll be setting mainstream research priorities just to acquire a non-library upgrade. Note that some nations receive

FIGURE 4.1: *The Greek research advantage is most pronounced in the early stages of the game.*

certain non-library techs and upgrades for free as national bonuses, but that all mainstream advances have to be acquired the hard way. Greeks and the Chinese enjoy important advantages that make things easier (see Figure 4.1).

One thing you should be very aware of: The A.I. conducts mainstream research with dazzling efficiency. You'll have to make an effort to keep up on all games but those played on the two easiest difficulty levels. Keeping up with the computer while playing on the two toughest difficulty levels is impossible unless your opponent is in a war that isn't going too well. Players who want to play a peaceful game at a high difficulty level are practically doomed to lose because of the A.I.'s research efficiency.

Understanding Research Costs

The one outstanding feature of research costs is that they can change drastically depending on both pre-game and game choices. Pre-game choices include setting Technology cost (pull-down menu on the Options panel) to one of the following:

 Cheap. All research costs are 50% of the Normal rate. This makes things so cheap it worsens the gameplay. Important advances end up costing less than a couple more military units (excluding knowledge costs). Computer opponents like this setting; it allows them to progress noticeably more efficiently than usual. At tougher difficulty levels, they'll murder you.

 Normal. Standard rates for everything. Research is still reasonably priced—*very* reasonably at times—however, it requires some budgeting, particularly in times of war. The computer opponent is very comfortable with this setting; at tougher difficulty levels, you'll constantly find yourself behind. All research costs quoted in this book relate to the Normal setting.

 Expensive. Age advance costs are increased 50%; all other research costs are increased 25%. This slightly slows the pace of the game; research requires budgeting, but doesn't present any great difficulties. Things might get tight in times of war. The computer opponent performs efficiently, although its edge is somewhat blunted. You might get ahead here and there without resorting to war.

 Very Expensive. Age advance costs are increased 100%; all other research costs are increased 50%. This requires careful budgeting of resources throughout the game and causes repeated resource-related crises in times of war, however, this is the setting the computer opponents like least. The A.I.'s strong focus on mainstream research means computer opponents might lack, or be unwilling to spend, resources needed for other important stuff, such as military units. This setting works well in games played on higher difficulty levels, and on larger maps where abundance of resources might make research costs semi-irrelevant.

> ### Note
>
> The game also lets you pre-set research speed. Unlike changing research costs, this doesn't carry serious consequences; setting the research speed to Very Slow is helpful when playing solo games because of the A.I.'s ruthless research efficiency. Arguably, it also gives things a nicer feel.

Once you start playing, your research priorities can significantly affect research costs. As you know from the game and the manual, each Science level reduces the costs of all research by 10%. This includes all the non-library research, so trying to calculate the savings just by looking at the library research costs might be very misleading.

Advancing to Classical Age drastically rearranges research costs (see next section). Timing it well is extremely important. The newly introduced resources—metal and knowledge—are instantly in great demand and nonexistent supply.

There's a quick way around the Classical Age research resource shortages. All you need to do is make a couple of extra advances while still in Ancient Age, paying with food and timber. In all cost-related cases, the game substitutes an existing resource for a resource that hasn't been discovered by your nation (see Figure 4.2). Here's which resource replaces which, and the ratio between the two:

FIGURE 4.2: *You can research all non-Age advances for just timber and food.*

- Food is substituted for knowledge. For example: Researching Science level 2 in Classical Age costs 120 wealth and 80 knowledge, but researching it in Ancient Age costs 120 wealth and 120 food. The ratio is three food for two knowledge.
- Timber is substituted for metal. This is primarily useful when constructing certain military buildings (see Chapters 6 and 8), but it also lets you research Military level 2 and pay 120 timber (Ancient Age) instead of 100 metal (Classical Age). Ratio: five timber for four metal.

Later on, the game also substitutes metal for oil as necessary (3:2 ratio), but that's of no importance to research. You cannot advance to Modern Age without researching Industrial Age.

The next sections discuss specific research, including their costs. Note that the cost given is base cost: It assumes you'll be researching an advance while in the corresponding Age. For instance, the base cost of Science level 2 is given as 120 wealth and 80 knowledge, but it would be 120 food and 120 wealth when researched in Ancient Age. Every Science advance reduces research costs by 10%, so staying ahead in that field will greatly cut research costs. Finally, selected rare resources can let you save plenty (see Chapter 3).

The Price of Knowledge

Knowledge is gained by building universities, creating scholars, and exploiting rare resources with a knowledge bonus (see Chapter 3). Your first university will set you back by 60 timber and 30 wealth; each subsequent university costs 20 timber and 20 wealth more. Scholars can get very expensive! Each university can accommodate just seven scholars; the first one costs 30 wealth, while each of the next six costs two wealth more. However, when you try to fill your second university with scholars, you'll find that the cost increase for each subsequent scholar is three wealth; with your third, university, four wealth; and so on. It can get very expensive, and on top of everything else scholars count toward your population limit.

The A.I. is always very keen to acquire knowledge; in the later game, a university is often the first building to be completed in a new computer-controlled city. Don't let it scare you too much! The A.I. often concentrates on the acquisition of knowledge at the cost of ignoring other issues; you'll often see nations that have advanced to a relatively late Age using earlier-Age military units. The golden rule is this: if you're not in a position to reap rewards from extra knowledge, don't invest heavy money in it until you are.

MAINSTREAM RESEARCH

The mainstream research panel is accessed by clicking on the library, and it displays a certain oddity. There are eight Ages in all (Ancient Age, in which you begin, counts as Age I), but seven levels in the four other research lines (Military, Civic, Commerce, and Science). This apparent imbalance is rectified once you research everything that's available. A new library research panel that appears features the "missing" eighth level for all four non-Age research lines (see Figure 4.3). You can get a quick preview by starting a solo sandbox (no opponents) game in Information Age.

The in-game tooltip texts already give exhaustive information about each advance. The following entries are meant to complement the game manual's and in-game info, not replace it.

Age Advances

The Age advances are the most important in the game because they let you update military units. It's as simple as that. Of course there are other consequences, all briefly reviewed here. Note that if any single opponent reaches a given Age before you, your cost to advance to that Age drops by 10%.

CLASSICAL AGE

FIGURE 4.3: *The game's four futuristic technologies become available only once all other library research is completed.*

- ◆ **Base Cost:** 250 food.
- ◆ **Prerequisite:** Two library advances.

This is the most revolutionary single advance in the game. Classical Age opens the door to important lines of non-mainstream research, and is a prerequisite for more new buildings than any other single advance: mines, universities, forts, stables, siege factories, all resource production-enhancing buildings (keep in mind many buildings require other advances too). It's wise to line up both resources and extra labor to begin construction of those that are most needed (universities and mines) immediately upon advancing to Classical Age. Ideally, you should have two or three cities before you advance to Classical Age; its new buildings mean you'll find it very difficult to concurrently found new cities.

Researching Classical Age requires just two level-1 techs, but is made difficult by the fact that Military, Commerce, and Civic level 1 all require food, too. And on top of that, the early stages of any game see you creating many new citizens.

MEDIEVAL AGE

> **Base Cost:** 250 food, 250 knowledge.

> **Prerequisite:** Classical Age, four new library advances.

The Medieval Age ushers in a new era in warfare: It lets you build supply wagons and employ spies, which are invaluable in planning and executing a military campaign (see Figure 4.4). It's also a prerequisite to some non-mainstream research of military relevance (Oath of Fealty, Tactics, and so on), and lets Small cities turn into Large cities as long as they've got the necessary five types of buildings.

FIGURE 4.4: *The science of war begins to bloom in the Medieval Age.*

Advancing to Medieval Age is necessary for an offensive war if your enemy has attrition techs; you'll need supply wagons to keep your army hale and healthy.

GUNPOWDER AGE

> **Base Cost:** 500 food, 500 knowledge.

> **Prerequisite:** Medieval Age, four new non-Age advances.

Gunpowder Age is misleading. It has less impact on military matters than it might appear—definitely less so than Classical or Medieval Age—but in any game, appearances count a lot, and Gunpowder Age brings about a big change in how things look. Cities acquire the glitter of cosmopolitan centers, and battlefields are lit up with bright muzzle flashes and wreathed in smoke. You'll love it, and it will probably influence you to advance into Gunpowder Age even when it isn't absolutely the best time to do so in game terms. The change in appearances includes caravans: They change into horse-drawn carts.

ENLIGHTENMENT AGE

⏩ **Base Cost:** 500 food, 1,000 knowledge.

⏩ **Prerequisite:** Gunpowder Age, four new non-Age advances.

Enlightenment Age is noteworthy for two big reasons. It's the last stop in an oil-less world, and smart players will double their efforts to bring a few more promising rocky patches (potential oil fields) under control. The other major change is in the firepower of military units equipped with firearms. You no longer need artillery to destroy buildings reasonably quickly; infantry can do the job against all but the toughest structures. Artillery remains attractive because it becomes noticeably less vulnerable as well as more powerful, so you'll be building plenty of cannon too, don't fear.

The net result is that Enlightenment Age allows you to engage in a war of maneuver. Chapters 6 and 9 have more details; for now let's just say you acquire a new flexibility that gives you more battlefield options. All these benefits don't come cheaply: 1,000 knowledge is a lot.

INDUSTRIAL AGE

⏩ **Base Cost:** 500 food, 1,500 knowledge.

⏩ **Prerequisites:** Enlightenment Age, four new non-Age advances.

Advancing to this Age will be the watershed of almost every game (see Figure 4.5). The first couple of players to reach it are automatically serious contenders for victory. The Industrial Age brings a military revolution along with the industrial one; all earlier-era military units are instantly completely obsolete (this is not the case with previous Age advances). The new resource needs (more metal, oil) might rearrange the order among the economic superpowers and grant new hope to the lucky losers who happen to have many oil fields on their shrinking territory.

FIGURE 4.5: *Industrial Age brings sweeping changes to the game economy.*

Be prepared! Stock up on all resources to trade for oil on the market as soon as you enter Industrial Age, and have citizens ready to start building oil wells and platforms. *Don't* wait for enough oil from your own sources; it costs too much time. It's best if your metal stocks are at least in the low thousands, and you should be able to afford purchasing at least 1,000 oil independently of that. Of course, games played at low difficulty levels are more forgiving.

> **Note**
>
> *Do not hoard resources! Unless you have a very good reason (such as an upcoming Age advance with all the military upgrades that follow on its heels), it's much better to spend them right away on units, buildings, and/or research.*

MODERN AGE

- **Base Cost:** 2,500 knowledge, 250 oil.
- **Prerequisites:** Industrial Age, four new library advances.

Cities change appearance yet again with glass and steel buildings. War acquires a new and terrible character in Modern Age. Weapons introduced an age earlier (tanks, planes) acquire greater effectiveness, and a tiny corps of half a dozen units can easily take a city. Long-range missiles and then nuclear warheads

appear on the scene, however, if you've started playing in Ancient Age, any major upsets are unlikely: It's more or less clear who has a chance of winning. The number of cities under control has decisive influence simply because it limits the number of universities and scholars you might have. If the outcome of the game hasn't been settled yet, knowledge can become extremely precious! Add almost chronic metal and oil shortages, and you've got a pretty exciting time even if you're sure of final victory.

INFORMATION AGE

- **Base Cost:** 3,500 knowledge, 500 oil.
- **Prerequisites:** Modern Age, four new non-Age advances.

Many games will end before you reach the Information Age. At this stage, the only nations still in the game will be its superpowers, desperately trying to edge each other out in the race for final victory. If you find yourself leading one of these superpowers (there rarely will be more than two), keep in mind that efficient management of your vast empire is vital! The final stages of the game are often about who researches Missile Shield (see next section) first, and subsequently about who can out-produce whom; you might say victory is won in the factory as well as on the battlefield.

Golden Rule of Age Advancement

It's no use advancing to the next Age if you can't take advantage of what it has to offer. Simply having enough resources to advance to an Age isn't a good reason to start research. For instance, you should budget for instantly researching subsequent military unit upgrades, and always have something set aside for emergencies such as a destructive enemy raid. Wise budgeting is the area in which the A.I. is prone to mistakes, which becomes especially evident if you set the research cost to Very High. You'll see games in which a computer opponent reaches Gunpowder Age, but still fights with Classical Age military units. Make sure you don't make the same mistake!

Military Research

The main function of Military research is somewhat unmilitary: Each military level increases your base population cap by 25 units. Additionally, each level over the level corresponding to your current Age on the library research panel reduces military unit and upgrade costs by 5%. Example: You're in Classical Age, but have already researched Military level 4. This results in a 10% bonus.

Military research also increases the speed of transports, that is, the ships land units change to when told to cross a body of water. Transports are extremely vulnerable to attack, so it's an important quality on sea maps, but of no value on land maps.

Finally and importantly, Military research is also a prerequisite to obtaining new types of military units. It shares that quality with Age advancement, and Age advancement is much more expensive; in most games you'll stay a Military level or two ahead of Age, anyway. The most frequent difficulty you might experience in planning Military research is budgeting enough knowledge, which is always much in demand. The metal costs are at least initially negligible when compared with the cost of creating armies. Here's the basic costs list of Military research:

Musketeer
Fusilier

- Level 1 (The Art of War). 120 food. Don't research it too early! It's little use if you haven't got enough resources to create military units, or haven't advanced in other areas so that you can research Allegiance at the tower.

- Level 2 (Mercenaries). 100 food, 100 metal. The metal translates into timber if you research this in Ancient Age, and on some maps (those with little metal), that can be a wise move. It's also a good option if you're following the recipe for rapid economic development described in the Age Jump. This is a groundbreaking level that opens up many new military possibilities, all listed within the game.

- Level 3 (Standing Army). 200 metal, 160 knowledge. Prerequisite for researching Tactics and Fortification at the fort, and thus rather important.

- Level 4 (Conscription). 250 metal, 360 knowledge. Prerequisite for researching Operations and Bombardment at the fort.

- Level 5 (Levee en Masse). 400 metal, 650 knowledge. This is the first occasion on which you might find the research cost meaningful (unless you choose the Very Expensive tech cost setting). This level is notable for letting you upgrade your artillery units.

- Level 6 (Nation-At-Arms). 500 metal, 1,100 knowledge. Prerequisite for researching Strategy and Strategic Reserves at the fort, which increases its importance.

- Level 7 (Selective Service). 750 metal, 1,500 knowledge. The final step to acquiring the game's most sophisticated military units.
- Level 8 (Missile Shield). 3,000 metal, 4,000 knowledge. Futuristic tech that's an option only after advancing into Information Age and researching everything up to level 7. Grants immunity from nuclear missile attacks, and turns Armageddon clock back by two.

Civic Research

Civic research brings you several political and economic advantages. Benefits include extra cities and expanding national territory. Most importantly, Civic advances let you research attrition and taxation techs at the tower and temple, respectively.

Civic research is of particular importance in the early stages of a game, when it's the prerequisite to founding new cities and thus to your nation's development. Once you run out of space to expand peacefully, Civic research loses some luster: A successful war tends to bring in more cities and income than any amount of research. Note that you do not need extra levels of Civic research to administrate conquered cities that put you over your Civics-determined city limit. You won't be able to start any new ones, that's all. It doesn't matter much once you've embarked on a path of conquest, anyway. Here's a list of Civic levels and their base cost:

- Level 1 (City State). 120 food. In games that start with Low resources, this is the very first advance you should research (see Figure 4.6). It lets you build your second city; the sooner this is done, the better. It also lets you research Allegiance at the tower and Taxation at the temple (other prerequisites: Military and Science level 1, Classical Age).

- Level 2 (Empire). 160 food. Another candidate for early research: In many games, it actually makes sense to do this before advancing to Classical Age (see Chapter 8 for strategy details). Allows the first of "religious" techs, Religion, at the temple (see "Temple Research" section).

- Level 3 (Feudalism). 160 food, 160 knowledge. It's still cheap despite the added knowledge cost: It allows Vassalage at the temple and Oath of Fealty at the tower.

FIGURE 4.6: *Founding a second city is your number one initial goal in almost every game.*

- Level 4 (Divine Right). 300 food, 300 knowledge. This is the level where you start to feel the research costs. It allows you to research Monotheism at the temple.
- Level 5 (Constitution). 450 food, 480 knowledge. This lets you research the final, third level of both the taxation and attrition line: Social Contract and Patriotism.
- Level 6 (Great Power). 600 food, 1,000 knowledge. This allows Existentialism and Income Tax at the temple.
- Level 7 (International Law). 900 food, 1,300 knowledge. This allows Nationalism at the tower.
- Level 8 (World Government). 3,000 food, 4,000 knowledge. This future tech becomes available after researching all standard mainstream advances.

In practice, most games will see you terminating civic research around levels 5–6; that's simply the way things play out most often. There's little incentive to research another level of Civic technology when you've got a dozen cities under your control.

Commerce Research

Commerce research raises production caps on resources, plus raises the initial bonus generated by caravans upon starting a trade route (10 wealth for each Commerce level). You'll be constantly striving to increase production, and so Commerce will stay high on the list of research priorities in practically every game. The rule of thumb is to stay ahead of your current Age by a single commerce level; for example, Commerce level 3 is commonly researched right before or just after reaching Medieval Age. Each new Commerce level raises the production cap for all resources. The amounts vary, and are listed here with research costs:

- Level 1 (Barter). 60 food, 60 timber; raises Commerce cap to 100 units. You'll research this before you advance to Classical Age; exact priorities will differ according to circumstances, but as a rule of thumb, the sooner you anticipate a war, the more urgent it is to set up some kind of cash flow. Researching level 1 is a prerequisite to building markets, and thus also to creating merchants and caravans.
- Level 2 (Coinage). 60 timber, 140 knowledge; raises Commerce cap to 150 units. The knowledge cost means it might sometimes make sense to research this before advancing to Classical Age, which substitutes food for a cost of 210 food, 60 timber.
- Level 3 (Trade). 100 timber, 260 knowledge; raises Commerce cap to 200 units. In spite of the relatively stiff knowledge cost, this is a number one priority as soon as you enter Medieval Age (if you haven't researched it earlier).
- Level 4 (Mercantilism). 150 timber, 500 knowledge; raises Commerce cap to 260 units. Note the bigger increase (by 60 units). Try to get here before researching Gunpowder Age.
- Level 5 (Finance). 250 timber, 900 knowledge. Raises Commerce cap to 320 units.
- Level 6 (Assembly Line). 350 timber, 1,300 knowledge. In spite of the stiff knowledge cost, get this before advancing to Industrial Age. Raises the Commerce cap by 80 units to a new total of 400.

Note

Note that Commerce advances do not act as prerequisites to any specialized (non-library) research.

Level 7 (Globalization). 500 timber, 1,800 knowledge; raises Commerce cap by a full 100 to a total of 500 units. There'll be significantly less pressure to research this level because in the meantime you'll have advanced to Industrial Age and will be preoccupied with getting oil production past Barter levels. Nevertheless, it becomes a necessity if a victor hasn't emerged by Industrial Age.

FIGURE 4.7: *Even a smoldering wreck of a city you couldn't care less about contributes something to your economy.*

Level 8 (Global Prosperity). 3,000 wealth, 4,000 knowledge. Note the change in resource costs. This future tech raises the Commerce cap to 999 units, and lets you create advanced fighters and stealth bombers. Researching it is necessary only in longer, drawn-out games.

The pressure on raising the Commerce cap remains fairly constant regardless of whether you pursue a peaceful or warlike policy. The only way to win a peaceful game is by out-producing your opponents, while a successful war will automatically increase production levels; each captured city automatically kicks in its bit even if you don't deploy a single worker (see Figure 4.7).

Science Research

Science research? That's right. Researching research pays big dividends, too. Each level of Science reduces *all* research costs by 10% as well as shortening *all* research times by 10%. Science advances also play a vital role in increasing the productivity of your industries and let you keep a better eye on your empire by improving unit and structure line of sight (LOS), or spotting, range. The military advantages are obvious. Here's a list of Science levels with their costs and especially noteworthy benefits:

Level 1 (Written Word). 120 timber, 50 wealth. This is the most expensive level 1 non-Age advance. It is also the most desirable, because it instantly cuts the costs of all subsequent research. It's advisable to research it first (before City State) if playing with Normal or better starting resources *and* if there's no urgent pressure. It lets you build temples, which confer numerous benefits including the ability to research taxation and "religious" techs.

CHAPTER 4 WHY RESEARCH IS POWER

- Level 2 (Mathematics). 120 wealth, 80 knowledge. This is cheap as dirt: Unfortunately, Commerce level 2 might lay first claim on what little knowledge you have. It's a strong candidate for researching prior to Classical Age: Its cost then amounts to 120 food and wealth each, and brings a meaningful decrease in Age advancement costs along with others. With advance to Classical Age, level 2 Science lets you build granaries and lumber mills, and opens the door to researching the techs available therein.

- Level 3 (Chemistry). 200 wealth, 160 knowledge. This is still cheap compared with the benefits it brings. You can now build smelters, which open new possibilities: more specialized research in industry buildings. As a rule, you should try to reach this level in Classical Age.

- Level 4 (Laws of Nature). 300 wealth, 300 knowledge. Usually it's best to research this upon entering Medieval Age and prior to the spate of specialized research Medieval Age makes possible; everything will be 10% cheaper. It allows specialized research at the granary, lumber mill, smelter, and most importantly, the university (Printing Press, which increases scholar productivity—see "University Research" section).

- Level 5 (Electricity). 500 wealth, 500 knowledge. This is best acquired in Gunpowder Age; rising research costs mean Electricity pays for itself very quickly. It lets you further improve scholar productivity, plus conduct still more research at industry buildings.

- Level 6 (Electronics). 900 wealth, 900 knowledge. This is a milestone advance that results in the entire map being revealed. Achieving this prior to Industrial Age can be key to winning the game! Other benefits include new research at industry buildings and at the university.

- Level 7 (Computerization). 1,500 wealth, 1,500 knowledge. This lets you see everything happening within your territory, including all unit movement. It also lets you research Logistics (the ultimate attrition-fighting tech) at the smelter, and improves scholar productivity.

- Level 8 (Artificial Intelligence). 3,000 timber, 4,000 knowledge. Note the resource switch in research costs. Making this final Science advance means you'll be able to see the whole game world at all times and create units instantly. Getting there first might just tilt the balance in your favor during an intense, prolonged end game.

Science research is sneaky and requires diligent monitoring. Its neglect does not result in an alarm flashing on screen (as it does when you hit population or production limits). What's more, games played at an easier level rarely let you feel the full effect of neglecting Science research. Don't let this make you complacent, or you won't stand a chance at the higher difficulty levels! Stunted Science research affects all other research badly.

SPECIALIZED RESEARCH

RoN features plenty of research activity outside the library. A significant part focuses on obtaining new and better military unit types, however, other specialized research is just as important. The in-game texts are exhaustingly informative about every advance available; the following sections add some comments, supply a cost comparison to help you plan research expenses, and organize info on research lines for reference purposes.

Temple Research

Faith is a powerful force in *RoN* (see Figure 4.8). It spawns two lines of research, the first consisting of Religion, Monotheism, and Existentialism, all of which enhance temple benefits. Here's the breakdown:

ADVANCE	BASE COST	PREREQUISITES	BENEFITS
Religion	70 food, 70 wealth	Civic 1 (Science 1 required to build temple)	National borders +4, city hit points +50%, city firing range +2
Monotheism	150 food, 150 wealth	Civic 4, Religion	National borders +7, city hit points +100%, city firing range +3
Existentialism	300 food, 300 wealth	Civic 6, Monotheism	National borders +10, city hit points +200%, city firing range +4

FIGURE 4.8: *The well-being of your empire rests on those pillars.*

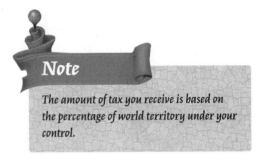

> **Note**
>
> The amount of tax you receive is based on the percentage of world territory under your control.

The taxation line consists of four advances. Note that the merchant and fisherman productivity bonuses apply only within your and any allied nation's territory; merchants and fishermen deployed elsewhere aren't affected.

ADVANCE	BASE COST	PREREQUISITES	BENEFITS
Taxation	80 food, 80 timber	Civic 1 (Science 1 required to build temple)	50% tax rate, merchants and fishermen gather 120%
Vassalage	160 food, 160 timber	Civic 3, Taxation	100% tax rate, merchants and fishermen gather 150%
Social Contract	320 food, 320 timber	Civic 5, Vassalage	Tax rate 200%, merchants and fishermen gather 200%
Income Tax	480 food, 480 timber	Civic 6, Social Contract	Tax rate 300%, merchants and fishermen gather 300%

In summary, temple techs are vital to your economy and greatly increase your security. Their impact increases as the game goes on. Note that fishermen also increase productivity following appropriate granary research (see later section).

University Research

This research doesn't mean the gathering of knowledge, but ways of increasing your scholars' productivity. Each scholar begins by contributing five knowledge to your knowledge gather rate. There are no less than five levels that bring increasing efficiency:

ADVANCE	BASE COST	PREREQUISITES	BENEFITS
Literacy	200 timber	Medieval Age, Science 3	Scholars produce +7 knowledge
Printing Press	400 timber	Gunpowder Age, Science 4, Literacy	Scholars produce +10 knowledge
Scientific Method	600 timber	Enlightenment Age, Science 5, Printing Press	Scholars produce +15 knowledge
Institutional Research	900 timber	Industrial Age, Science 6, Scientific Method	Scholars produce +20 knowledge
Supercomputers	1,200 timber	Modern Age, Science 7, Institutional Research	Scholars produce +25 knowledge, research speed doubled

University techs play an increasingly important role as the game goes on. They let you continuously increase knowledge gather rate without creating new scholars, which in turn lets you create more military units within your population limit. Most importantly, they let you maintain a brisk pace in mainstream research, which otherwise is slowed to a crawl by the steeply rising knowledge costs of most later-game advances.

Scholars don't come cheaply. The first scholar costs 30 wealth; each extra scholar costs two wealth more if the total is seven scholars or less. Once you have seven scholars, the cost increase is three wealth; once you have 14, the increase is four wealth, and so on.

Granary Research

Granary advances include two research lines. One of these focuses on increasing food production, the other on the health of your military units. Food production boosters include the following:

ADVANCE	BASE COST	PREREQUISITES	BENEFITS
Agriculture	150 timber, 150 metal	Science 3 (Classical Age needed to build granary)	City farm food production +50%, fishermen gather +50%.
Crop Rotation	250 timber, 250 metal	Science 4, Agriculture	City farm food production +100%, fishermen gather +100%
Food Industry	450 timber, 450 metal	Science 6, Crop Rotation	City farm food production +200%, fishermen gather +200%

The other granary research line makes for hale and hearty soldiers and sailors. Note that LOS stands for line of sight or unit spotting range, and that the techs affect just stable units; auto plant unit creation is speeded by other techs researched at the smelter.

ADVANCE	BASE COST	PREREQUISITES	BENEFITS
Herbal Lore	80 food, 80 wealth	Classical Age, Science 2	Barracks and stable units +1 LOS; barracks, stable units, and ships created 10% faster. All garrisoned units heal 25% faster.
Medicine	250 food, 250 wealth	Gunpowder Age, Science 3, Herbal Lore	Barracks and stable units +2 LOS; barracks, stable units, and ships created 20% faster. All units heal 50% faster.
Pharmaceuticals	450 food, 450 wealth	Industrial Age, Science 5, Medicine	Barracks and stable units +3 LOS; barracks, stable units, and ships created 30% faster. All units heal 75% faster.

This "medical" line of research is far more important than it might seem. As explained in Chapter 9, your military success largely depends on the timely withdrawal of heavily battered units, and returning them to battle once they've regained full health (see Figure 4.9).

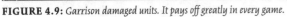

FIGURE 4.9: *Garrison damaged units. It pays off greatly in every game.*

Lumber Mill Research

The two lines of research available at the lumber mill increase timber production and improve building hit points and construction times. Timber production boosters include the following techs:

ADVANCE	BASE COST	PREREQUISITES	BENEFITS
Carpentry	150 food, 150 metal	Science 3 (Classical Age needed to build lumber mill)	City camp wood production +50%
Logging Industry	250 food, 250 metal	Science 4, Carpentry	City camp wood production +100%
Paper Mill	450 food, 450 metal	Science 6, Logging Industry	City camp wood production +200%

The lumber mill building-improving line of research includes the following advances:

ADVANCE	BASE COST	PREREQUISITES	BENEFITS
Construction	80 timber, 80 wealth	Classical Age, Science 2	Building hit points +10%, building construction 10% faster
Architecture	150 timber, 150 wealth	Gunpowder Age, Science 3	Building hit points +20%, building construction 20% faster
Engineering	350 timber, 350 wealth	Industrial Age, Science 5	Building hit points +30%, building construction 30% faster

These three advances are particularly helpful when waging war. Increased building hit points and quick construction of new structures in freshly captured cities help in both defense and offense because the structures are then so much more difficult to destroy.

Smelter Research

Smelter research exerts a special influence on your military capabilities. One line traditionally boosts metal production, while the other decreases and finally erases the effect of attrition on your forces, plus endows your supply wagons with new powers! Metal production boosters include and the following:

ADVANCE	BASE COST	PREREQUISITES	BENEFITS
Metal Alloys	250 food, 250 timber	Science 4 (Classical Age needed to build smelter)	City mine metal production +50%
Cold Casting	350 food, 350 timber	Science 5, Metal Alloys	City mine metal production +150%
Steel	450 food, 450 timber	Science 6, Cold Casting	City mine metal production +200%

Now you can see how important it is to designate at least one city as a metal mining center. The second smelter research line is also very important. It carries big consequences for the military side of things. Note that researching just the first of the three techs (Forage) means your units do not receive any attrition in enemy territory unless they're moving or fighting.

ADVANCE	BASE COST	PREREQUISITES	BENEFITS
Forage	150 metal, 150 wealth	Medieval Age, Science 3	Attrition damage reduced 25%, none when idle; supply wagons gain +20% hit points, +2 healing radius, and move 25% faster; auto plant units created 10% faster
Supply	300 metal, 300 wealth	Enlightenment Age, Science 5, Forage	Attrition damage reduced 50%, none when idle; supply wagons gain +40% hit points, +4 healing radius, and move 50% faster; auto plant units created 20% faster
Logistics	450 metal, 450 wealth	Modern Age, Science 7, Supply	Attrition damage reduced 75%, none when idle; supply wagons gain +60% hit points, +6 healing radius, and move 75% faster

Chapter 9 has additional comments on attrition and supply wagon management. For now, let's just say that attrition is a real problem primarily in multiplayer games; it's not that hard to avoid it when playing in solo mode.

FIGURE 4.10: *The Industrial Age wave of change turns stables into auto plants.*

Specialized Military Research

Specialized military research that takes place outside the library has a great impact on your military. It's greater, in fact, than mainstream Military research, because it includes the all-important, practically constant activity of upgrading military units. This is done at the building where you create the units (barracks for infantry, stable for mounted troops, and so on; see Figure 4.10).

The art and costs of modernizing military units is discussed as appropriate in Chapters 6, 7, 8, and 9. Direct upgrade costs are given in Chapters 6 and 7, which list all the military units in the game; while related general and strategic issues are covered in Chapters 8 and 9. Here, let's just note that timing military unit upgrades is an art form.

In addition to upgrading military units, specialized military research also includes techs researched at the tower (which later becomes the keep, stronghold, and so on) and the fort (castle and so on). These are reviewed in the following sections.

Tower Research

Tower research is particularly important in the early to middle stages of the game. It features two lines of research: the attrition techs, and advances that let you turn your citizens into (rather poor) soldiers. The attrition techs are definitely more important:

ADVANCE	BASE COST	PREREQUISITES	BENEFITS
Allegiance	80 metal, 80 wealth	Classical Age, Civic 1	Level 1 attrition to enemy units in your territory
Oath of Fealty	150 metal, 150 wealth	Medieval Age, Civic 3, Allegiance	Level 2 attrition to enemy units in your territory
Patriotism	300 metal, 300 wealth	Enlightenment Age, Civic 5	Level 3 attrition to enemy units in your territory
Nationalism	450 metal, 450 wealth	Modern Age, Civic 7	Level 4 attrition to enemy units in your territory

Attrition techs are of immense help in defense early on in the game, and of lesser help later on, when everyone has researched a level or two of anti-attrition techs at the smelter, plus built a large number of supply wagons (see Chapter 9).

The other line of tower research concerns itself with turning citizens into military units (militia, minutemen, and so on). These are discussed along with all the other military units in Chapter 6.

Fort Research

Fort research features the customary two lines; one focuses on forts, the other on units created in forts: generals and spies. The first line greatly enhances your forts: Note especially the effect on national borders (normally a fort increases these by two).

ADVANCE	BASE COST	PREREQUISITES	BENEFITS
Fortification	150 metal, 150 wealth	Medieval Age, Military 3	National border +5, fort and tower firing range +1, +2 LOS, max. garrison size +5.
Bombardment	300 metal, 300 wealth	Gunpowder Age, Military 4, Fortification	National border +8, fort and tower firing range +2, +4 LOS
Strategic Reserves	450 metal, 450 wealth	Industrial Age, Military 6, Bombardment	National border +5, fort and tower firing range +1, +2 LOS, max. garrison size +10

As you can see, the border bonus alone is well worth all this wealth and metal. The other line of fort research greatly improves the quality of your generals and spies, which qualify as special units rather than military units (neither can fight, that is, cause damage to enemy units or structures). Here are the advances available:

ADVANCE	BASE COST	PREREQUISITES	BENEFITS
Tactics	50 timber, 50 wealth	Medieval Age, Military 3	Generals and spies created 100% faster and receive +3 to craft range, +2 LOS, +50% hit points, and move 25% faster; generals' unit armor bonus +4
Operations	150 timber, 150 wealth	Gunpowder Age, Military 4, Tactics	Generals and spies recover craft 100% faster and receive +6 to craft range, +4 LOS, +200% hit points, and move 50% faster; generals' unit armor bonus +6
Strategy	300 timber, 300 wealth	Industrial Age, Military 6, Operations	Generals and spies cost 50% less and receive +9 to craft range, +6 LOS, +450% hit points, and move 75% faster; spies bribe enemy units and plant informers twice as quickly

> **Tip**
>
> It's almost criminally stupid to wage war in Gunpowder Age without researching Operations, which can make your army incredibly tough when led by a general.

Smart Research Moves

The smart research move always depends on your particular game situation. There is a very broad strategy you can follow (detailed in Chapter 8) and some general moves that always work (listed here). What always matters most, however, is the set of circumstances you're facing at any given time. Don't ever get into the habit of researching advances in a given sequence because it's worked in the past few games. Sooner or later it won't work, and you'll have egg on your face and enemies at your gates (see Figure 4.11).

FIGURE 4.11: *Guess I didn't need that next level of Civics after all.*

Some nations enjoy natural advantages in research; they just have more up there, apparently. The Greeks lead the pack with a set of research bonuses that truly make advances a snap, closely followed by the Chinese (detail in game and in Chapter 1), but these national bonuses are very misleading. True, Greeks will enjoy a marked initial advantage (especially if technology is set to Very Expensive), however, in the longer run, you'll find that an economic advantage invariably translates into a research advantage, no matter what nation you play. Smart research moves might also put you ahead without any help from national bonuses. Here's a list of those:

- As hinted often, don't do research before you're in a position to take advantage of its benefits. For instance, don't research the next level of Commerce before you've even gotten near your current production cap. Don't spend resources on a unit upgrade when you don't have any units of that type, and cannot afford any. Use foresight and common sense.
- Minimize research costs by aggressively pursuing Science advances.
- Increase scholar productivity as soon as the option becomes available.
- Make maximum use of rare resources (many provide a knowledge bonus). Increase merchant productivity through researching the taxation line.

Finally, and most importantly, don't waste resources. Waste not, need not; you'll automatically be able to afford all the research you can handle—really.

The next chapter takes a look at a very special way of putting resources to good use: building Wonders, and the benefits this brings.

CHAPTER 4 Why Research is Power

THE WONDERS
OF WONDER

5

Rise of Nations features 14 very special structures. These are its Wonders of the World: semi-mythical, gigantic edifices that endow the nation that owns them with special powers. In a standard Quick Battle game, Wonders are simply selected from a citizen's build menu; however, in a campaign game, they can be acquired only through playing a special Bonus Card (see Chapter 10 for more campaign game details).

Building the right Wonder at the right time can be a winning move. This chapter explains why, and reviews all the Wonders from a practical point of view. The Wonder descriptions will help you decide which Wonder is right for your empire, and when; each Wonder has a special character that fully shines in a defined set of circumstances. Note that a Wonder is always a good investment in terms of return. The only time this isn't true is when you begin building a Wonder and someone else completes it first. Each Wonder may be built only once in a game, and if it's destroyed, it's gone forever.

THE BEST THING SINCE...

Many players hold Wonders of any kind, from any game, in slight disdain. They build a strong economy, a strong army, and proceed to capture whatever Wonders others might have built. They build their own Wonders only when they happen to have more than the necessary resources on hand, and they're not needed for anything else. This approach could be a mistake when playing *Rise of Nations*, because the Wonders in *RoN* have wonderfully practical qualities:

- ▷ They are affordable. Early Wonders cost less than half a dozen military units. They get more expensive with time, but stay roughly in step with your growing economy.

- ▷ They help the economy. It doesn't make sense to build a Wonder in the very early stages of a game. A Wonder built before your nation has grown to at least a couple of well-developed cities is of little practical value and constitutes an economical effort that will critically hinder development in all other areas of nation-building. But building a Wonder is an option that you should consider as soon as you've founded a couple of cities, built them up a little, and possibly also advanced to Classical Age. Most Wonders in *RoN* carry economic benefits that make their cost well worth it.

- ▷ They help create stronger armed forces. Many Wonders are truly helpful in a military sense (not as many are as helpful economically; occasionally you get both). Some are particularly useful in defense, and others in offense; see the Wonder descriptions in the next section.

- ▷ They earn victory points. You enable this particular option on the pre-game Options panel; you can also set the number of Wonder points separating the winner from the runner-up. It's an option that might not be at its best in some types of games (Assassin, Survival of the Fittest); nevertheless, its presence adds a splash of color to any game. Later Wonders earn more points, so it's hardly possible to win quickly in this manner.

- ▷ They meet your special needs. This last quality is what should always tip the scales when you're trying to decide whether to build a particular Wonder.

As you can see, building a Wonder in *RoN* should not be considered a gesture of prestige, but a sound, practical move that either meets an acute need or reinforces a special advantage you have, hopefully making your nation unstoppable.

You may build only one Wonder per city (Egyptians may build two). Naturally, you should choose a city that is relatively safe from attack—the safer, the better. The A.I. does not make a point of targeting Wonder cities, but cunning human players do; take that into account when playing a multiplayer game. What's more, you'd better move fast if you find an opponent is building the same Wonder you are.

There can be only one Wonder of a kind in a game, and initially at least, it belongs to the player who finishes it first. Any Wonders of the same kind that are still under construction are destroyed, and there is no refund on the resources spent. It's a good idea to allocate a team of half a dozen citizens and build your Wonder quickly.

Tip

In solo games, the A.I. usually assigns just one or two citizens to building a Wonder. It's easy to overtake the A.I. nation and build the same Wonder first if you have a sufficient number of Wonder builders. The added benefit is that the A.I. opponent in question loses the resources spent on starting construction.

The following sections review Wonders in their order of game appearance: their timing, cost, benefits, and possible weak points. Yes, in this imperfect world, even a Wonder might have a weak point.

THE WORLD OF WONDERS

The 14 Wonders of *RoN* enter the stage in pairs. Each new Age brings another pair of Wonders; due to an accounting gimmick, Ancient Age and Classical Age count together as Age I. The first pair of Wonders (the Pyramids and the Colossus) thus appears at the very start of the game, and you'll have to wait till the Medieval Age to see new entries.

Note

In most games, circumstances will limit you to building one Wonder per Age. It's often a matter of building the Wonder you can handle rather than the one you'd like to. It's quite acceptable; all Wonders are very good value.

Note that the cost of building a Wonder can be significantly affected by your national economic bonus—or even simply a stroke of luck. For instance, if you forgo an offensive policy while playing the Romans, you'll find it extra easy to build the Colossus: You'll automatically accumulate the needed wealth from your city or cities. Exploiting certain rare resources might be helpful too: The 10% across-the-board reduction in food costs conferred by sugar, for example, saves plenty of food when building a Wonder that requires it (see Figure 5.1). Naturally, marble is the rare resource most helpful in Wonder building: Exploiting this rare resource brings a 10% reduction in Wonder cost.

FIGURE 5.1: *Oh, sugar! You're the best thing in this world.*

Wonders of the Ancient and Classical Ages

The first two Wonders you may build are both very attractive choices, but of different character. Both are very reasonably priced in proportion to the probable strength of your young economy. As a rule, both of them get built in almost every game. The computer-controlled nations make revealing choices: The Egyptians are always hot for the Pyramids; the British go for the Colossus. These choices let them exploit their national advantages (Egyptian food bonus, British commerce cap bonus) even more effectively.

These two initial Wonders are worth a single Wonder point each.

The Pyramids

▷ **Standard cost:** 200 food, 200 timber.

▷ **Benefits:** City limit +1, food and wealth Commerce cap +50, food gather rate +20%.

This is a very useful, very affordable Wonder that greatly helps solve food problems for the remainder of the game. It compensates for its cost by allowing you to build an extra city the moment you complete the Wonder. Because of this, building the Pyramids doesn't significantly delay the growth of your empire, and it provides production cap bonuses that help defray construction costs within the space of a single Age. This Wonder is practically custom-made for the Egyptians (seven farms per city, +2 wealth per farm), greatly useful for nations with appropriate economic bonuses (such as the Bantu, Japanese, Mongols, Germans), and truly useful for every other nation in any Age. Consequently, it gets built early on in the vast majority of games. It doesn't carry much heft toward a Wonder point victory, though.

The Colossus

▷ **Standard cost:** 200 timber, 200 wealth.

▷ **Benefits:** Population limit +50, timber and wealth Commerce cap +50, wealth gather rate +30%.

The Colossus is another eminently affordable Wonder with very solid and game-lasting benefits. It is a

particularly good choice for aggressive players, allowing them to build armies far bigger than any contemporary opponent's. Its benefits let you make up for its construction costs with sharply increased production, and it will start making you money (in a manner of speaking) within a single Age. The Colossus is also a good escape hatch if your metal supply isn't capable of supporting energetic Military research, however, don't count on it being conveniently available whenever you want it; this Wonder is built fairly quickly by one of the players in most games. It is particularly well matched to nations enjoying timber and wealth production bonuses, and very good value regardless of national choice. Looks good, too (see Figure 5.2).

FIGURE 5.2: *The Colossus is hard to beat in terms of awe-inspiring appearance.*

Wonders of the Medieval Age

The Medieval Age marks a big jump forward in all matters military, so in a way it's no surprise the Terra Cotta Army and the Colosseum both bring military benefits. Both are primarily helpful in defense, although the Colosseum brings new effectiveness to an offensive Border Push strategy. Finally, there's a pronounced difference in affordability: The metal needed for the Terra Cotta Army might be a problem in some games. Medieval Age Wonders are worth two Wonder points.

The Terra Cotta Army

- **Standard cost:** 300 food, 300 wealth.
- **Benefits:** A new light infantry unit created every 30 game seconds (+0.5 second delay for each infantry unit you already have).

The Terra Cotta Army is sure to be very popular with many players because of its charming quality: a spanking new light infantry unit turned out every so often, ostensibly free of charge (except for the inevitable increase in next-unit costs). This rather spectacular benefit obscures some drawbacks. Even though free units are an undeniable bargain, you might feel frustrated when you unexpectedly hit the population limit while trying to assemble, let's say, a cavalry corps. Paying special attention to your population cap is wise. The military benefits brought by the Terra Cotta Army are primarily useful in defense (see Figure 5.3); players who aren't particularly skilled at managing military matters will be especially happy. The effect of this Wonder's benefits tends to wane with time, as the value of light infantry shrinks toward the end of the game.

Predictably, it works best for nations that have unique light infantry units; the British with their Highlanders are particularly advantaged.

The Colosseum

- **Standard cost:** 300 timber, 300 metal.
- **Benefits:** Attrition to enemy units in your territory +50%, national borders +3, forts and towers cost 20% less.

The Colosseum is a bit pricey, and unless your military situation is fairly comfortable you'll find it hard to afford; it costs a lot of metal! It's definitely not a good idea to cripple army growth trying to save up for that Wonder. If you do build it, you'll find that this Wonder is very useful in the

FIGURE 5.3: The Terra Cotta Army Wonder works well for nations of a defensive character, such as the Koreans.

early stages of the game, helping to easily contain any enemy attacks on your territory. Naturally it works best for large empires, albeit its national border bonus and reduced cost of forts can be helpful to smaller nations trying to muscle onto others. Not surprisingly, it's tailor-made for the Romans but will also suit any other player using the Border Push strategy (see Chapter 9). The Coliseum loses a little of its attrition value once the game progresses into Industrial Age and beyond: Air and missile strikes can be as lethal as an invading army. Still, it's so inexpensive that it's always worth it.

Wonders of the Gunpowder Age

The Gunpowder Age Wonders both carry sizeable economic bonuses. In addition, the Temple of Tikal strengthens your nation's infrastructure, while the Porcelain Tower provides an extra marginal advantage on all sea maps. Its unique rare resource bonus is sure to make it popular among many players. Gunpowder Age Wonders continue to be worth only two Wonder points; they're a little disappointing in that respect.

The Temple of Tikal

▶ **Standard cost:** 400 food, 400 timber.

▶ **Benefits:** Timber gather rate +50%, timber Commerce cap +100; increases temple effect on national border, city hit points, and city firing range by 50%.

The Temple of Tikal greatly helps out with major timber shortages that might occur once you advance into Gunpowder Age. Arquebusiers don't replace crossbowmen and will put your timber industry under severe strain. This can be felt badly even if you're waging a successful war: Repairing captured cities and constructing extra troop-producing buildings ratchets timber demand even higher. Naturally, given the benefits of the Temple of Tikal, you'll be making sure you've got a temple in every city. The improved temple bonuses carry special defensive benefits. This is another Wonder that fits well into a Border Push strategy. It's tailor-made for the French with their timber production bonus, but also works well for any nation with a defensive profile: Maya, Chinese, Koreans, and so on. Other good fits: Romans, Germans. This Wonder has a couple of minor weaknesses: It's still worth only two Wonder points despite higher construction cost. Predictably, the timber-associated bonuses of the Temple of Tikal fade slightly in the game's last two Ages.

The Porcelain Tower

▶ **Standard cost:** 400 metal, 400 wealth.

▶ **Benefits:** Income from rare resources and markets +200%, allows exploitation of all rare resources' bonus abilities in player territory (but not in allied territories) without sending merchants, ships created 50% faster.

This is one of the most charming Wonders in the game. It appears with perfect timing, just as you need a bunch of markets, merchants, and rare resources to really make use of this Wonder's potential. That will definitely be the case by Gunpowder Age. Note that its usefulness can vary wildly from map to map; a small map that has just four or five rare resources might make this Wonder something of a luxury. Nubians are the exception to all of these rules: Their national economic bonuses complement the Porcelain Tower's ideally. When playing any other nation, you should evaluate the potential profits carefully before committing to this Wonder's construction. The ship creation speed bonus isn't very meaningful; ironically it makes itself felt most on smaller sea maps.

Wonders of the Enlightenment Age

The Enlightenment Age introduces two stylish Wonders that bring great military benefits. The Angkor Wat is the more valuable of the two; its metal production bonus sets up your economy perfectly for the coming Industrial age. Still, the Versailles Wonder is also a very attractive choice for players waging offensive war; it's especially useful on larger maps. Both Enlightenment Age Wonders are worth three Wonder points.

The Angkor Wat

➤ **Standard cost:** 500 timber, 500 wealth.

➤ **Benefits:** Metal gather rate +50%; metal Commerce cap +100; barracks, stable/auto plant, and docks units cost 25% less.

The Angkor Wat is one of the most desirable Wonders in the game. Unlike the Temple of Tikal, it comes at a perfect time: Its metal production bonuses make it simply ideal for the challenges of Ages that lie ahead. If you want to own this Wonder (and you do), accumulate the needed food and timber ahead of time to begin construction the moment you advance to Enlightenment Age (see Figure 5.4), otherwise someone else might beat you to it, especially in multiplayer. Owning the Angkor Wat means any metal problems are greatly diminished, if not outright solved, for the remainder of the game. Its metal bonus and lower unit costs combine to allow you, in practice, to double the rate at which you can create tanks (an all-important unit). When you con-sider this Wonder's advantages, its cost is extremely reasonable: By Enlightenment Age, 500 food or timber isn't a big deal. The Angkor Wat is equally useful to all nations; the only circumstances in which it might be inappropriate are when you're losing the game anyway. This Wonder is absolutely priceless on maps that are scarce in metal! When built by the Mongols or the Japanese, it results in extremely cheap military (which can be made cheaper still by exploiting the right rare resources, such as Horses and Salt).

FIGURE 5.4: *Enlightened rulers should try to own the Angkor Wat Wonder.*

The Versailles

➤ **Standard cost:** 500 food, 500 metal.

➤ **Benefits:** All research costs reduced 50% (knowledge, university knowledge-gatherings techs, and unit upgrade costs excluded); supply wagons heal troops (French supply wagons' healing speed doubled); artillery and supply wagons move 25% faster.

This is the ideal Wonder for the warmonger. It makes offensive war a real snap. There are huge savings hidden behind the supply wagon healing ability: You won't have to build numerous forts, barracks, and so on to heal troops. This benefit will have less significance in multiplayer games, where other players will target enemy supply wagons first and foremost. The reduced research costs are very helpful, as they include a lot of specialized research, however, all military unit upgrade costs are unaffected. Also, owning this Wonder calls for some careful planning: You don't want its construction to wipe out your metal stocks right before the metal-hungry Industrial Age. At the same time, if you want to have it, you have to run: Delaying construction might mean someone else will snap it up (especially in a multiplayer game). It's equally useful to all the nations in the game except the French, for whom its qualities are (ironically) a little bit less helpful.

Wonders of the Industrial Age

The Industrial Age ushers in the Statue of Liberty and the Kremlin. The Statue of Liberty effectively cancels attrition; if the enemy has built the Kremlin, it erases the second Wonder's attrition bonus. In a nutshell, the Statue of Liberty provides you with unparalleled freedom to wage offensive war, while the Kremlin greatly helps in a defensive war. Both these Wonders can be tie-breakers in many games, pushing their owners ahead of others when the race for victory is closely run. Each of these Wonders is worth four Wonder points.

The Statue of Liberty

- **Standard cost:** 600 food, 600 wealth.
- **Benefits:** Reduces owner's attrition in enemy territory by 100%, effectively countering the Kremlin attrition, all Airbase and ground unit upgrades are free, anti-aircraft structures and Bombers cost 33% less.

The Statue of Liberty is the Modern Industrial Age's answer to the Kremlin. It is the ideal Wonder for the warmonger and extremely useful to any player engaged in a war. It comes at a time when it might help an underdog suddenly emerge as a valid contender for the winner's seat; this is because it makes war cheaper while helping develop new weaponry. It is equally helpful to all nations, although it must be said it works particularly well for the Russians. Coupled with the Kremlin, it gives you an edge on any battlefield. It's very affordable: Once you've got the oil situation under some control, 600 wealth is small change. Capturing a couple of Industrial Age cities just about pays for the whole thing.

The Kremlin

- **Standard cost:** 600 food, 600 metal.
- **Benefits:** Food, timber, and metal Commerce cap +200; attrition to enemy units in national territory +100%; receive an immortal spy unit that doesn't count against the population limit. All spies are created instantly.

This is a very attractive Wonder for players who want to keep up the momentum in an offensive war. The raised Commerce caps mean you'll be able to put all the captured cities to economic use; in most games, production limits restrict captured cities to the role of military outposts. The attrition bonus means you can still count on attrition as a valuable deterrent; otherwise, high unit hit points and smelter advances weaken its impact significantly as the game goes on. The immortal spy is a unit that is revived each time it's killed; it's a hoot as well as a considerable irritant to your opponents, although its real value depends on the amount of time you're willing to spend on micromanagement. The pressures inherent in the later stages of a winning game don't leave any spare time. Predictably, the Kremlin is a perfect fit for the Russians, reinforcing further their national attrition bonus, however, it's also very helpful for any nation that needs a little extra steam to keep winning. Its weak point is the high metal cost coming at a time of peak metal demand. If you can weather that, the newly raised production levels will make this Wonder pay for itself very quickly.

Wonders of the Modern Age

The Modern Age breaks with tradition: Its two Wonders have widely different characters. The Statue of Liberty is a riposte to the Kremlin and the ideal Wonder for the dedicated warmonger. The Eiffel Tower primarily brings economic benefits in the area that needs them most: oil industry. Each of these two Wonders is worth six Wonder points.

The Taj Mahal

▷ **Standard cost:** 700 timber, 700 wealth.

▷ **Benefits:** Wealth production and building hit points increased 100%, wealth Commerce cap +300. Players who love wealth will love this Wonder. Its economic benefits are also felt in the military sphere of things: You'll greatly appreciate the extra flexibility all this wealth brings. The building hit points are helpful in both offensive and defensive wars, since a successful war also means having more buildings to defend, however, all in all this is more of a "comfort" than "breakthrough" Wonder. The cost can make your economy stutter; if you can deal with this, the Taj Mahal earns back your investment in record time. This is a versatile Wonder with benefits that increase slightly over time; it might make the difference in a tight end game. It's equally suitable for all nations, and especially suited for those who enjoy a national wealth bonus (Egyptians, Romans, and others).

The Eiffel Tower

▷ **Standard cost:** 700 timber, 700 metal.

▷ **Benefits:** Oil production +100%, oil commerce cap +200, national border +6.

The Eiffel Tower is an extremely useful Wonder. It has the potential to eliminate any oil-related problems at a stroke. In addition to doubling your oil output, it can bring new oil fields within your national territory. All this adds up to a real booster for any nation. The seemingly purely economic bonus has enormous impact on the military scene, where oil supply often defines how many new military units you can create (see Figure 5.5).

FIGURE 5.5: *A small armored army easily costs 1,000 oil (plus other costs).*

In most games, the Eiffel Tower is by far the most desirable of the Modern Age Wonders. Every player should plan to build it if possible; it's even important enough to be a factor when planning advancement into the Modern Age. Be ready for enemies launching furious attacks with the aim of capturing or destroying your Eiffel Tower! The oil production bonus makes it easier to assemble an arsenal of nuclear weapons, so your owning it creates considerable excitement among your opponents.

Wonders of the Information Age

Information Age Wonders feature a new twist: They both cost knowledge. Although this knowledge cost isn't high, it might make an important difference in an age where most advances carry high knowledge costs. The Supercollider Wonder brings strong economic and research advantages, and these always have at least some military implications. The Space Program Wonder is very military in character; in fact its benefits make it perfect for players who want to wage a nuclear war. Information Age Wonders are worth eight Wonder points.

The Supercollider

▶ **Standard cost:** 800 food, 800 knowledge.

▶ **Benefits:** Market price to buy maximum 125, to sell minimum 50; all techs researched instantaneously.

This is the right Wonder to build if you've missed out on the Eiffel Tower. The market price bonus basically means you'll never be painfully short of any economic resource (unless you're losing heavily). Instant tech research makes a meaningful difference only if you've set Technology to Very Expensive/Slow. Nevertheless, there's no other Wonder in the game that can match the Supercollider in terms of sheer value: This particular Wonder earns its investment back in a minute of game time. The Supercollider is tailor-made for the Nubians, but remains very helpful to all nations that are still contenders in the final stages of the game. However, if you get to that stage think carefully before using nuclear weapons; the embargo on market trading that follows each nuclear strike will mean you cannot take advantage of this Wonder's benefits until the embargo is lifted.

The Space Program

▶ **Standard cost:** 800 wealth, 800 knowledge.

▶ **Benefits:** Map and everything on the map becomes visible, aircraft and missiles cost 50% less and are created 100% faster, owner is immune to effect of Nuclear Embargo.

This might be the last-minute upset Wonder of the game: It lets you wage nuclear war effectively and with impunity. Nothing can hide from your missiles, which this Wonder makes very affordable and available under all circumstances. The Space Program is the more valuable of the two Wonders available in the Information Age, however, having it can be dangerous for the owner when playing against intelligent opponents in a multiplayer game. Capturing it might become priority number one for everyone concerned, however, it's a very safe bet in all solo games.

THE ARMY

6

Land army units compose the vast majority of the units featured in Rise of Nations. This simply reflects the role your army plays in the game. It's vital to victory, for only land units can capture cities, and winning the game largely consists of capturing cities. By now, you might be a little confused; Chapter 3 says that a strong economy is essential; a little later, you're told that research is crucial too, and that Wonders help as well. Prepare for the awful truth. The main reason economy, research, Wonders, and so on are all so important is this: They all enable you to field big, modern armies, or at any rate, armies that are stronger than those of your opponents.

This chapter discusses the army in detail, beginning with explanations of basic concepts for new players. It goes on to examine army units, the respective roles they play, and the changes they go through with consecutive Ages. It advises you how to combine units into viable operational groups, and alerts you to tactical possibilities that result. It concludes with a review of the national armies in RoN, which includes comments on nation-specific battle tactics and war strategy.

GETTING TO KNOW YOUR MEN (AND HORSES)

In *Rise of Nations*, military land units are created in special buildings. These are:

- Barracks. This is the most basic of military buildings; it becomes available in Ancient Age upon researching Military level 1. Barracks allow you to create foot units: infantry and scouts.
- Stable/Auto Plant. The stable becomes available upon researching Military level 1 and Classical Age, and lets you create cavalry. It changes into the auto plant with Industrial Age, and its units turn into armored cars and tanks.
- Siege factory. At first, this merely lets you create a single type of artillery unit and supply wagons. With Industrial Age, this building changes into the factory with a new unit line of anti-aircraft weapons in addition to artillery and supply vehicles.
- Fort. Forts allow you to create generals, which are perhaps the most valuable single unit on the battlefield. Forts also let you create spies, whose activities are necessarily quasi-military in character.

In addition, researching the appropriate line of techs at the tower will let you turn your citizens into combat units. The militia, minutemen, or partisans obtained in this manner are of negligible military value unless used in very special circumstances, such as an ambush on a group of severely damaged enemy units on their way back to garrison and heal themselves; however, ordinary citizens do have a moment of military glory, when the efforts of a single citizen can affect the course of the entire game. This is when you start with Nomad, discover a rival nation building their first city, and detail one of your citizens to beat up on the enemy builder(s). Confident and skillful players might want to apply this tactic in multiplayer games, but be mindful it will cause some resentment.

The following sections discuss the game's land military units by building of origin, as established earlier. Note that the game is full of information on each unit: Simply turn the tooltip help detail to High, and pick a unit to learn all its vital stats plus hints as to its optimal use (see Figure 6.1).

The stats shown in tooltip help include:

◆ Unit cost. This changes drastically during the course of the game. The more units you have, the more expensive they get.

◆ Unit use. You'll be told which enemy units the selected soldiers perform well against and which badly.

FIGURE 6.1: *Learn all about military units with the game's excellent tooltip help.*

◆ Hits. This is the number of hit points the unit has. A unit loses hit points as damage is inflicted through combat or attrition—see the following entries.

◆ Attack. This is the amount of damage the unit can inflict during a successful attack on an enemy unit.

◆ Armor. This determines the unit's resistance to damage. When calculating damage received, the strength of the armor is subtracted from the attack value. For instance, a unit with an attack of 13 will inflict 12 damage when attacking a unit with an armor of 1.

◆ Range. This is the maximum range measured in map coordination tiles. Melee units have a range value of 0; some units also have a minimum range, meaning they cannot hit targets close by.

◆ Population cap contribution. This shows how many points the unit contributes to the population count (one or two).

◆ Speed. This is the speed with which the unit moves over terrain (note that land units crossing bodies of water turn into transports; see Chapter 7).

◆ Upgrades. This entry lists the future military upgrades to the selected unit, obtainable after researching the prerequisites listed (Age, sometimes also mainstream Military research).

In addition, units also have many "hidden" qualities. One of the most important of these is attack frequency; as a rule, light units inflict less damage than heavy units, but attack more often. In addition to movement speed, all units have a turn speed, which lets them face an attack more or less nimbly; this is important inasmuch as flank attacks (from the side) carry a 50% damage bonus (attacks from the rear carry a bonus of 100%). Units are also differently affected by terrain (as you might guess, mounted and light infantry units move faster and are affected less; heavy infantry and artillery move slower and are affected more). Finally and very importantly, units might have special qualities and/or abilities; when that occurs, it's highlighted within the game and explained in the tooltip help.

Note that the unit qualities listed here also apply to naval and air units discussed in Chapter 7 as well as civilian units (although some qualities obviously won't be applicable).

Barracks Units

From Ancient through Medieval Age, the barracks units fall into four easy-to-distinguish classes:

- Light infantry. These units have the highest mobility of all combat infantry units. They work well as a front guard for armies, raiders (Ancient Age only), and replacements. Strong against ranged attack infantry, in the late game light infantry tends to be used as cheap, expendable front guard/replacement units. This line of units costs food and timber throughout the game.

- Heavy infantry. These units are powerful but very slow. They work well as main army body troops, providing protection from cavalry to artillery units and supply wagons. They're also useful for storming cities in the early game. Strong against cavalry, heavy infantry makes your armies tougher throughout the game. This line of units costs food and metal starting with Classical Age, food and timber in Ancient Age.

- Ranged attack infantry. This line includes bowmen, archers, and crossbowmen. Very effective against heavy infantry, ranged attack infantry is an important factor in defense. It's also invaluable as part of an individual army, significantly weakening any engaged enemy force. This line of units is quite expensive; it requires timber and wealth. It merges with the light infantry line in Enlightenment Age (crossbowmen turn into musketeers).

- Scouting/reconnaissance units. The scout (Ancient Age) and explorer (Medieval Age) have no combat abilities; these are acquired in Enlightenment Age, when the explorer turns into the commando. Note also that the explorer is invisible to enemy units when it is not moving, enabling you to spy on enemy activities. The commando can be used as a sniper (one shot kills any infantry/mounted unit) as well as a saboteur (damage to targeted building equals 200 hit points to start with; subsequent unit upgrades raise this amount by 200 damage per upgrade, up to a maximum of 800 hit points, or half remaining hit points, whichever is greater). With Modern Age, the commando turns into a special forces unit (more craft to use on unit abilities, higher sabotage damage as previously noted); later on, it undergoes one more change in Information Age. Unfortunately, the elite special forces unit that becomes available then arrives too late to make a big difference in the game in spite of new skills (jam radar ability, which can clear the way for an air assault on cities with strong anti-aircaft defenses). Note that the scout line units are immune to attrition in enemy territory.

Following advancement into Gunpowder Age, light infantry receives firearms (see Figure 6.2). With Enlightenment Age, ranged attack infantry as such disappears: There are only light and heavy infantry, both with ranged attack capability. Industrial Age introduces a new and very powerful infantry unit: the flamethrower, and the machine gun after you research the anti-tank rifle. The machine gun is extremely effective against all other infantry;

> **Note**
>
> Even though scouts and explorers have no combat abilities, they're worth their weight in gold. No game played at Moderate or higher difficulty level can be won without extensive and early reconnaissance of the game world. Scouts are also excellent at finding ruins and the goody boxes within; more than likely, the first scout you build will quickly repay its cost. Later in the game, the explorer's/commando's (upgraded scout) ability to spot hidden units and decoys becomes very useful.

heavy infantry mutates into anti-tank rifles, thus keeping its anti-cavalry capability (by that time, cavalry turns modern with armored cars and tanks).

All in all, barracks units carry the greatest weight in the early game (they're the only military units available in Ancient Age). They undergo a renaissance of sorts in Gunpowder/Enlightenment Age, with the acquisition of firearms. The flamethrower is an absolutely lethal though short-range unit that becomes the special operations unit of choice, being often more effective than the commando/special forces unit. It is equally good against buildings (it ejects all garrisoned units from the attacked structure) and military units; note that when it appears, it has better anti-tank capability than the anti-tank rifle, although it does need to be much closer to the target to launch an attack.

FIGURE 6.2: *Quite apart from military considerations, the arrival of firearms means plenty of neat sound and visual effects.*

Barracks units are well suited for both offensive and defensive actions. They are best grouped together to form armies for both offense and defense, because it's very easy to wipe out a small group of foot units on their own. Once Enlightenment Age comes around, consider forming special operations groups composed of one or preferably more generals and five to six commandos. These can wreak great havoc behind enemy lines, sniping enemy units and sabotaging buildings.

> **Note**
>
> *Regardless of the Age you're in, infantry always retains a special role because it's the only unit type affected by the General's Entrench ability.*

Once Industrial Age comes along, you'll be able to form the ultimate special ops team by including flamethrowers in the mix. This combination can even take cities. All you have to do is approach unseen (a general using Ambush skill, possibly another general for Forced March), and flush any defenders garrisoned inside the city with flamethrowers. Once the city can't fire at your units, you can reduce it at will, unless the enemy rushes an army to the scene. In the meantime, your generals will have regained their craft, so by the time an enemy army shows up, you'll have the option of staying to fight it out (only if extra support is available) or perform another quick, invisible retreat. Note that air units, especially missiles and bombers, can be very helpful while attempting to take a city in this manner.

Naturally, infantry works great as protection for your artillery units; see the "Siege Factory/Factory Units" section later in this chapter.

Stable/Auto Plant Units

There are three types of mounted units created at the stable from Ancient through Enlightenment Age. All of them are invaluable for waging offensive warfare and very useful in defense. Here's who's who:

▷ Light cavalry. This is the unit line that becomes available earliest; the first mounted unit you can create is the light horse (Classical Age and Military level 1 required). Light cavalry is the most mobile unit available for most of the game, until airplanes appear on the scene. It's good for raiding, patrolling, mobile defense, though not very good for reconnaissance because of its short line of sight. It performs best when it's part of a cavalry group that includes ranged attack cavalry. The light mounted units are replaced by armored cars in Industrial Age, which changes unit creation costs from food and timber into food and oil.

▷ Heavy cavalry. Those are your shock troops for much of the game. This line begins with the cataphract (Classical Age and Military level 2 required), and morphs into the tanks line in Industrial Age (that's when unit creation costs change from metal and wealth to metal and oil). Heavy cavalry combines good armor with mobility; a group of these units is equally useful in offense (as the army shock corps) and defense (a group of heavy cavalry can finish off the artillery of a besieging army even more quickly than light cavalry). This class of unit also works very well as part of a cavalry corps.

▷ Ranged attack cavalry. This line begins with the horse archer (Classical Age, Military level 2), switches to firearms in Gunpowder Age (dragoons), and eventually morphs with light cavalry into the armored car line with the beginning of Industrial Age (which changes unit creation costs from timber and wealth to food and oil). Ranged attack cavalry is invaluable as an offensive unit; its high mobility makes it dangerous and difficult to deal with. When grouped together with light or preferably heavy cavalry, it effectively protects the other mounted units from heavy infantry; at the same time, the other mounted units can intercept any force aimed at the ranged attack cavalry.

Forming cavalry-only corps and occasionally even armies is very helpful toward winning the game. A corps or army like that led by a general is very dangerous, and can be fought off only with a full-sized army or a similar, stronger cavalry group. It is perfectly capable of conducting swift marches to the target and back without a supply wagon as long as you pull it back to heal after achieving the mission objective. What's more, its mobility allows it to break contact and retreat safely when faced with a stronger enemy.

> **Note**
>
> *A general that wins a battle but fails to pursue retreating enemy forces has won only half a victory.*

You can also use cavalry in a defensive role to good effect. Its high mobility means it can be rushed as reinforcements to the endangered part of your empire, and subsequently used to outmaneuver attacking enemy forces and destroy their artillery (see Figure 6.3). Whether it's used offensively or defensively, cavalry also has an extra ultra-important role: It's the type of unit best suited to pursuit. A freshly won battle is a unique opportunity to destroy many badly damaged units; always grasp this opportunity even though a smart enemy will set up an ambush or two to cover the retreat. Cavalry is ideal for that task: It's fast enough to catch up with retreating enemy units, and swift enough to extricate itself from trouble when it runs into an ambush.

Forming a few small cavalry corps early in the game and using them to conduct raids can make the final victory surprisingly easy; you can virtually bring enemy economies to a standstill by massacring farmers and lumberjacks and retreating before enemy forces can intervene effectively. Once Industrial Age arrives and cavalry units turn into armored cars and tanks, your cavalry corps turns into the armored division. Tanks accompanied by armored cars aren't good at reducing city defenses, but they are great at virtually everything else. Just as when handling cavalry, don't press attack when faced with a dangerous resistance. The biggest asset of your mechanized corps is its mobility; use it whenever it can give you an advantage (as in swift retreat or a flanking maneuver).

A group of tanks and armored cars that enjoys the support of anti-aircraft units (see "Anti-Aircraft Defense" later in this chapter) and/or air cover/support is extremely dangerous. Make sure you assemble a couple yourself; when you see one approaching, use delaying tactics while you assemble an army to deal with the threat.

FIGURE 6.3: *Cavalry's biggest advantage lies in its mobility.*

Siege Factory/Factory Units

Building a siege factory requires advancing to Classical Age and researching Military level 2. At first, the only thing on offer is a primitive artillery unit: the catapult. With Medieval Age, the range expands to include:

> **Warning**
>
> *Do not send out tanks on their own; they might fall prey easily to flamethrowers and anti-tank weapons if not accompanied by armored cars.*

- Artillery units. This line begins with catapults in Classical Age; unit costs are timber and metal, and atypically change to metal and oil only in Modern Age, with the self-propelled howitzer. The main function of artillery is to destroy enemy buildings and reduce the defenses of enemy cities, however, it can also be used as a support weapon in field battles (by targeting a certain spot on the ground) and in an anti-ship role (note that shore bombardment ships have a marginally longer range than contemporary land artillery units). Artillery is very fragile to begin with, acquiring some toughness only with Enlightenment Age; subsequent models might actually be difficult to destroy unless you use tanks and aircraft. All artillery requires a nearby supply wagon to maintain its standard firing rate, but in the early stages of the game the sub-standard fire rate works for capturing small cities.

- Supply wagons/trucks. The presence of a supply wagon protects your army from attrition damage; if you play the French or build the Versailles Wonder, supply wagons also heal damaged combat units. They are an obligatory component of siege armies; you might also need to set up a relay chain of wagons in games on large maps to protect units from attrition on the way to and from the battlefield. In multiplayer games, supply wagons will draw enemy attacks like honey draws flies, also because destroying one is rewarded with 50 wealth.

◆ Mobile anti-aircraft weapons. This line appears only in Industrial Age, which turns the siege factory into a modern factory and introduces the anti-aircraft gun. Interestingly, unit creation costs are food and wealth. Anti-aircraft units quickly become an essential part of any army that hopes to arrive at

its objective without being shredded on the way by enemy aircraft. Sadly, they do not work well against other targets than aircraft.

As a rule, siege factory units are created to be included in an army, however, it also pays to keep one or two artillery/supply wagon teams in reserve. This will let you quickly exploit any opportunities your scouts, spies, and cavalry discover while going about their stuff. Games on large maps abound in opportunities to capture smaller enemy cities without any opposition—provided you can pull up the artillery quickly enough (see Figure 6.4).

Deploy anti-aircraft artillery with an eye to existing anti-aircraft capabilities. The whole question of who is allowed to shoot at aircraft and who isn't is dealt with in the next section.

FIGURE 6.4: *Stay flexible, and take advantage of strategic opportunities when they appear.*

Anti-Aircraft (AA) Defense

The air force doesn't become a really potent force until the Modern Age (see the next chapter), however, even the biplane fighters that appear in Industrial Age can grow to be a nuisance if you let them rage unchecked. You can, and should, build airbases of your own; however, if the enemy has a strong air force, don't neglect building anti-aircraft defenses in the shape of permanent structures (the lookout building line morphs into the air defense gun in Industrial Age, and subsequently into radar air defense and SAM installation). Enemy air strikes directed at buildings of economic significance are particularly dangerous, so place AA defenses accordingly.

Don't build too many permanent AA defenses; this role can also be played by mobile AA defense units. Once the enemy air threat is contained, these mobile units can then be used to protect your advancing armies from aircraft. Distribute them among your armies according to the armies' existing AA potential, as some "ordinary" military units have AA defense capability.

Understanding AA Capability

There are only two kinds of aircraft for targeting purposes. These are aircraft on their way to a target or airbase, and aircraft that are actively attacking a target. The game assumes the first group is flying high and out of harm's way if possible; attacking aircraft need to get close to their targets, thus fly low and into range of ground units.

The majority of the land and sea units in the game can target only low-flying (attacking) aircraft. Each AA-capable unit has its own chance to hit the enemy aircraft:

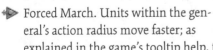 Light infantry gains AA capabilities with the musketeers (Enlightenment Age, 25% chance to hit low-flying aircraft). It retains that capability, with chance to hit increasing to 30% (Industrial Age infantry) and subsequently to 33% for Modern and Information Age light infantry.

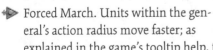 Enlightenment Age heavy infantry (fusiliers) are the first to have AA capability. Both the fusiliers and all subsequent units in this line (anti-tank rifle, for example) have a 20% chance to hit attacking aircraft.

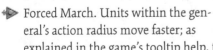 Ranged attack cavalry (horse archer line) gains AA capability very early: in the Gunpowder Age. Dragoons and carabineers have a 20% chance to hit attacking aircraft; subsequent models of armored cars a 33% chance.

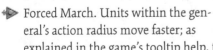 Units in the factory mobile anti-aircraft line have an incomparably greater AA capability. All of them, starting with the Industrial Age-era anti-aircraft gun, have a 90% chance to hit attacking aircraft *and* a 50% chance to hit high-flying aircraft on their way to the target or airbase.

Keep in mind that tanks and artillery are defenseless against air attacks. Also, many sea units have good AA capability; see Chapter 7.

General Truths and Tips

As mentioned earlier, forts let you create generals and spies. Spies and their role in the game are discussed in detail in Chapter 9; this section focuses on generals. They're certainly worthy of all this attention, for although the general does not have any direct combat abilities, it is probably the most valuable single military unit in the game. This is because a general has special skills, which work not unlike a magician's spell, affecting all friendly units within the general's action radius (see Figure 6.5).

In the order of appearance on the general's orders panel, the special abilities are:

FIGURE 6.5: *Forced March can make your pikemen run like Jesse Owens. Well, almost.*

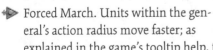 Forced March. Units within the general's action radius move faster; as explained in the game's tooltip help, this effect is weaker on mounted units/vehicles. The advantages are obvious: Forced March enables you to move your armies and task groups that much faster. Use it both defensively (for example, to break contact with the enemy and retreat) and offensively (for any kind of offensive maneuver that really needs to be completed quickly). Lasts for 30 seconds of game time.

- Entrench. This ability affects heavy and light infantry most, and only within your own national territory. It's explained in the tooltip help. Note that heavy infantry gets +3 armor, and light infantry gets +1 armor; all other troops get no armor bonus, however, all are protected from the extra damage meted out by artillery projectiles, bombs, and missiles. This ability is useful only for desperate death stands; hopefully you won't get to use it at all.

- Decoy. As the tooltip help explains, this creates a group of "fake" military units; the type is determined by the type of your real units in the vicinity. They last for 150 seconds of game time, which is plenty in game terms. This ability is especially useful in multiplayer games, but remains good value in solo play (for example, when used to stage a diversion or to cover a retreat).

- Ambush. This extremely useful ability renders units within the general's action radius invisible to the enemy. It's very valuable in both solo and multiplayer games.

When you review the general's skills, it quickly becomes obvious that there is much to be gained by using them in conjunction with each other. For instance, Ambush coupled with Forced March will let you insert special operations teams deep inside enemy territory without being detected on the way. Naturally you'll need more than one general assigned to a group of units for this. For optimum flexibility, you need three: The effects of Forced March and Ambush last 30 seconds, but a general takes 60 seconds to regain the 1,000 craft spent on using either ability (prior to researching Operations, which lets generals recover spent craft 100% faster; see Chapter 4 for other fort research details).

These special abilities all have a limited time span; however, a general also provides units within his action radius with an armor bonus. This initially amounts to +2, but can be significantly improved following appropriate research at the fort (see Chapter 4). All in all, you can never have enough generals; they're that good. They're not inexpensive, starting at 100 metal and 100 wealth; however, they're worth every penny. Note also that fort-based research helps you reduce general creation costs.

Tip

Having three generals with a task force or an army means you can have one of them using a special skill at all times.

MILITARY UNIT UPGRADES

Military unit upgrades play a very, very important role in the game; the whole Age Jump strategy laid out in Chapters 4 and 8 revolves around military upgrades. Their cost is always the same: twice the basic unit cost plus any other extra costs stemming from the fact that the new unit is more expensive (this happens mainly during the transition from Enlightenment to Industrial Age). If extra costs apply, they are calculated for each and every unit of the affected type in your possession. Now you know why upgrading cuirassiers into light tanks can be so expensive.

A Short History of the Army

The following sections examine the changes your land forces go through with the Ages. They also contain comments about army composition and size. Treat those comments as very general guidelines, remembering that army composition and size in your particular game is always defined by that game's circumstances, first and foremost. For instance, this guide repeatedly recommends forming a number of cavalry-only corps and sending them out to damage the enemy economy. When you play a sea map such as the East Indies, you need to adapt this approach accordingly (see Figure 6.6).

Ancient Age

This is the Age that supposedly separates the men from the apes, so military options are limited. You may build a barracks once you research Military level 1, and a tower; that's it. The barracks lets you create infantry; usually, you'll want to restrict new unit creation to a scout or two, bowmen for garrisoning cities, and at most, a couple of slinger units for reconnaissance and raiding (slingers cost precious food, which you need for the Age Jump). If

FIGURE 6.6: *A small cavalry corps finishes off the defenses of a city damaged by naval bombardment. Infantry isn't visible, but it's on its way.*

there's a nearby enemy capital you have to capture right there and then, form a strong force of heavy infantry (four to five units) to assault the city; add slingers for protection from enemy bowmen if that threat exists. Also, consider using the city-defense bowmen if it's safe to do so; every little bit helps in capturing that first city more quickly.

Classical Age

This Age brings a revolution to your armed forces. Upon reaching it and researching Military level 2, you can build stables, siege factories, and all the combat units therein. You can also build forts and create generals; in fact, the only army item missing is the supply wagon, which doesn't become available until the Medieval Age. If you're in the process of executing an Age Jump, restrict creating new military units to two to five cavalry, depending on the threat to your nation. If you've already embarked on a war of conquest, add a general and a couple of catapults to your army, and consider creating your first independent cavalry corps. Use these both for independent operations and in support of your main army (general, infantry, catapults). If you have Science level 2, Herbal Lore (granary research) will let you create and heal units faster.

Note

Don't neglect to research Allegiance quickly once you reach the Classical Age. It's particularly useful in high difficulty solo games and all multiplayer games.

Medieval Age

Your army blooms fully with the Medieval Age. Supply wagons finally appear on the scene, making protracted offensives feasible. Catapults upgrade into trebuchets with markedly increased destructive power, and a similar wave of change sweeps through your entire army (see Figure 6.7). If you haven't stepped out on the warpath yet, now is the time; spies, newly available at the fort, will be very helpful in determining whom to attack.

FIGURE 6.7: *A medieval army in combat*

Your main offensive army should consist, roughly, of at least one general, half a dozen units of pikemen, four each of crossbowmen and elite javelineers, a couple (three is better) of trebuchets, and a couple of supply wagons (three in multiplayer games). Also have at least one (and preferably two) strong cavalry corps led by another general, plus half a dozen miscellaneous units acting as reserves (crossbowmen garrisoned inside cities, towers, and/or forts; a few cavalry as a mobile defense force; and so on). Medieval Age also lets you conduct some useful specialized military research: Forage at the smelter (decreased attrition to your units) and Oath of Fealty at the tower (increased attrition to enemy units). Generals and spies can be improved by researching Tactics.

Gunpowder Age

You finally get a real bang for your buck. The new generation of military units that appears is still somewhat medieval in character (elite pikemen, heavy knights). Light infantry and ranged attack cavalry greatly increase in value thanks to firearms (arquebusiers, dragoons). Generals greatly increase in value thanks to Operations researched at the fort. Most players will greet the appearance of firearms with great glee and immediately plunge into war with new enthusiasm; so it bears repeating that this is your only chance to execute the Age Jump for the second time (from Medieval to Enlightenment). Enlightenment Age offers even greater military benefits. At this stage of the game, your army composition and size will be dictated strictly by the situation that has developed in the meantime; however, in the vast majority of games, you'll want to add at least a few arquebusier and dragoon units to your army or armies. Don't forget to research Medicine at the granary.

Enlightenment Age

Your heavy infantry finally becomes enlightened and switches to firearms, merging with the crossbowmen line. There's a big improvement, across the board, in the firepower of all land units; the only melee units that remain are hussars (light cavalry) and cuirassiers (heavy cavalry). Researching Patriotism at the tower and Supply at the smelter boosts your attrition/anti-attrition capability. By the time Enlightenment Age comes around, you should definitely have at least two main armies and three to four smaller corps, mostly cavalry-only, along with at least half a dozen generals. Heavy infantry comes into particularly sharp focus, and you'll probably want to add some fusiliers to your land forces. Fusiliers also make possible the infantry-only corps; half a dozen musketeer and fusilier units supported by a single cannon/supply wagon combo can easily take a small city, or inflict considerable economic damage.

Industrial Age

As you know by now, Industrial Age brings about a military revolution. All the weapons of modern war—tanks, airplanes, machine guns, flamethrowers—make their first appearance (see Figure 6.8). The tank upgrade is a priority: The tank is a weapon that immediately transforms the face of battle. This does not mean you can ignore the other novelties, particularly the flame-thrower. Beginning to develop an air force is a non-army priority, but it's a priority nonetheless and will affect the pace at which you can modernize and expand your army. The profound changes that take place are headed by the transformation of the cavalry corps into the armored army,

FIGURE 6.8: *The changing face of war*

which emerges as a lethal threat when backed by the new supply trucks, which are faster than the wagon. Most importantly, you must now give your armies and corps anti-aircraft capability. Special operations acquire a new lethality with flamethrowers. Researching Strategy at the fort further boosts the abilities of your generals, while Pharmaceuticals (granary) boost the recovery rate of damaged units.

Modern Age

In Modern Age, the recently reborn army undergoes yet another fundamental change. Self-propelled artillery (howitzers) transforms the armored army into a very capable conqueror of cities (as long as you take along a symbolic infantry unit to actually capture the reduced city). The need for extra AA defense units rises sharply, airplanes become much more dangerous, and an army lacking in AA protection is at a great disadvantage. Research the last levels of the attrition and anti-attrition techs, and make sure you upgrade your armor quickly once in Modern Age; the Industrial era light tank cannot compete with the Modern Age models. Although the first missiles make an appearance, they do not as yet affect army operations to any significant degree. The commando changes into the special forces unit with enhanced capacity for mayhem. A special operations task force supported by a handful of conventional infantry is powerful enough to take a city. The biggest single change is the impact made by the new air force, which now boasts tank-killer helicopters; combined operations that involve close coordination of land and air units become the new modus operandi.

Information Age

The Information Age is the age of MAD: mutually assured destruction. Any runner-up that feels frus-trated at not winning the game may destroy the world, leaving no winners; all that's needed is a few missile silos, sufficient resources to make a number of nuclear ICBMs, and some time. Used in modera-tion, ICBMs can play a major tactical role by instantly reducing the defenses of enemy cities or crippling large armies. It's a good idea to split your land forces into a number of medium-sized armies rather than keep them in a couple of behemoth-like army corps. Successful land operations are very difficult without strong AA presence; control of the air is assured only if you destroy the enemy airbases (another target for an ICBM strike prior to an offensive). It's not many games that will still be undecided by the time you reach Information Age; if you find yourself in that situation, your best bet is to push the Armageddon clock as fast and far forward as possible without actually causing Armageddon. The game lets players use a limited number of nukes, so make sure you're the one to use them; it's that simple. If you manage to do that and select targets well, the rest is a walkover (unless someone decides to go MAD).

National Armies

Each and every *RoN* nation receives a few unique units as part of its national bonuses. When considered together with other national bonuses, a nation's unique units might give that nation a little extra advantage when pursuing a particular strategy. The following sections review the national armies and comment on using them to their best advantage.

Aztecs

Aztec unique units: Five models of light infantry: Atl-atls (Ancient Age), Royal Atl-atls (Classical Age), Xopilli Atl-atls (Medieval Age), Jaguar infantry (Modern Age), Jaguar assault infantry (Information Age).

FIGURE 6.9: *A medieval Aztec army lays siege to a German city. Note the city info provided by a planted informer.*

Comments: The Aztec national bonuses include free light infantry with every new barracks, plus resource gifts for every slain enemy unit. The five Aztec unique units consist of light infantry that's slightly tougher and more powerful than the standard model. Altogether, the Aztec path to victory is clearly marked: Attack as early as you can, and keep attacking until you win (see Figure 6.9).

Bantu

Bantu unique units: Three models of light infantry: Umpakati (Ancient Age), Yangombi Umpakati (Classical Age), Impi (Medieval Age). Two models of unique fighter aircraft: Hawk fighter (Modern Age), Eagle fighter (Information Age).

Comments: The Bantu light infantry are faster and cheaper than regular light infantry; coupled with the +1 city bonus, this predestines the Bantu for an offensive path from the start of the game. The Umpakati and Yangombi Umpakati are faster and slightly cheaper than regular models; Impi are also tougher and slightly more accurate. The two fighter types have stronger attack capability than regular fighter aircraft, but by the time they arrive on the scene, the Bantu should control the world anyway.

British

British unique units: Three unique units in the ranged attack infantry line that are upgraded free of charge: Longbowmen (Classical Age), King's Longbowmen (Medieval Age), and King's Yeomanry (Gunpowder Age). Two models of light infantry: Highlanders (Enlightenment Age) and Black Watch (Industrial Age).

Comments: The three archer-line unique units are extra effective against enemy heavy infantry; the two later-age light infantry models are very effective against all enemy infantry. The British unique unit lineup suggests a defensive policy to start with, with optimum offensive units appearing in Enlightenment Age, however, don't let this dictate your policy. The British are arguably the most versatile nation in the game, and perform well when led well regardless of strategy, which you should chose solely on the basis of game circumstances.

Chinese

Chinese unique units: Three types of light infantry: Fire Lances (Medieval Age), Heavy Fire Lances (Gunpowder Age), Manchu Musketeers (Enlightenment Age). Two models of light infantry: Manchu Riflemen (Industrial Age), and Manchu Infantry (Modern Age).

Comments: The Chinese are unique in receiving a unit equipped with firearms in the Medieval Age. The Fire Lances are especially effective against enemy heavy infantry; the Heavy Fire Lances have better range than arquebusiers; and the Manchu Musketeers are real killers, having better range, moving faster, and also being cheaper and quicker to create. The later two models of light infantry have increased firepower and are cheaper and quicker to create than standard light infantry. Altogether, the Chinese are very well adapted to the Age Jump, which is made even easier by the Chinese research bonus; it's best to delay the main offensive until Medieval Age, and exploit the slight edge offered by infantry firepower over the next couple of Ages.

Egyptians

Egyptian unique units: Four types of ranged attack cavalry: Chariot (Classical Age), Heavy Chariot (Medieval Age), Mameluke (Gunpowder Age), and Royal Mameluke (Enlightenment Age). Three types of light cavalry: Light Camel (Classical Age), Camel Warrior (Medieval Age), Elite Camel Warrior (Gunpowder Age).

Comments: The Egyptians are one of the luckier nations in the game: In addition to whopping economic and Wonder bonuses, they get no less than seven models of excellent cavalry. The Chariot and Heavy Chariot are especially good against enemy ranged attack cavalry; the Mameluke and the Royal Mameluke are better raiders than standard dragoons and carabineers. The three light cavalry types (Light Camel, Camel Warrior, Elite Camel Warrior) are very versatile: They have superior line of sight, which makes them good scouts, and work well against enemy cavalry and artillery. Overall, the Egyptians are very well suited for the Age Jump; having two good, unique cavalry units in both Medieval and Gunpowder Age indicates the optimum time for an all-out offensive.

French

French unique units: Four types of heavy cavalry: Chevalier (classical Age), Heavy Chevalier (Medieval Age), Horse Grenadiers (Gunpowder Age), and Horse Guard Grenadiers (Enlightenment Age).

FIGURE 6.10: *The French are easy to lead gracefully to victory.*

Comments: The most important of French military bonuses lie elsewhere: A free general with every fort and supply wagons that heal your troops are as valuable as a large number of unique units. Things are helped a little further by the four unique heavy cavalry models, which all have a slightly better attack, better speed, and more hit points than standard heavy cavalry. The French are made for continuous offensive warfare, preferably starting with Medieval Age; they are ideally positioned to take advantage of the Age Jump (see Figure 6.10).

Germans

German unique units: Four types of heavy infantry: Solduri (Ancient Age), Barbarians (Classical Age), Vandals (Medieval Age), and Landsknechts (Gunpowder Age). Two types of tanks: Tiger (Modern Age) and Leopard (Information Age). Also, a unique type of light infantry: Volksgrenadiers (Modern Age) and a unique machine gun unit—MG42, both Modern Age.

Comments: The Germans are arguably the most advantaged of all the nations in *RoN*; in solo games, they invariably emerge as a leader when controlled by the A.I. Their great economic bonuses are complemented by an array of heavy infantry with better armor and slightly more hit points then standard contemporary units; in case that isn't enough, there are two heavily armored and powerful tanks later on. The unique infantry is extra icing on the cake: The Volksgrenadiers have better armor, speed, and rate of fire than their standard light infantry counterparts, while the MG42 is a machine gun that's even more deadly against infantry than the standard unit. In summary, the Germans are so strong that attacking from very early on is both feasible and recommended; however, they'll perform well led to any strategy that fits the circumstances.

Greeks

Greek unique units: Four heavy cavalry models: Companion (Classical Age), Royal Companion (Medieval Age), Striatotai (Gunpowder Age), Royal Striatotai (Enlightenment Age).

Comments: The main Greek advantage lies in their big research bonus; by comparison, the unique unit lineup is almost immaterial. The Greek heavy cavalry is distinguished by its speed (faster than French unique units). Extra mobility is always a big asset, and this slight edge will be helpful both in offense and defense. Generally speaking, the Greek military advantage lies in fielding more modern units than those of their opponents (see Figure 6.11), not in unique unit types. The Greeks are a very flexible nation that performs well on any map and in any circumstances; every strategy works well as long as it fits the situation.

Inca

Inca unique units: Two light infantry models: Inti Clubmen (Classical Age) and Inti Macemen (Medieval Age). Two artillery models: Mortar (Enlightenment Age) and Siege Mortar (Industrial Age).

Comments: Inca unique units feature an interesting twist: Their unique light Inti infantry have no ranged attack like their contemporary counterparts. Instead, they have a stronger melee attack and more hit points. The mortar and siege mortar are extremely accurate, much more so than standard cannon and artillery units. All in all, the most significant Inca military bonus is the 25% unit cost refund you get when one of your units is destroyed. The Inca are not a nation that's especially well equipped for warfare, however, their economic bonuses are helpful in meeting wartime economical demands. Strategy should be dictated entirely by circumstances.

FIGURE 6.11: *The Greek military advantage consists mainly of maintaining a technological edge.*

Japanese

Japanese unique units: Five types of heavy infantry: Ashigaru Spearmen (Ancient Age), Bushi (Classical Age), Elite Bushi (Medieval Age), Samurai (Gunpowder Age), Gun Samurai (Enlightenment Age).

Comments: The Japanese enjoy powerful military bonuses that include cheaper and quicker-to-create barracks units that are especially effective against buildings. The unique unit lineup makes Japanese barracks troops even better: All five special heavy infantry models have a slightly better attack capability and more hit points than their standard counterparts. In summary, the Japanese are a nation made for conquest; the sooner this starts, the better. Their national farm and food bonuses provide extra help in quickly creating large infantry armies.

Koreans

Korean unique units: Four ranged attack infantry: Hwarang (Ancient Age), Elite Hwarang (Classical Age), Royal Hwarang (Medieval Age), Elite Royal Hwarang (Gunpowder Age). Two artillery models: Flaming Arrow (Classical Age), Heavy Flaming Arrow (Medieval Age).

Comments: The Korean ranged attack infantry line boasts a better attack capability and more hit points than standard contemporary units, while the artillery offers increased effectiveness against buildings. All in all, this is not much when compared with the other Korean bonuses, which favor a relatively peaceful policy. Choose a strategy that fits the circumstances without being influenced by the availability of the unique units.

Maya

Maya unique units: Three types of light infantry: Balamob Slingers (Ancient Age), Royal Balamob Slingers (Classical Age), Eagle Balamob Slingers (Medieval Age). Two types of anti-tank weapons: Recoilless Gun (Modern Age), Dragon AT Missile (Information Age).

Comments: Maya military bonuses tend to favor defense (cities without a garrison can still fire at enemies, buildings have 50% more hit points), therefore, the three unique light infantry types are a welcome boost to the Maya offensive ability: They perform equally well against ranged attack infantry and light infantry. The two later unique units are defensive in character, and thus don't quite have the same impact. If you want to put the special Maya slingers to good use, it's better to attack early; however, don't let this dictate your overall strategy, which should be determined by your specific circumstances.

Mongols

Mongol unique units: Four models of ranged attack cavalry: Nomad (Classical Age), Steppe Nomad (Medieval Age), Horde (Gunpowder Age), Golden Horde (Enlightenment Age).

FIGURE 6.12: *The Mongols are lethal in the hands of an aggressive player.*

Comments: The Mongols are tailor-made for offensive warfare (see Figure 6.12); national bonuses include free ranged attack cavalry with every stable. Appropriately enough, Mongol ranged attack cavalry is composed of unique units that, unlike their standard counterparts, are effective against enemy light infantry. The player who leads the Mongols should exploit this advantage to the hilt: Forming and leading cavalry-only corps has never been more rewarding.

Nubians

Nubian unique units: Three types of ranged attack infantry: Kushite Archers (Classical Age), Royal Kushite Archers (Medieval Age), Apedemak Archers (Gunpowder Age). Four types of ranged attack cavalry: Camel Archer (Classical Age), Heavy Camel Archer (Medieval Age), Camel Raider (Gunpowder Age), Camel Corps (Enlightenment Age).

Comments: The Nubians get the best of both worlds: Terrific national economic bonuses are complemented by a rich lineup of unique units. The unique archer units are deadly against enemy ranged attack infantry (other archers) as well as the usual heavy infantry; the mounted Camel Archer and Heavy Camel Archer are especially effective against enemy light infantry. Thus, the Classical Age sees the Nubians on the threshold of a unique opportunity to exploit their economic bonuses (which have just begun kicking in) and the beginning of two lines of good unique units that are rounded off by two improved mounted raider models (Camel Raider, Camel Corps). Note that the Nubian economic bonus makes them very well suited for the Age Jump and comfortable with any strategy that addresses specific game circumstances; you're not necessarily committed to offensive play.

Romans

Roman unique units: Three types of heavy infantry: Legions (Classical Age), Caesar's Legions (Medieval Age), Praetorian Guards (Gunpowder Age).

Comments: Roman national advantages include a city wealth bonus as well as free heavy infantry with new barracks; both are very helpful in waging an early war. Add in forts with an increased effect on national borders, and the stage is set for a slow, steady offensive. The unique heavy infantry is lethal against enemy heavy infantry as well as cavalry, so it becomes a truly versatile and dangerous unit. Roman advantages tend to wane in the later game; getting an early offensive start is recommended.

Russians

Russian unique units: Three types of light cavalry: Rusiny Lancer (Medieval Age), Cossack (Gunpowder Age), Don Cossack (Enlightenment Age). Two types of light infantry: Red Guards (Modern Age) and Shock Troops (Information Age). One unique tank: T80 (Information Age), as well as one unique artillery type—Katyusha Rocket (Modern Age).

Comments: The big Russian military bonus is the doubled attrition to enemy units, plus free attrition techs. Come Industrial Age, the oil production bonus assists in the modernization and expansion of the army. The long and varied array of unique units doesn't hurt. Among those, the light cavalry and infantry lines include units that attack with greater frequency than standard models and cost less to create; the unique tank is a heavily armored, powerful, and tough, and the Katyusha artillery is especially effective against infantry. The Russians are very flexible; the optimum strategy involves the Age Jump and attacking in Medieval Age (Russian borders increase with every Age, so waiting has extra advantages besides gaining unique units). The oil bonus and four unique units in Modern and Information Ages combine with the border bonus for a particularly strong position in the late game.

Spanish

Spanish unique units: Four heavy infantry types: Scutari (Classical Age), Royal Scutari (Medieval Age), Tercios (Gunpowder Age) and Royal Tercios (Enlightenment Age).

Comments: The Spanish enjoy a unique advantage: They can see the geography of the entire world from the start (enemy cities and units remain hidden). This gives them a great military advantage when they are led by a player experienced enough to quickly draw the right conclusions about possible enemy approach routes, strategic spots, and so on. The lineup of unique units includes four models of heavy infantry that are even more effective against enemy cavalry than what is standard for the type. What's more, the Spanish are unique in that their heavy infantry receives firearms in Gunpowder Age. This makes Spanish infantry-only armies a much more dangerous proposition than is the case with other nations. Other notable military advantages include a free heavy ship with every new dock, which makes the Spanish at a double advantage on sea maps (sea maps are inherently harder to explore). The Spanish are flexible, but concentrate on exploiting their exploration advantage to the maximum in the early to middle game (see Figure 6.13). The self-sufficient infantry will of course perform even better when aided by cavalry.

Turks

Turkish unique units: Two types of light infantry: Janissaries (Gunpowder Age) and Royal Janissaries (Enlightenment Age). Two models of unique artillery: Basilica Bombard (Gunpowder Age) and Basilica Cannon (Enlightenment Age).

FIGURE 6.13: *The Spanish perform particularly well on large sea maps.*

Comments: The Turkish national bonuses predestine them for offensive war after a period of intensive economic development; they are very well suited for the Age Jump. The national bonuses include a +3 bonus to the range and line of sight of artillery units, plus two free artillery units with every new siege factory or factory. Add free artillery upgrades and the fact that captured cities assimilate 200% faster, and you've got a truly dangerous war machine. The unique light infantry units have a slightly more powerful attack capability, move faster, and are more accurate than their standard counterparts. The two Basilica artillery pieces are extremely accurate.

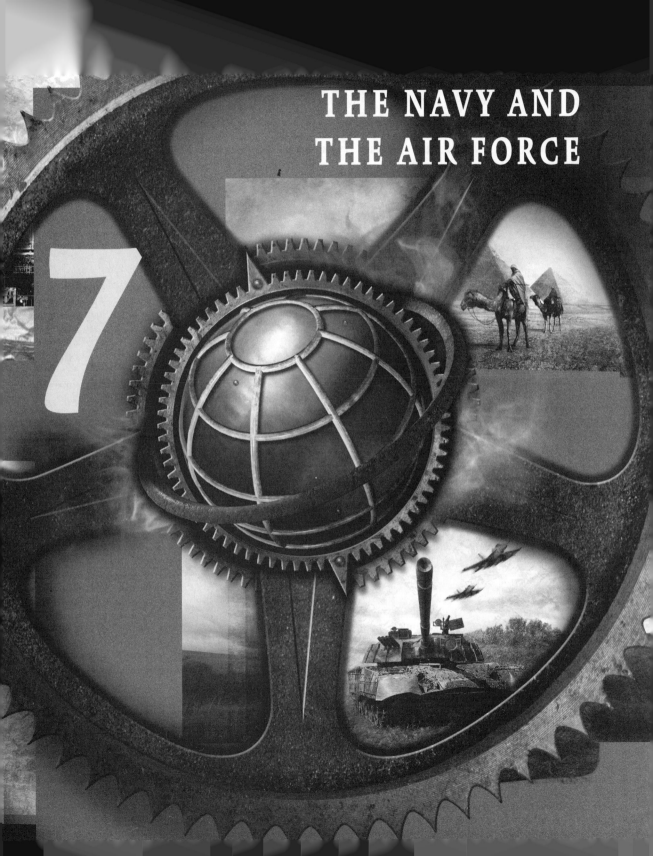

THE NAVY AND THE AIR FORCE

7

As you know from the preceding chapter, your army is the most important branch of your armed forces: Cities are captured by land units, not ships or planes; however, the remaining two branches of RoN armed forces—the navy and the air force—do play a significant role, and in certain circumstances might decide which player is victorious.

This chapter begins by examining the game circumstances in which your ships and aircraft can play a decisive role. It goes on to discuss the impact using sea and air units can have on your strategy, and subsequently to review the changes that transform the two services with the passage of Ages. Age advancement has great impact on your naval and aerial capabilities, invariably expanding the number of options at your disposal; this chapter evaluates these new options, and comments on their strategic value. It also includes practical advice on forming an effective navy and air force, and tips on using them in battle.

SEA AND AIR IMPERATIVES

You'll be creating an air force in any game that extends to Industrial Age and beyond, while you'll need a navy only when playing a sea map, or a land map with lakes. In a way, the air force is the more important of the two services; this is particularly true if your game extends into Modern Age. Once you pass into Information Age and nuclear ICBMs appear on the scene, aircraft and missiles might become the most important units in the game. True, you still need land units to capture cities, but in practice, this might translate into a symbolic couple of infantry units taking over the ruin that remains after repeated missile strikes and bombing missions.

Many players will be shocked at the importance a navy assumes in a game played on a sea map. This importance will be especially pronounced in multiplayer games. Your armies will need to cross water to take enemy cities, and sea transports are extremely vulnerable. An otherwise unbeatable army can be sunk by a handful of light ships in a fraction of the time it took to create it. What's more, ships boast good anti-aircraft defenses, which means that a large navy handled by a skillful opponent can be countered only with another navy; destroying it with air power and missiles alone is so difficult it is impractical. You can build ships from the moment you research Military level 1 in Ancient Age, and their importance grows steadily as time goes on. Keep in mind you can only build fishing ships. Military ships appear at Classical Age.

The sections that follow examine each service in more detail.

THE NAVY

For the most part, the game's naval units consist of ships that are built in the dock, however, the game also features other naval units: troop transports and merchant fleets. Both the transports and merchant ships are "temporary" units: Simply speaking, they are land units that change into sea units when ordered to cross a body of water (see Figure 7.1).

Civilian Ships

They don't cost anything, and they change back into land units upon striking land. Here's who changes into what:

- Citizens, merchants, and all military land units change into transports. Note that merchants change into transports only when ordered across a body of water to set up a trading post on terra firma; rare resources that appear on sea are exploited by fishermen, not merchants.

- Caravans change into merchant fleets.

Both transports and merchant ships undergo transformations as time goes on. Troop transports begin with the transport barge, which is replaced by the transport galleon in Gunpowder Age, and by the transport freighter in Industrial Age. The new varieties have more hit points, but speed doesn't change; it remains abysmally slow. What's more, the increase in hit points merely keeps pace with the bigger damage meted out by newer ship types.

FIGURE 7.1: *Land units automatically change into sea-going transports if you've checked the appropriate option on the unit panel.*

Sending your caravan to an overseas city is possible only with Classical Age (remember you need Commerce 2 to colonize overseas, too), which introduces the merchant fleet; this is upgraded to modern merchant fleet in Industrial Age. Both types of merchant fleets are much tougher than the troop transports, but they're dreadfully slow, even slower than the troop transports. This makes them vulnerable to attacks by enemy corsairs.

This leaves us with just one more non-combat sea unit: the fisherman. Fishermen are waterborne merchants that qualify as part of your navy inasmuch as they're created at a cost in a dock. A fisherman's vessel has no military use other than a somewhat short-sighted waterborne observation post; its value lies in enabling you to fish the seas for rare resources. Needless to say, fishermen are extremely fragile.

Tip

Fishermen steadily increase in productivity thanks to specialized research, and by the late game, constitute a very valuable source of food and wealth. Their fragility makes them ideal targets for air strikes or raids by light naval units.

Military Ships

All the other units created at the dock are military units. They include the following unit types:

- Light ships. This is the most versatile category of them all. Light ships are relatively inexpensive and very fast, making them ideal for exploration (see Figure 7.2). They do not do much damage with each attack, but have a relatively high fire rate, which coupled with their high speed, makes them the optimum enemy-transport interceptors. Light ships are also very effective against fire ships (see the following paragraph) and as sub hunters (they can spot submarines). In addition, they're also the only type of naval unit to count as a single population point toward the population limit. All other military ship types cost you two population points.

▶ Heavy ships. The ships in this line have more hit points, better armor, and inflict more damage; however, they're also considerably slower than light ships, and have a relatively low firing rate. Beginning with the dreadnought in Industrial Age, they're also well suited for bombardment of land targets. You'll be using heavy ships whenever you need plenty of firepower coupled with the ability to take damage. This will occur mainly when you're fighting large enemy fleets, intercepting enemy shore bombardment ships, or supporting troop landings.

▶ Fire ships. These appear in Classical Age, and mutate into submarines with Industrial Age. Fire ships have only one use: to damage and break up fleets of heavy enemy ships. All of them inflict damage within a certain radius; the effect decreases with distance, and the size of the area affected roughly resembles that of a city surrounded by farms. Fire ships are expensive, and since they're one-shot deals, use them very selectively; later models inflict more damage while boasting more hit points and marginally higher speed. Submarines are, of course, reusable; they have a relatively short range and a long reload time, but inflict considerable damage. This makes them the ultimate corsairs as well as a major threat to heavy ships.

▶ Shore bombardment ships. This ultra-short line of ships begins with the bomb vessel in Gunpowder Age and ends with the bomb ketch in Enlightenment Age. As the name indicates, this ship type is useful for bombarding shore targets; it has much more hitting power than heavy ships of the same Age. Note that your shore bombardment ships upgrade into dreadnoughts (heavy ships) upon advancing into Industrial Age.

There's also a single ship that is in a class all by itself. This is the aircraft carrier, which appears in the Modern Age and costs as much as a Wonder (base cost is 600 wealth, 600 oil), but comes with a complement of seven fighter-bomber aircraft (a unique type that cannot be built at airbases). It's an extremely powerful unit that can deal out meaningful damage to other ships as well as very good anti-aircraft defenses. Its aircraft live up to their name: They can shoot down other planes, though they are not effective at this as pure-bred fighters; and they can bomb targets to somewhat less effect than dedicated bomber planes.

FIGURE 7.2: *Explore the seas with light ships early in the game.*

Note

You may have only seven fighter-bombers per aircraft carrier. Extra fighter-bomber planes may be created on the carrier only when one of the original set is destroyed.

Fighting Fleets

You need ships to explore on sea maps; it's as simple as that. While you may explore with a scout that has turned into a transport barge, a ship is much faster and not as easy to destroy (which is particularly important in multiplayer games). As you know from earlier chapters, you should start exploring as soon as you can afford it, and even before you can really afford it in multiplayer games. Your first ships therefore will almost inevitably be light ships: barks (Ancient Age) or dromons (Classical Age; of course things will be different if you begin playing in a later Age). As mentioned earlier, light ships are ideal for exploration; also they're good at sinking enemy transports, and thus are very effective at preventing enemy nations from colonizing new lands.

Fleet Priorities

The number of light ships you need initially differs according to game difficulty, map size, and the number of opponents as well as their proximity to your nations; you might require anything from two (easier difficulty level, small map, couple of opponents) to eight (higher difficulty level, large map, many opponents). Assuming a higher level of difficulty, you need to divide your light ships between the following duties: exploration (two or three), interception of enemy transports at source and harassment (one to four), and finally your own coast guard (one to three). You want to build as many as you really need and no more; the premium you have to pay for every new ship increases with every ship you own; it costs 30 food and timber to build the first light ship, and 31 of each for the second, but the third costs 33 food and timber, the fourth 36 of each, and so on.

If you can, avoid building heavy ships in Ancient and Classical Age; they're very expensive (particularly in Ancient Age, when a single trireme costs as much as a new building). Sometimes, however, things can't be helped (see Figure 7.3). The discovery of nearby enemy presence instantly pushes all other considerations into second place.

FIGURE 7.3: *A trireme provides support for raiders about to land on the enemy shore.*

Building a Battle Fleet

If things are safe and secure, wait until the carrack in Medieval Age before beginning to build heavy ships in any numbers. The carrack still isn't great shakes: It's relatively slow and easily damaged, and lacks real firepower, but your opponents won't wait till you're satisfied with the current ship model, and you need to have a main battle fleet of heavy ships. Numbers vary for the same reasons as mentioned earlier; most of the time you'll need from three to six, depending on size of map, number of opponents, and so on. This main battle fleet ideally always operates as a single group; keep it in a strategic spot and send it out whenever your light ships cannot cope with something, or when you undertake an offensive operation such as transporting an army to an enemy-held land.

Note

Note that shore bombardment ships can target other sea vessels, although their slow speed and reload time makes them a less than ideal choice when fighting enemy ships.

Further fleet development is strictly dictated by circumstances. For example, there's no need to build fire rafts if you're the player with the superior fleet. What you'll need then are extra light ships to protect your fleet from enemy fire rafts. Shore bombardment ships are very useful when they finally appear in Gunpowder Age; all previous and concurrent models of heavy ships simply don't have enough firepower to do much damage to enemy buildings (destroying a dock takes forever), although they do work well against weak enemy land units such as citizens.

The Industrial Age brings far-reaching changes to naval forces: The dreadnought is the first versatile naval unit with meaningful punch, and the appearance of the submarine (into which all fire ships all upgraded) means a new threat to all heavy ships and merchant fleets. All surface ships acquire anti-aircraft ability (in fact the Enlightenment Age sloop is the first ship with AA capability), which makes them even more valuable as support for seaborne invasions of enemy lands.

THE AIR FORCE

Players who start every game in the Ancient Age will inevitably remain unaware of the possibilities created by owning a large air force. Airplanes appear on the scene only with the Industrial Age, and an aggressively played Ancient Age game played on a small- to medium-sized map will most likely be over by then.

The first aircraft are represented by fighter biplanes that are of little more than nuisance value unless used in very favorable circumstances (strafing artillery, supply wagons and tanks). It's probably wise not to invest too heavily in an air force until all the other Industrial Age military priorities are taken care of; remember you'll be spending a lot of oil on unit upgrades, and you'll be eager to build a few new tanks. Nevertheless, air power quickly acquires more significance as the game progresses into Modern Age, so unless you're convinced you're going to win very soon, build a couple of airbases. Position them strategically and in accordance with your situation; if you're planning an offensive, put them closer to the front line.

Tip

One of the best uses of the early biplane fighter is to hunt enemy flamethrowers—but only if you really have the time for the micromanagement involved.

Modern Air Power

The biplanes change into the more dangerous monoplanes with Modern Age, which also introduces the bomber. Early bombers work best against buildings; they're not very accurate and cannot be expected to achieve anything meaningful quickly if not supported by land forces. At the same time, they are useful in the tactical support role, weakening enemy units that are subsequently easier to kill (see Figure 7.4). Bombers are also helpful in bringing city sieges to a faster conclusion. All in all, use the first generation of Modern Age fighters and bombers primarily for tactical support. On occasion, air power can be used in conjunction with a special operations group to knock out a strategic target, such as a Wonder.

FIGURE 7.4: *Use bombers against buildings and to provide tactical support on the battlefield.*

If you have researched Military level 5, Modern Age lets you upgrade your aircraft into jet fighters, strategic bombers, and attack helicopters. Upgrading to stealth bombers and advanced fighters requires researching a future tech (Global Prosperity). All that trouble is worth it, because the last two generations of aircraft have great capabilities. Fast, tough, and with superior range, they are very hard to shoot down; in fact stealth bombers cannot be targeted by ground units or anti-aircraft structures at all. You have to shoot them down with aircraft.

> **Note**
>
> *Acquiring monoplane fighters, bombers, and helicopters requires Military level 3 as well as Modern Age, however, this is a concern only if you start the game in a late age (Enlightenment or later).*

> **Note**
>
> *Aircraft cost wealth and oil, while missiles cost oil and knowledge.*

Missiles and Nuclear Business

Missiles become available in the Modern Age once you build a missile silo and research Military level 6. The first missile type is the V2; a medium-range weapon with somewhat limited destructiveness but nice shock value in multiplayer games. Researching Military level 7 lets you acquire cruise missiles, which are great improvement in terms of destructive power; however, the first nuclear missiles become available even easier: It's enough to meet the prerequisites for a V2 and then conduct appropriate specialized research at the missile silo. These are eight times more destructive than the V2 and can destroy weaker buildings while meaningfully damaging others. On the minus side, they also start the Armageddon clock ticking plus bring about a temporary market trading embargo unless you've built the Space Program Wonder. If you intend to engage in extensive missile warfare, seriously consider acquiring this Wonder; it reveals the whole map, thus providing plenty of great targets.

Upon advancement to Information Age you'll be able to acquire nuclear ICBMs. These can instantly reduce cities; you'll still need to have troops standing by to capture the defenseless city, however. The conventional-warhead missiles definitely don't qualify as a strategic weapon, especially since missiles as such are difficult to use en masse; you can store only one missile per missile silo. All in all, missiles are at their best when used in conjunction with other weapons, or in an anti-shipping role when on their own.

Ruling the Air

Creating an effective air force is an expensive undertaking that has to be financed with plenty of oil along with wealth and knowledge. Since you'll also need plenty of oil for other exciting new toys, such as tanks and modern fighting ships, building a strong air force right away is rarely possible. Most of the time, you'll be having trouble keeping three to four airbases full of airplanes (the limit is ten per airbase). If you're able to afford more, it most likely means you've won the game anyway, and don't really need to invest in extra planes. Note that building new airbases to transfer existing planes might save plenty of airbase-to-target travel time, and thus increase the effectiveness of your air force without investing in new airplanes.

The size of your air force should correspond to the needs of the game. Playing on a large map, you'll most likely be able to do nicely with just a couple well-placed airbases in Industrial Age; however, definitely build a third right after advancing into Modern Age at the latest, and immediately fill it with bombers. You need a full flight of seven bombers to achieve anything meaningful; many players will also opt to build a second airbase right beside the bomber base, and fill it with fighters to provide convenient fighter escort for bombing missions. Consider also converting one of the airbases built earlier to a bomber station, moving the fighters stationed there to another location.

Warning

Don't site a new airbase too close to the front in multiplayer games. If there's one target that's really ripe for a missile attack, it's an airbase stuffed to full with refueling airplanes.

Although airplanes will continue flying the ordered mission without further attention on your part, you'll need to check on the situation fairly often in solo games and very often in multiplayer games; human players won't waste time pulling units out of harm's way, and you'll need to issue fresh orders to your pilots. This need of micromanagement is another reason why maintaining more than four active airbases simultaneously might prove difficult (especially if you're also conducting fighter-bomber combat missions from an aircraft carrier as well as arranging the odd missile strike). Besides, there's also a lot of fun to be had with helicopters.

Using Helicopters

Helicopters are one of the most fun units in the game (see Figure 7.5), and it's a pity they inevitably can be acquired only with Modern Age (and Military 3, which you'll have most likely researched a long time earlier). To begin with, unlike airplanes, helicopters never run out of fuel; they can hover endlessly over the same spot until they're destroyed. Helicopters work very well against vehicles (better than any other air unit), and they can also spot and attack submarines, which makes them doubly great for patrolling and border-watching duties on sea maps. They perform nicely though not spectacularly against buildings; the problem is that helicopters are rela-

FIGURE 7.5: *Helicopters are both extremely useful and fragile; they need looking after.*

tively fragile, and might get easily shot down during the long time they take to destroy a building. Naturally, using combat groups numbering three to five helicopters helps; any more and they tend to get in each other's way.

Advancing to Information Age and having Military level 5 lets you upgrade helicopters into attack helicopters, which perform slightly better in all respects. In games that see you reaching Modern Age, make sure to form an attack group of helicopters. They can be invaluable both as a tool for diversionary attacks and while lending tactical support during tank battles and any other encounters with enemy vehicles. Helicopters might also be helpful in taking out artillery during an enemy siege; however, the presence of numerous other ground troops with anti-aircraft capability might necessitate some deft micromanagement.

CHAPTER 7 THE NAVY AND THE AIRFORCE

BUILDING THE PERFECT EMPIRE

8

This chapter does not pretend to be an omniscient oracle. The game allows too many options to make a single approach the best for every game and game type. Instead, this chapter describes winning strategies for playing the game in Quick Battle mode, featuring a walkthrough of a full-fledged Survival of the Fittest game stretching from Ancient to the Information Age with a large number of opponents. This type of scenario is the hardest to play, particularly on a land-only map, and what will work there has an excellent chance of working well in any other game. This chapter also contains comments, as appropriate, on how things work in other types of games, such as Assassin and Diplomacy.

Note that this chapter discusses solo Quick Battle games. Chapters 11 and 12 deal with multiplayer, while Chapter 10 offers advice on how to win the Conquer the World campaign game. Both the campaign game and multiplayer, however, share many traits with Quick Battle solo games. The Quick Battle is the mother of all the other battles, so wherever your interests lie, you'll find the advice in this chapter useful.

STARTING OFF ON THE RIGHT FOOT

Let's start with a tip about selected pre-game settings: You'll put yourself at maximum advantage against the computer opponents if you start the game with Nomad, Low resources, Technology cost/research speed Very Expensive/Slow. The A.I. has been optimized at standard settings, and naturally you'll deal with the extra difficulty more skillfully than it can. The strategy in this chapter has been developed while playing the game with these settings at Tough, Tougher, and Toughest difficulty levels. Note, however, that games on small maps (Arena, even Standard when playing a sea map) can become uncomfortably drawn out with these starting settings.

As explained in Chapter 2, carefully consider your choice of nation. You can't miss by choosing a nation with a strong economic bonus coupled with miscellaneous advantages. Although the nations in *RoN* are finely balanced and each of them has a good shot at victory, some nations are, well, more equal than others. The safest national choices are the British, Egyptians, and Germans; the French, Greeks, Japanese, and Spanish also are quite safe, although their national advantages do require some skill to be put to good use. All the other nations can be deadly even when led by an experienced player (the Aztecs and the Turks can be particularly lethal).

The following walkthrough starts with a small bunch of nomad citizens wandering the map to begin building their nation's first city (see Figure 8.1). If your new game settings are different and you're starting with a Large city, for instance, you can skip through the text until you come to the part where it becomes relevant. The same does *not* apply if you started a game in a later Age (the walkthrough begins with Ancient Age). Regardless of your starting Age and the amount of resources you

Warning

Things really start hopping as the game goes on; once you have a couple of cities, the fastest practical playing speed is Slow. Setting game speed to Normal or Fast means either pausing it often or overlooking a lot of things. At higher difficulty levels, that will lose you the game.

begin with, you'll still have to research
new advances, fight enemies, and build up
your nation's economy (the few buildings
that come with a Large city make for a
slightly quicker start, that's all).

Note that if you start a new game
with a city center or a city instead of
Nomad, the starting locations of all the
competing players will be fairly evenly
distributed: typically, at roughly equal
distances around the edges of the map.
You're guaranteed to have some space to
yourself in the game's early stages, however, the starting locations chosen by the
computer often have little timber (a spin-
ney that can accommodate five lumberjacks is pretty common). Playing the
French or the Germans with their
national economic bonuses helps a little; leaders of any other
nation will just have to grit their teeth and make sure their second
city is a major timber production center.

FIGURE 8.1: *There's a special dangerous charm to beginning the game in Nomad mode.*

Finally, something to keep in mind at all times: If you play
every game to a tried and true pattern, you might become a competent player, and even win most solo games, but you won't be
able to prevail consistently in multiplayer. Your specific circumstances are the most important single factor determining your
strategy in any game, however, it also pays to compare any
options you might think of with a template of sorts; it helps you
see which revolutionary plans are unrealistic. This is where this
chapter will really help.

First Steps

Your first priority when beginning a game with Nomad is to
choose a good site for your first city, which automatically becomes
your capital. Don't waste time exploring the whole map with your
citizens. Time is very precious—it always is when you're playing a real-time strategy game. If you take
too long, even the most perfect site in the world won't help. You cannot hope to win a game in which all
the other players are busy looking for a site for their second city while you still haven't found the right
one for your capital.

You're facing additional time pressures because it's also important to complete construction fast.
Capital cities take an extra long time to build, and it's very helpful if all your citizens are working on the

> ### Warning
>
> *Starting the game with Nomad means some
> nations forfeit national benefits. The
> Spanish won't see the entire map until their
> first city is complete; the French won't get a
> free lumber mill, and the Koreans won't get
> a free temple. This won't mean much to an
> experienced player, since being able to
> choose the city site outweighs all other bene-
> fits in the long run. Other players, however,
> might feel disappointed. City Center Only is
> the second best starting choice because it lets
> you put farms and so on where you want
> them.*

site, so be sure to make them explore the map in such a way so that their paths converge in an area that suits your placement strategy (as illustrated earlier in Figure 8.1).

The ideal site for your capital has the following characteristics:

- Decent forests nearby. The reason is obvious: More timber means accelerated progress while building your empire. Metal-bearing mountains and cliffs close by are great too, but not as important as forests; metal isn't as vital in the initial development of your empire. Of course, this will change if you start later than in Ancient Age.

- Good strategic location. There are several considerations here. The first is ease of defense. If your capital is tucked away in the corner of the map, it's going to be easy to keep a tight watch on your border, however, the worth of the location depends also on the type of map/game you play. It might be better to have a capital in the center of the map when you're playing the East Indies map, for example (better chance of finding a rich island), or an Assassin game (enemies are easier to eliminate). Using common sense and some imagination, you won't have a problem recognizing a good strategic location when you see one.

- Lots of space for city buildings. This is a concern mainly on sea maps, where the amount of good real estate is limited. You can easily squeeze in plenty of buildings within city limits—but the key word is "squeeze." Allowing enough space between structures is crucial to the ease with which you'll be able to move your units, more specifically, armies. At the same time, strive to build as many structures as you can well within city firing range, especially in a multiplayer game.

- Defensibility. It's much easier to successfully fight off enemy forces if there are few possible approaches to your city. Rivers help too; remember that units crossing a river take heavier casualties. This also means that it's difficult to destroy enemy artillery pounding your city from the other shore. The best spot to build is right on the banks of a river (enemy units have to cross it to take a city reduced by bombardment) or some distance away, so that the circle showing city firing range runs through the water. This will let you hit enemy units attempting a river crossing, yet makes it difficult for enemy artillery to bombard your city; they'd have to be placed right on the other shore, making them extremely hard to defend against counterattacks.

- On sea maps, you also need to be able to build a dock quickly, thus your initial national territory needs a stretch of coastline that's appropriate for that purpose.

Keep in mind that any discoveries made by your nomad citizens take precedence over everything else; if a citizen comes across a whacking big forest, for instance, consider locating your capital nearby then and there (see Figure 8.2).

Tip

You can view your city's firing range by opening the city display, and holding the cursor over the range entry (red-and-white target shield). You'll see a white circle appear on the map. The same procedure applies to all structures that can fire on enemies (tower, fort, and so on).

The other exception to the "every citizen is working on the capital" rule is if you have a competitor nearby. Sending a single citizen to interrupt your rival's construction process can pay off in a big way. It's practically impossible to destroy the enemy building site; a citizen unit cannot inflict much damage, but it's definitely possible for your intruder to keep interrupting enemy construction until you're way ahead with your own capital. Naturally any close-by competitors are primary targets for conquest; making them fall behind right at the start will let you conquer them easily later.

A final reminder: Spending too much time on initial exploration will kill any chance of victory when playing at a higher difficulty level. You have to build that first city pretty fast! It's a crapshoot, too: Taking 60 seconds of game time to find a great site is better than finding an average site in 20 seconds. Also, things vary wildly depending on the difficulty level of the game. It's possible to spend literally minutes wandering around and still win on the Easiest level, while on the Toughest level, you should start building your capital within 20 seconds; however, there are no cast-iron rules because every game is different; a lot rides on the placing of rival nations' citizens on the map. They'll be looking for great sites just like you, and just like you, they might be lucky or unlucky.

FIGURE 8.2: *In the beginning, the name of the game is Get More Timber.*

Capital Progress

The speed of your nation's initial development is largely determined by the amount of starting resources you chose. If you've set them to low, you have to build up stocks of food and timber first; if you've set both starting resources and research costs to Normal, you can embark on the ambitious expansion policy described here right from the start.

The moment your capital city is ready, you'll hear an appropriately majestic sound effect as all of your new national territory is revealed. In solo games, hit Pause and take a moment to examine things, and choose a possible site for your second city. Have two of your three starting citizens build a woodcutter's camp in the optimum location. This location is determined by distance from the city as well as the size of the forest you want to exploit.

Note

In Diplomacy games, your neighbor is also very likely to propose an alliance (particularly when weaker than you). Evaluate this offer carefully. You just might get an offer from a stronger, better-placed nation later; and you probably can put the neighboring city to better use than the A.I.

A woodcutter's camp for 6 workers right next to the city is better than a camp on the borders of your empire accommodating 12. Your initial Commerce limit doesn't allow you to produce more than 70 units of timber per game half-minute, anyway, and the city already produces 10. Woodcutter's camps in remote locations are very vulnerable to attack (if you see any belonging to your foes, target them). Also, a faraway camp means sluggish production growth; it will be a while before a newly created citizen gets to work. Tell the third of

Tip

Given Normal starting resources and research cost, you can build the library right away and then send off a citizen to found your second city. Low starting resources and high research costs don't allow this.

FIGURE 8.3: *Don't waste any time getting started on your second city.*

your initial trio of citizens (more for Koreans) to build a farm. Low starting resources let you create just one citizen before food stocks bottom out, so have this second citizen build a second farm. The +20 food bonus you get upon completing a farm will instantly let you create more citizens. Alternate new workers between food and timber; you want to have enough timber to build new farms and enough food to continue creating new citizens until you reach maximum possible production: 60 food for a single city plus farms (no special national bonuses) and 70 timber (initial production cap).

Once you've hit the production cap in timber and built as many farms as you're allowed, create one extra citizen and build the library. It takes long, and by the time you're done, you'll have accumulated a nice stock of food and timber. Send off the library builder immediately to build the new city even if you haven't started to research Civics 1 (see Figure 8.3). It always pays to explore the area around your proposed city site a little.

City Planning and Placement

You already know what to look for when founding your first city: good timber, good strategic location, and so on. Very similar considerations apply when founding subsequent cities. There are also some important differences:

- Border location. It makes obvious good sense to site a city right on the border, because that will result in the greatest increase of your national territory and resources. Bigger distances between cities translate into more money both from taxation and from caravan routes.

  You'll be able to place a city right on the border most of the time; however, sometimes the following considerations will take precedence.

- Good metal supply. You have to start thinking about the coming Classical Age, which ushers in metal. Unless your capital is literally surrounded by mountains and/or cliffs, you can always use some metal. If the woodcutter's camps around your capital can supply plenty (100 units or more) of timber, forests aren't very important. Use common sense throughout the game, and always try to place a city where it pays best in economic terms (e.g., if your capital is poor in timber, build the second city near a big forest).

- Enough space for city buildings. Obligatory structures in every city include the temple, the market, and the university. You definitely don't need a second library unless you have a very large and rich empire and can afford to research two mainstream advances at the same time (usually a consequence of overlooking a specialized tech that would be quite useful). You'll know in advance whether you want any of the production-enhancing buildings.

Occasionally, other considerations enter the picture—defensibility is always a high priority. You don't want your new city right next to an enemy city except in special circumstances (mainly when implementing the Border Push strategy). You might want to build a city in a certain spot just so the enemy doesn't get to build nearby, too. Sometimes you'll find yourself planning a "hidden" city: Most often, an industrial center in an area free of enemy raiders. This last necessity is often also a signal that something's going wrong, and that you need to re-evaluate your policy: If your opponents are dictating where you can found cities, something's seriously wrong. Finally, although cities are of such great importance, it's also important to keep things in perspective and avoid focusing completely on building new ones, to the exclusion of every other activity. In particular, don't let it distract you from an equally important activity: research.

Research Variations

If you've been extremely lucky with timber (a few goody boxes inside ruins, big woodcutter's camp completion bonus), consider researching Science level 1 before anything else and building a temple in your capital before a second city. Thanks to the temple's border-expanding qualities, you'll be able to site your second city a little farther away from the capital. Over time, that means plenty of extra caravan income.

The presence of a couple of very attractive rare resources can be a strong reason to research Commerce level 1 and build a market before anything else. However, consider carefully given rare resource qualities before adopting this course: Metal and knowledge, for example, won't be any use to you in the Ancient Age.

Researching Military level 1 very early is rarely a good move: You cannot really afford to build an army anyway, at this stage. Building a barracks and a scout quickly is an option only if you've allotted yourself generous starting resources. Things are a little different in multiplayer, because multiplayer games abound with madmen whose goal in life is to build plenty of military units and send them off against other players. *Rise of Nations* makes adopting a Rush strategy very risky; the final section of this chapter discusses this and other strategies (Boom, for example) as applied in *RoN*.

Things are different when playing at the Toughest level. This level gives the computer-controlled nations a big production advantage, and they invariably manage to raise big armies before you can. You'll have to research Military level 1 early, and build a tower quickly to help protect your industry plus offer a sanctuary to your citizens. Survival of the Fittest games played at the Toughest level are simply about brutal, constant war from start to finish; this aspect of *RoN* is discussed in Chapter 9.

To sum up: Research the first level of Civic, Science, Commerce, and Military quickly, but the sequence in which you research these advances is determined by your situation. From the point of view of optimum development, it's best to research Science 1 first (lower research costs, temple); then Civic 1 (second city); Commerce 1 (markets, caravan route); and finally Military 1. If you don't start the game with Nomad, you'll get a free scout; given a big map and absence of enemy nations nearby, you may sometimes even postpone researching Military 1 until forced to do so by your population cap.

Exploration on Land and Water

Knowing where you are in relation to the rest of the game world is simply invaluable in making any strategic plans. Fortunately, the unknown world can be explored by any unit; the A.I. in particular often likes to use citizens in that role. However, exploring with citizens is like eating with knitting needles: plenty of entertainment, little profit. Of course, occasionally a citizen gets lucky (see Figure 8.4).

FIGURE 8.4: *A herd of bison, and timber! It's the perfect spot for a city.*

No unit can explore as well as the scout (which later upgrades into very attractive special units). Many players will balk at the sizeable cost of creating one, but this is a unit that pays for itself very quickly. In an average game, a scout released on Auto-Explore will find at least ten goody boxes in addition to locating resources, enemy cities, and so on. On higher difficulty levels that start with Nomad, creating a scout is an Ancient Age priority. Quite often, your scout runs into an enemy army that is about to descend on your capital and lets you divert enemy attention while you complete frantic defense preparations.

Finally, something to remember. If you set the scout to Auto-Explore while he's in the middle of your territory, he'll explore in a circle expanding outward, and seemingly waste a lot of time repeatedly crossing through your territory. Nevertheless, there are often a couple of ruins (goody boxes) and rare resources hidden inside your territory (Spanish excepted), so this isn't such a waste of time as it might seem. If you want to quickly reveal a certain area of the map, it's best to send the scout there manually before switching to Auto-Explore. Note that if you have just a single scout, he'll insist on exploring around and in your territory first. Build at least two if playing at Tougher/Toughest level.

Tip

Exploration is more difficult on sea maps because it means investing in a dock first. Exploring seas with a scout is a very bad idea: Light ships (dromons, caravels) are very affordable, much more efficient, and can engage the enemy (transports are totally defenseless).

You may also instruct your scout to explore the map by following a route you laid out. This is done by shift-right-clicking (Shift + right click with your mouse), which sets waypoints for the scout. The next stage consists of implementing a strategy especially developed for *Rise of Nations*. It's called the Age Jump, and it's a lethal move in both solo and multiplayer games; it's practically your only hope when playing a solo game at the Toughest difficulty level. The next section discusses what Age Jump is all about.

The Secrets of Time Travel

As you know from preceding chapters, Age advancement brings important benefits. The ability to upgrade your military units is the arguably the most important of these, and also very expensive. The total costs of upgrading every type of unit are especially overwhelming early on in the game and roughly add up to the equivalent of building a Wonder or founding and building up a new city. Yet the very next Age forces you to go through the whole process again, and again…Well, there is a shortcut: the Age Jump.

The Age Jump consists of advancing a couple of Ages very quickly, without spending resources on a full set of military upgrades in between. Military upgrades are unique in that they don't require the prior advance like other research. You cannot research Science level 3 without Science level 2; you cannot research Vassalization without Taxation; but you can upgrade your Ancient Age bowmen into Medieval Age crossbowmen without spending resources on researching Classical Age archers in between.

Naturally, advancing two Ages in a row requires preparation. You must have a very solid industrial base, and your empire must consist of no less than three cities (see Figure 8.5). You'll know you have a solid industrial base when you'll see resource stocks begin to grow slowly in spite of constant ongoing expenditures (building your new cities, conducting research, and so on). The following sections outline what needs to be done to quickly reach this happy point in the game.

FIGURE 8.5: *The Age Jump requires building a strong economic base that includes three cities.*

Note

The beauty of the Age Jump is that you cannot be prevented from it unless your opponent commits to a full-scale early attack on your empire (the Rush). Such attacks are very risky in RoN; Ancient Age units aren't very effective. At this stage, heavy infantry is the only unit that can effectively attack buildings, but it suffers badly from the arrows fired by city garrisons.

Building a Time Machine

This invention consists of three cities, each with a suite of basic city buildings: market, temple, farms, and woodcutter's camps as appropriate/needed to hit the level 2 Commerce cap (150 units).

You've already founded your second city, and researched level 1 Commerce, Civics, and Science. Here's what to research and what to build next:

◆ Military level 1. This is needed to raise your population cap, a barracks, and a tower. You may research it after Civic level 2 when playing at Tough or lower difficulty level.

- **Civic level 2.** It will almost break your heart to spend all this food, but do it anyway. Instantly send out a citizen to start a third city. Ideally it will be situated on the opposite side of your capital, since that's best for security, but special map considerations come first.

- **Commerce level 2.** Again, it's going to cost a lot of food. But the food will be accumulating nicely even as you build up your two nice new cities. Naturally building extra farms as needed to hit the production cap has priority. Also, look around for rare resources that could bring in extra food. Once you've maximized food production, build markets and temples as appropriate. Don't forget about caravans!

- **Military level 2.** You'll want to build a single stable quickly. At high difficulty level you'll also want to create a few of light cavalry units right away for mobile defense—they don't do that well in reconnaissance because of short line of sight (LOS). See Chapters 6 and 9 for more military details.

> **Tip**
>
> *If attacked by an enemy while you're waiting to advance to Medieval Age (Tougher, Toughest), rely on light cavalry to destroy any enemy catapults. A Classical Age army deprived of catapults is easily prevented from doing serious damage.*

This gives you the level 2 advances needed for Medieval Age. Building a tower in Ancient Age is a wise security move (it takes quite a long time!), and saves you precious metal in Classical Age. Building a single barracks situated in between your three cities is a necessary security move. Build a scout and set him loose because he'll start finding goody boxes, which are very helpful in the early game. If you have a talent for micromanagement, you could try handling your scout manually instead of Auto-Explore; it's particularly advisable to scout out the proposed location of your third city.

While you're accumulating and spending all that food, you'll most likely achieve a slight timber and wealth surplus, even with all the construction going on in your new cities. Use it to build bowmen, one unit to each of your cities (at the Toughest level, also the tower). It's not absolutely necessary if playing at the Tough or lower level, but as mentioned you'll probably have a few spare resources anyway.

Classical Age Priorities

At this point, you'll be getting messages that some of your opponents have advanced to Classical Age. Don't panic. You have three cities and a production level of 100+ units of food and timber, plus at least 60 wealth (two caravan routes and two or three markets). Besides, if someone else advances an Age before you, the price for your own Age advancement

FIGURE 8.6: *The Age Jump in action. Here, a capital city is at the threshold of Classical Age.*

instantly drops 10%. You'll definitely be able to start Classical Age research yourself within moments of hearing someone else did (see Figure 8.6).

Start creating extra citizens with any food left over from investing in Classical Age. Your priority is to build a university in every city and enough mines to produce around 100 metal (plus/minus 20, as your circumstances dictate). Research Taxation at the temple next. Having three cities makes it a great source of extra wealth. Other priorities: Research Allegiance in the tower; the first attrition tech is a powerful deterrent early on, when units have less hit points, and researching it doesn't cost any food.

You'll be glad you've researched Commerce level 2 in the Ancient Age, because this will let you quickly start saving up knowledge for advancing to Medieval Age. In the meantime, build a few military units as resources allow; remember you'll be spending a lot on the military upgrades in Medieval Age, so don't go wild just yet. You'll be creating military units solely to defend yourself (Tougher and Toughest) or to begin probing enemy territory (Tough and lower difficulty level, all multiplayer games). You'll find military strategy discussed in detail in Chapter 9.

Begin researching Medieval Age the moment you have enough knowledge (see Figure 8.7). If you haven't yet formed an idea of whom to attack, do so now. The next section discusses related considerations, plus putting plans into action in the Medieval Age.

FIGURE 8.7: *The same scene a few minutes later. Medieval Age research is just beginning; note the number of new buildings.*

Tip

While waiting for knowledge to accumulate, build a fort and a siege factory (at Toughest level, two forts). Use the market to raise cash or make small (100 unit) purchases of needed resources such as metal. Don't sell off too much; there's a wave of military upgrades coming.

Medieval Age Choices

Upon reaching Medieval Age, your priority is to upgrade all types of military units instantly (see Figure 8.8). Also create a couple of spies and at least one general. If you haven't built a fort yet, it's high time you did! A general greatly extends the life span of your military units by giving them an armor bonus that can be tripled by doing fort-based specialized research. Also build a supply wagon, even when you're sure your intended victim hasn't researched any attrition techs. This is because supply wagons increase the firing rate of your artillery (trebuchets, bombards, cannon, and so on).

All those military upgrades will also cost some time; spend it confirming your choice of target. This choice is defined by three factors:

- **Your needs.** If you have few mountains/cliffs within your territory and are short on metal, go get metal. If you're short of timber, go get timber. It's that simple. Naturally you also need to apply other standard considerations, such as strength of enemy relative to yours, ease of operations, threats to your empire, and so on.

- **National security.** If another nation has begun raiding your territory in the meantime, obviously it needs to be stopped. If there's a small, weak empire on your flank that nevertheless might make things more difficult for you, it needs to be taken out quickly. These are just two of the innumerable security-related reasons that might influence your target. The golden rule is not to get too fixated on conquest; it always has bad consequences.

- **Emerging winners.** There'll be big differences between the players within a couple of Ages. The pattern is set very early on, and of course the earlier you attack a potential winner, the better your

FIGURE 8.8: *Reaching Medieval Age signals the start of a series of military upgrades.*

chances of winning the game yourself. Sometimes, however, (often at the Tougher/ Toughest difficulty levels) you simply won't be strong enough without conquering a weaker empire first. Note that in Assassin games, you are directed to attack a designated target nation; when you defeat it, you are assigned its target. This doesn't give you any freedom of choice, and a spot of bad luck might lose you the game despite your best efforts. A rival you can't attack might be consistently assigned easy victims; and keep in mind that throughout an Assassin game you'll also be the subject of attacks from someone who has been given *you* as a target.

In Diplomacy games, watch out for situations where two relatively strong nations enter an alliance. A pairing like that can be too much at high difficulty level, especially if your own ally is a weakling. You'll increase your chances of a strong ally if you send out a scout early, make contact with all the players as quickly as possible, and subsequently take the initiative in negotiations instead of waiting for offers. Don't be reluctant to offer a bribe if you can spare the resources, and the potential ally is also the ideal one.

It all boils down to this: You have to beat up on people who hurt your chances of victory. Whether they're attacking you or being passive doesn't matter. A tiny one-city state that has managed to corral a couple of good rare resources and a big mountain right next to you hurts your chances of victory as badly as a big nation that's rapidly conquering new cities. You won't be able to stand up to a monster nation if you don't lead at least a semi-monster nation, however, don't get carried away by easy conquests (see Figure 8.9). It's punished especially swiftly in multiplayer.

Note that the relatively peaceful period preceding your first grand offensive is basically your last chance to found a new city. If that's what you'd like to do, quickly research Civics and found a new city before you capture any from the enemy. Once you embark on war, you'll quickly find yourself owning many more cities than allowed by your Civic level. In most games you'll end up having more cities than you can ever hope to build peacefully. Civic research loses a lot of its importance and becomes necessary only as a prerequisite to another tech (for instance, to improve taxation) or for its minute territorial gains (they can be very important on the battlefield).

FIGURE 8.9: *Once an offensive gathers momentum, it might be difficult to stop.*

Marching to Victory

Don't expect to start and stop fighting as you please. Once you start fighting, chances are you won't stop until the game is over. Because of this, prior to sending your army out, quickly run a check on your empire. Are all resource-gathering structures, particularly mines, working at full capacity? Did you build production-enhancing buildings in the right cities? Is there anything else that really needs to be researched before you create that final pair of knights? Things are going to be very, very busy from now on.

It's a good idea to have a small bunch of citizens following in the footsteps of your conquering army. You'll need them to perform several tasks:

Warning

Pause the game and review things from time to time. It's very easy to get caught up in the excitement of a military campaign to the point where no research is being done even while accumulating thousands of units of resources.

▷ Build new military buildings. You'll need barracks, stables, and siege factories close to the front lines. You'll also need quite a few new forts in which to heal your troops; it's often a good idea to build one in the right spot before embarking on a major offensive. A new tower or two is often useful as well.

▷ Repair captured cities/buildings. Although cities in *RoN* repair themselves over time, buildings don't, and anyway it's in your interests to begin repairing a city even before it's assimilated (cities need to be at 10% health to garrison units inside). Note that building numerous new barracks, stables, and so on ratchets their costs incredibly high; consider razing some in your original cities; a troop-producing building far away from the front is basically useful mostly for researching military upgrades.

FIGURE 8.10: *The Age Jump can be repeated to advance to Enlightenment Age quickly.*

Tip

You'll find winning considerably easier if you remember to trade resources regularly. Market trade lets you greatly speed up research and Wonder construction, however, don't rely on it to pay for your troops.

Don't forget to work the Age Jump gimmick again! You have just one more chance to do so, by skipping through Gunpowder Age to Enlightenment Age (see Figure 8.10). You cannot jump three Ages in a row—it's just not feasible. Unfortunately, Industrial Age puts such big demands on the economy that's it's simply too difficult to repeat the Age Jump with Modern/ Information Age, unless you've won the game anyway and are leisurely coasting toward final victory.

Start Summary

Many new players might feel slightly overwhelmed by the wealth of the gameplay and nervous because of the time pressure. The following table contains a rough template for getting off to a good start. Keep in mind that priorities might change depending on your starting conditions. The scenario assumes high game difficulty as well as starting with Low resources and Very Expensive/Slow technology cost and speed. Things won't be so strict on more generous settings.

ACTION	COMMENT
Locate site for capital city.	Select a strategically well-placed area and converge upon it with your citizens; if any citizen discovers timber on the way, investigate.
Build city.	Turn all citizens into builders to complete city faster.
Build woodcutter's camp, farm, create first new citizen.	Assign two citizens to the woodcutter's camp, the new citizen to build a second farm.
Continue creating citizens as food allows.	Alternate new labor between woodcutter's camp and building new farms to hit production cap quickly.
Once you have 30 timber, create a new citizen to build library.	Let resources accumulate while a single citizen is building the library.
Upon completing library, send the builder off toward optimal second city site; research Civic 1 as soon as resources allow.	If your citizen reaches city site early, explore city site area.

continued

ACTION	COMMENT
Found second city; as soon as resources allow, research Commerce 1.	Pick sites for second woodcutter's camp to hit 100 timber quickly; pick site for market.
When second city is ready, build second woodcutter's camp, market, new farms as resources allow.	Building woodcutter's camp first gives helpful timber bonus.
Build caravan, also merchants as appropriate; create citizens until you hit production caps.	Caravan comes first; merchants are great at raising food and timber output; make sure you send them to resources that provide immediate benefits.
Research Science 1, create new citizen.	Do not create many citizens to use as builders; start hoarding food for the Age Jump.
Build temple(s), second market.	Examine the map to determine whether any enemy nations are nearby; "dented" national border, or a border of a different color next to yours, signifies nearby enemy presence.
Research Military 1, build barracks between the cities, create scout.	If no enemies are nearby, use scout to find goody boxes and boost resource stocks; determine site for third city before switching scout to Auto-Explore.
Research Civic 2, build bowmen, and garrison one unit inside each city.	Building bowmen not necessary at lower difficulty levels.
Build third city, research Commerce 2.	Don't build more woodcutter's camps if production is 120–130; hoard food, build third unit of bowmen at higher difficulty levels and garrison third city.
Repeat city buildup process.	Increasing food supply is a priority, preferably with merchants; build new caravans.
Build stable, second barracks.	Locate second barracks by third city unless impractical; build stable by first barracks, allowing space for unit assembly.
Create 4-5 light cavalry; build tower to protect barracks-stable combo.	Plan your upcoming strategy.

At this point, you'll be able to decide what to do next:

- Optimize the economy and go straight into the Age Jump
- Attack a nearby enemy you had discovered in the meantime
- Compromise between these two choices

Note that if you *haven't* come across an enemy nation by this time, you should give this high priority; creating more scouts might be wise. Every minute spent in isolation increases the chance another nation will discover you first. Note that at high difficulty levels, the A.I. nations conduct explorations with formidable armies in addition to any scouts they deploy.

Independently of who discovers whom first, what usually follows is war. This is the subject of the next chapter.

Tip

Don't forget to establish caravan routes manually. You'll be paid the new trade route wealth bonus at the beginning of the route instead of at its end. The size of the new trade route bonus depends on your Commerce level: +20 wealth to start with (Commerce level 1), then 10 extra wealth for each extra level (Commerce level 2 results in +30 wealth, and so on).

Timing Your Moves

Rise of Nations features a great tool that lets you see exactly how well you've performed in a game. This tool is a button on the victory panel; it's labeled Achievements, and by clicking it you access a mine of information on every aspect of the just-finished game in table or graph form, as preferred. The Achievements screen features tabs that lead to data illustrating the players' respective military machines, economies, research, and so on; most importantly, a tab labeled Timeline compares the progress of the nations in the game (see Figure 8.11).

The Timeline tells you a lot about what happened when in the game. Figure 8.11 illustrates the Timeline from a relatively relaxed game (Survival of the Fittest, Tough level, seven opponents, Big Old World map, Low starting resources, Technology Very Expensive/Slow) played by the author (the white or brightest line, second from bottom). As you can see, in this Nomad start game, one of the participants (Egyptians, middle line) didn't even get to build a city. All remaining players *completed* building their capitals within three minutes (a strong argument against prolonged initial exploration), with me being the first. I was also the first to build a second city (by a whisker, after roughly five minutes) and subsequently the third (by a mile, after roughly 10 minutes). Around 12 minutes into the game, the first player (Germans, second line from top) advanced into Classical Age.

Tip

The information accessed through the Military tab includes the number of enemy units killed and own units lost. To win at the Toughest level, you must achieve a ratio of at least five to one regardless of other circumstances.

As the Timeline shows, I then performed the Age Jump, advancing into Classical Age about 15 minutes into the game and into Medieval Age just five minutes later (ahead of every other player). What followed was the almost simultaneous capture of two enemy cities (24 minutes) followed by a third (27 minutes); advance to Gunpowder Age took place after

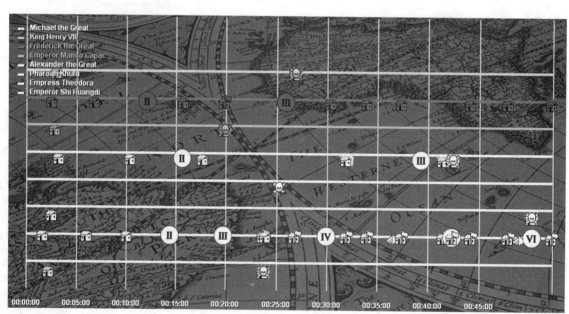

FIGURE 8.11: *The Timeline shows when all important game events occurred.*

30 minutes. Following a series of city captures and Age advances (up to Industrial Age), the game was won after roughly 60 minutes of game time with a 90% territory victory. No other player progressed beyond Medieval Age—testimony to the effectiveness of a number of small cavalry-only corps roaming the game world.

Tip

Use the game's Data Display (Political) to keep an eye on the progress of your rivals. It's particularly useful when the game allows a territory victory: It shows the percentage controlled by each player. A sudden increase in number of points can mean a research advance, or a new/captured and assimilated city (with the corresponding increase in territory). You get a special announcement whenever someone else advances an Age, begins/completes a Wonder, or is eliminated from the game.

Remember that trying to adhere strictly to a pre-set timetable in all games might be disastrous, if not impossible. For example, if you begin on a small island (East Indies), it could take quite a while before you even find a site for your second city because finding it might involve building a dock first. Game difficulty level, type of map, map size, technology cost and research speed, starting resources—almost everything, including type of nation chosen—can affect the optimum speed at which things get done, and the *relations* between those factors can affect it still further (for instance, the relation between technology cost and starting resources).

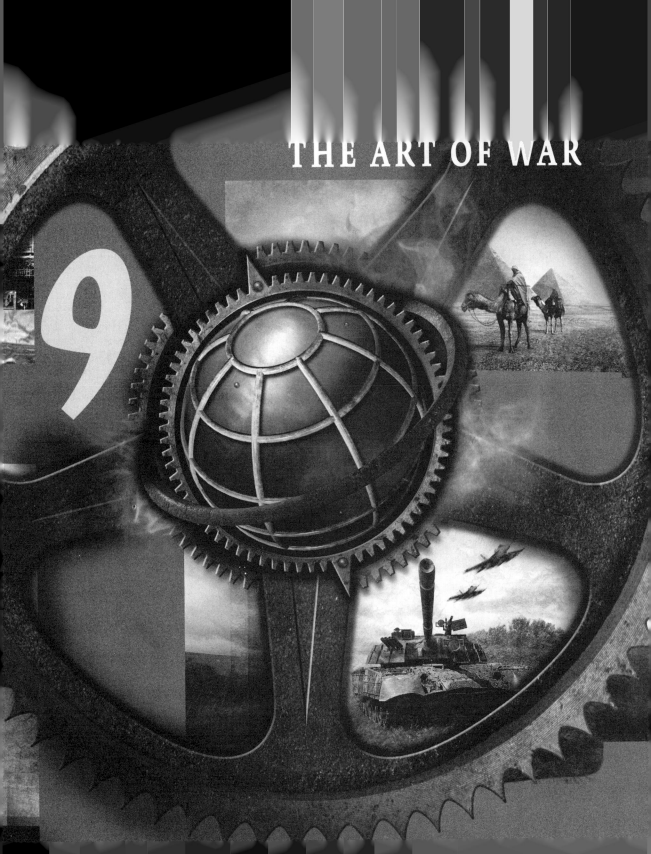

9

Some people say waging war is an art, others that it's a science. Both sides are right; it's simply a question of temperament. Regardless of which group you belong to, you'll find that Rise of Nations truly spreads its gaming wings in war. It features plentiful strategic and tactical options, which are the subject of this chapter, and a multitude of military units that change with the Ages (reviewed in Chapters 6 and 7). Note that army composition and size are discussed in Chapter 6.

This chapter goes beyond discussing individual units: It discusses war. You cannot win a war in RoN without laying a solid economic foundation first, therefore, this chapter begins by examining the level of economic development that is a prerequisite for a successful war, and goes on to discuss a working war economy. Subsequently, it examines what elements add up to victory in war. It concludes with a discussion of tactics that contains a section on special operations: tactical moves that can assume crucial importance in a war, out of all proportion to the forces involved.

ARE YOU READY FOR WAR?

Your ability to wage war successfully is determined by four main factors:

- Economic strength. This is measured in relative rather than absolute terms. Yes, being able to create four units per game minute is better than being able to create only two; but being able to create two units per minute when the enemy can create only one is just fine, thank you. When you play at a high difficulty level, the computer-controlled nations almost invariably have much stronger economies than yours; delaying a war only makes them stronger.

- Reconnaissance quality. There's a big difference between knowing the location of enemy nations and knowing the location of all their cities. Being aware of their economic strength, what wars they're currently fighting, and with what forces, makes you potentially unbeatable.

- Military quality. This is mostly determined by research, but other factors come into play, too. The Age you're in is the most important single factor, but only if you're up to date with military upgrades (see Figure 9.1).

FIGURE 9.1: *Getting a technological edge over an opponent must be translated into technological superiority on the battlefield.*

Mainstream Military research comes second: It allows cheaper units and larger armies. Don't underestimate specialized techs (attrition line at tower, anti-attrition line at smelter, healing line at granary, fort research, and so on). All together, they can be as important as the Age you've reached. Other important factors include the composition of your armed forces (see Chapters 6 and 7) and the number of generals you can field.

▶ Your leadership skills. This is the most important single influence of them all. A talented military leader can easily defeat a much stronger opponent. You have to polish your skills to win at the higher difficulty level: a five-to-one kill is very helpful if you want to win at the Toughest difficulty level. And these are just the tactical skills: You also have to have the strategic smarts to pick the right target and fight at the right time.

The sections that follow examine each of these points in more detail.

The War Economy

The single outstanding characteristic of a well-run wartime economy is that it allows you to continuously create new units and build new military structures without crippling research and other peaceful development areas. As you know from Chapters 6 and 7, military units are expensive, and can get horrendously expensive if you have many.

Your economy is able to support a war the moment you notice your stocks are growing despite vigorous economic development and continuing research. Usually this occurs only after researching Commerce level 2 and subsequently hitting the production cap. As recommended throughout this guide, however, you should build a few units as soon as possible, particularly when playing at a high difficulty level. If you've been developing the timber industry as recommended in Chapter 8, you'll begin seeing a timber surplus around the time you start researching Classical Age (first stage of the Age Jump). At the higher difficulty levels, it's good to create a unit of bowmen to garrison each of your cities.

The onset of Classical Age forces you to focus on building mines and universities even as you accumulate food for completing the Age Jump into Medieval Age. Nevertheless, at higher difficulty levels, sacrifice some resources to build a small light cavalry corps. Fast and highly maneuverable, light cavalry is handy when dealing with enemy ranged attack units (including artillery). Just don't let it get into rumbles with heavy infantry or heavy cavalry.

In most games (those played at Tougher and Toughest excepted) you can then afford to wait for Medieval Age before creating more military units. Instead, undertake a series of ancillary moves: Research the first of attrition techs, build a fort (see Figure 9.2), and immediately create a general. In practical terms, the presence of a general with his craft abilities and armor bonus brings the same benefits as doubling the size of an army.

Tip

During an enemy attack, pop the garrisoned bowmen out of your city (citizens hiding there will continue firing at the enemy) for extra arrow-power, then pop them back in again when they're badly damaged.

Since post-Classical Age Commerce research involves timber and knowledge, you'll easily afford to advance to Commerce level 3 even while accumulating food for the advance to Medieval Age. Continue this approach, researching new Commerce levels as you prepare to advance to subsequent Ages, and simply make sure you hit the new production cap as soon as you can. Running research and economic development in tandem in this manner will ensure your economy becomes more and more capable of supporting a big war effort.

Finally, remember that winning battles is crucial to your economic development, too. A lost battle can result in killed citizens, destroyed buildings, and the like, plus interrupted economic activity as your citizens take shelter from the enemy. On the other hand, capturing a city can give you a great economic boost. The amount and type of plunder you receive is based on very many factors that even include the type of game you're playing; however, as a rule

FIGURE 9.2: *Place a fort where it has most strategic value: in a location that's both convenient for healing your troops and which commandeers the approaches to your cities.*

of thumb, it increases with city size and Age. Note that cities that are captured and re-captured yield smaller amounts of plunder. Capturing a capital city brings the greatest rewards.

Using Reconnaissance to Determine Where and When to Fight

The successful general tries to pick his battles carefully. Of course at high difficulty levels, many of them will be forced on you: Even then, you can manipulate the situation a little by intercepting the advancing enemy army, and if your forces are inferior, retreating in a manner calculated to postpone the enemy attack on your city. Retreating skillfully is crucial to winning at the Toughest level. Always attempt to distract the enemy army from its objective (unless it's something stupid), and lead the pursuing enemy units into a couple of ambushes you've set up along the retreat route. It's always nice to succeed in luring an enemy army right into the firing range of a fort packed to bursting with troops.

This graceful maneuver, and many more, are possible only if you take the trouble to reconnoiter the game world thoroughly and post permanent or temporary sentries (structures such as lookout and tower, fort, as well as military units with good LOS). In the vast majority of your games, you'll begin by sending out a scout or preferably two. While the scout units are busy finding goody boxes and locating the colorful borders of neighboring nations, set up a patrol route for light cavalry along your own border. Click the Patrol command icon on the unit actions panel, and then simply click on a destination for a two-way route, or shift-right-click before left-clicking to add extra waypoints in between. You can refine things further by adjusting unit stance (Defensive, Offensive are the most sensible options). Note that advancing to Enlightenment Age turns scouts into commandos with combat abilities. You'll find more details in the "Special Operations" section.

Tip

If you can afford it, replace your border patrol cavalry with horse archers later on; they have better spotting range.

While you're busy with all that, your scout(s) will have probably located an enemy nation. Investigate while continuing to explore the map; don't commit yourself to an attack on the first enemy you come across. Of course don't let that stop you from creating military units. Take the time to explore at least a big, healthy area beyond your borders (to see how this is done on a sea map, refer to the next section). Good reconnaissance becomes especially important in Survival of the Fittest games. There's nothing worse than capturing an enemy city at great cost and effort only to see a different nation's army advancing to take that city from you.

FIGURE 9.3: *Look before you leap. The A.I. likes to hide powerful armies, ready to counterattack in the event of a serious threat.*

Keeping tabs on what's up becomes much easier with the Medieval Age, which lets you create spies. Planting a network of informers in enemy buildings and cities is a very high priority. You might be tempted to place informers in cities only because of the big sight radius (your informer has the same LOS as the building in which he's hiding); however, remember that informers inside such buildings as barracks or stables will also tell you how many units are garrisoned inside and what unit(s) are currently being created, if any.

Note

Spies can be detected only by scouts, lookouts, towers (plus their subsequent upgrades), and other spies.

To sum up: By the time you advance to Gunpowder Age, you should have a very good idea of what is happening in the game world (see Figure 9.3). You should have been able to locate every nation in the game, plus all the cities of nations neighboring yours. You should also have your entire border under watch through a combination of informers, sentries, and patrols.

Scouting the Seas

Sea maps put a different order on things, because you need to explore with both ships and land units. Once you've developed your capital a little (full set of farms, market, temple) you should build a dock, and create a couple of light ships (barks, dromons), perhaps three to four on larger maps. Light ships are very efficient explorers, and if you take the trouble to space them far apart before switching them to Auto-Explore, they'll have explored the seas and oceans of your world in no time at all. You can also set up an exploration route by shift-right-clicking on the map to set waypoints through which your ship must pass.

That's only half the job, for now you'll have the lands whose shores have been discovered by your ships. By this time your scout (it rarely makes sense to build more than one when playing a sea map) will have explored your landmass. Send him to the most promising of the unexplored lands, and have a dromon shepherd the scout transport across the water: Transports are so easily sunk, it isn't funny. An early, pre-galleon transport requires only three hits from a light ship to go down. By now, you might be nodding and promising yourself to set up light ship patrols around your shores, and you're right. That's what you should do next.

Concentrate on building inexpensive, light ships until you're actually ready for some offensive action, or when there's a threat to your shores. Heavy ships are very expensive, and the first couple of generations (trireme, galley) aren't that great. Your coastal defense fleet should consist of light units, reinforced by a couple of heavier ships when and where as needed. Assigning heavy ships to a specific fleet generally doesn't work well: They slow down the lighter units.

CREATING THE BEST ARMED FORCES IN THE WORLD

There are several things to attend to here. As you already know, always keep your military up to date with your current Age, and compose armies and naval battle groups along the principles laid out in Chapters 6 and 7. A lot rides on your attending to these details:

- Creating plenty of generals (see Figure 9.4). You cannot have too many generals; create as many as you can without actually hurting progress along other avenues. Having two generals lead an army gives it plenty of extra punch (although the armor bonus isn't cumulative). It enables you to issue Forced March and Ambush commands simultaneously, for example, letting your invisible army easily break contact with a superior enemy. Now, if you have *three* generals with an army, you can also simultaneously release decoy units that *will* be visible to the enemy, and—see the possibilities? There are plenty, so spend some time experimenting with various combinations. Also, do not neglect to upgrade your generals by researching the tactics line at the fort.

- Healing units. It's been said before, but here it is again: Healing units is the secret ingredient of many seemingly startling victories. Every war fought in *Rise of Nations* is a war of attrition (in the general sense, although the attrition line of techs certainly helps). You'll be amazed at how many resources you can save if you care after your military units. Don't forget to research anti-attrition and healing

FIGURE 9.4: *The general is a non-combat unit with a hero's powers.*

techs (smelter, granary). There's only one situation in which it is allowable to throw damaged units into a battle: if there are plenty of them and it's an important battle. Even then, try to rescue units that are critically low on hit points. Selecting the whole fighting army (hot key, by dragging a box) and then rapidly control-clicking on the relatively healthy units will leave you with those that need to be immediately withdrawn (short red health bar). Garrison them immediately. If you have an appropriate structure nearby, they might heal quickly enough to rejoin the fray.

- Good army/navy force composition. This has been discussed earlier, so here's just a brief reminder: It's a waste of fine mobility to group fast, mounted units (or, later, vehicles) with foot and artillery units. Instead, form infantry-and-artillery armies and all-cavalry (motorized) armies or corps. A couple of the smaller corps provide perfect protection for a big infantry army, and buy you extra time for maneuvering in case of unexpected encounters. Rotate the corps when attrition takes its toll, since all-cavalry armies tend to operate out of supply wagons' support radius at least part of the time. At sea, form several battle groups of light ships and reinforce them with a heavy ship squadron/shore bombardment vessels as appropriate.

Tip

Flanking attacks carry a 100% damage bonus; attacks from the rear, a 50% damage bonus. Now you know why the A.I. soldiers turn around so smartly to face any threats!

- Referring to in-game text. *RoN* is unique in having the most comprehensive help system in RTS game history; the tooltip texts will tell you what type of unit is best against a given type of enemy unit, when an artillery unit is out of supply, and so on.

Becoming Nelson and Napoleon in One

Skillful leadership is the factor that decides many a battle. If you adhere to the advice in the game, the preceding sections, and Chapters 6 and 7, you'll be more than halfway there. Some extra pointers:

- Know yourself. Take your emotions, wrap them in brown paper, and put them away in a pocket for use at another time. You have to keep cool at all times. Players who let themselves be frightened into adopting a passive stance are playing into the hands of the enemy. For instance, if you keep getting raided from a particular direction, arrange a nice ambush instead of building a protective tower (see Figure 9.5). If you're being defeated, retreat instead of fighting to the death. He who fights and runs away lives to fight another day: That's your motto. Use your ingenuity to turn a retreat into a punishing

FIGURE 9.5: *Sometimes building a tower is like setting a rally point for enemy armies.*

experience for the pursuing enemy: Maximize enemy troops' exposure to attrition in your territory, lead them into an ambush or two, and so on. Both of these examples show how to make a sad situation (getting raided, losing a battle) work in your favor.

➤ Know the enemy. The importance of knowing what's going on has already been explained: You have poor chances of winning without knowing what's going on in the game.

➤ Don't fear the result of a hundred battles. Don't play defensively, even when playing at the Toughest difficulty level. Remember that acting first gives you the initiative. What's the worst thing that will happen? You'll lose. If you watch carefully, you'll start winning quickly.

➤ Stay flexible. This is especially important in multiplayer games, however, it's also an invaluable quality in high-difficulty solo games. You might be committed to the Age Jump, but if you're in danger, you might want to make a couple of Classical Age military upgrades after all (javelineers, then archers if really necessary). If you see you're advancing into a tricky situation, don't advance. Retreat, rethink, and try again. A lot of RTS battles are fought on the mindless brawl principle: *RoN* does not reward that style of gameplay.

The following sections offer some practical pointers. Note that Chapters 6 and 7 contain advice on army, navy, and air force composition and size.

Battle ABCs

RoN lets you form your troops in several types of formations; making your troops face the attack always reduces your losses. All of these formations have one thing in common: They are useful only when your troops are stationary. When an army moves, it invariably loses cohesion, often stretching into a long snake when there are numerous obstacles present. It's very easy to wipe out an army like that, so take precautions.

As mentioned earlier, start by splitting an army into a core group (foot units, artillery) and a couple of operational groups (cavalry), assigning every group a separate hot key. This is especially important if your army reaches a meaningful size (around 16 units), as this is also the size at which armies might become difficult to maneuver. Naturally the presence of all types of units (say six infantry, two artillery, four cavalry, a general, and a supply wagon) further complicates matters. Splitting the four units of cavalry off to form a small corps will let you conduct reconnaissance ahead of the advancing army body, thus avoiding ambushes and getting good warning of any enemy armies on collision course.

> **Note**
>
> *The terrain in RoN features gentle swells and slopes: Note that units ascending a slope move slowly. Units on top of a rise have a slightly longer line-of-sight, while infantry units in rocky patches (future oil fields) enjoy a defensive bonus.*

There are endless variations on the slow group–fast group motif employing various units, but the theme stays the same: The slowest units are grouped together; the most mobile units are grouped separately. One of the mobile groups always marches in advance of the main body; the other mobile group covers the advance of the main body. This gives you maximum flexibility both in the case of an unexpected enemy attack and prior to an anticipated battle. Once you've arrived at the destination, you can group everyone together again if you so desire.

When you form up your army in battle order, your center will ideally be composed of heavy and ranged attack infantry, with artillery in the back row (if any). Light infantry usually ends up supporting heavy infantry once Gunpowder Age arrives; in earlier Ages, it's usually best to put it on the flanks so that it can get at enemy ranged attack infantry from the side. *RoN* arranges cavalry in front of infantry when all units are grouped together. This is a mistake. Always put cavalry on the flanks to make sure it has freedom to maneuver. Cavalry should not participate in a battle (except for ranged attack units) until it's actually time to charge: This might be to intercept enemy cavalry, attack enemy flanks (do it with light infantry if no cavalry is available), or make any other maneuver that lets you attack the enemy from the flanks or from the rear. When dragoons appear in Gunpowder Age, ranged attack cavalry gains enough power to lend extra firepower to infantry-artillery siege armies (see Figure 9.6).

Tip

Forming your army into three groups (main body with artillery, two corps of highly mobile units) makes maneuvering much easier. It also lets you easily execute attacks on the enemy flanks and rear—a highly desirable maneuver that always tilts the battle in your favor.

FIGURE 9.6: *Carabineers supporting an Enlightenment Age army storming an enemy city.*

In addition, always keep a small group of units as reserves. Lacking anything better, it may be composed of damaged units that for one reason or another hadn't been sent back to heal. Many a battle has been won by a small bunch of fresh (if weaker) units joining in at the appropriate time, and many a rout has been turned into an organized retreat by their timely intervention. Remember that every unit can fire at only one target at a time. Your damaged units *can* destroy healthy enemy units that are targeting something else.

The top priority in all battles is to destroy enemy units. As you know by now, a damaged unit can always be healed at no cost; a destroyed unit has to be replaced at a significant cost. Your units automatically target enemy units they can do the most damage to. Keep an eye on things and occasionally intervene, re-targeting your units onto enemy units that are close to death. Remember, however, that using the wrong unit to attack a certain type of enemy unit is a waste of time. For instance, a bowman shooting arrows into a javelineer will do little damage. When you select a unit, its panel lists types of enemy troops it's most effective against; use this info in practice and you won't be sorry.

Tip

Exploit the A.I.'s obsession with facing the danger by making feints with cavalry down the flanks. When enemy units react to the threat and turn, attack from the front—and get the 50% flank attack damage bonus.

Naval and Aerial Operations

You already know that a sea map requires you to build a dock and a couple of light ships relatively quickly. Once these have finished exploring the map, they'll form the nucleus of your new naval battle group (in the meantime, you should have also built a light ship or two to patrol your coastline). Build a few more light ships until you have four or five in addition to the coast guard; try to avoid building heavy ships until Medieval Age (galleys aren't very good value, being slow and low on firepower). When Medieval Age arrives, consider forming a squadron of carracks (two to four, depending on circumstances) and beefing up the light forces to six or more ships. This combined naval force should be sufficient to protect your troop transports

Overall, protecting your own troop transports and destroying the enemy's continue to be the main function of naval forces throughout the game. Most fleet battles will take place for one of two reasons: to protect a troop movement by sea, or to disrupt it for the enemy. With time, tougher models of troop transports (galleon, freighter, and the like) make it necessary to deploy increasingly powerful navies. In spite of the existence of a whole line of shore bombardment ships, the firepower of these units is a little disappointing, and they are useful mostly against units and weak structures (especially farms). Ships in general are more effective against units than buildings, though oil platforms are the exception: They are relatively easy to destroy by naval bombardment. The line of fireships is of limited usefulness: They're expensive and only pay for themselves when used against heavy and shore bombardment ships. For more details on ship classes and their usefulness, see Chapter 7.

Note

To use nuclear weaponry and have it make a difference in a solo game, you'll likely have to start a game later than in Ancient or Classical Age; most solo games are decided one way or another by their fifth Age.

Aerial forces are much more important. The first airplanes— the fighter biplanes that appear in Industrial Age—are reasonably effective against artillery and tanks, but not much else. They're sometimes capable of supplying the winning edge in a battle, softening up selected targets for ground forces. Primarily they have great harassment value, being the ultimately mobile unit, and for this reason if no other, exert a surprisingly strong influence. Successive generations of aircraft strengthen that influence until it's pervasive, with the new bomber

FIGURE 9.7: *The first bombers aren't very accurate: Here, a strike fails to destroy a flimsy trading post.*

line bringing new means to strike enemy structures and foot units (see Figure 9.7). Eventually, the development of rocket weapons (starting with V2 in the Modern Age) culminates with the Nuclear ICBM in the Information Age, at which point the significance of aerial weaponry reaches its peak.

If you do get to use nukes, remember that each use is penalized by a market embargo: You won't be allowed to buy or sell resources on the market for a certain time. Note that only a limited number of nukes may be used before the game world is wiped out by an Armageddon, leaving no winners. The number of nuclear missiles that may be used is displayed on a special counter in the upper right corner of the screen.

Special Operations

There's more to war than taking cities. In other words, do not form and maneuver armies solely for the purpose of capturing enemy cities or defending yours from an enemy attack. There are many other options open, and they include building smaller-sized, highly mobile corps instead of armies equipped with slow-moving artillery and supply wagons. This and other options are discussed in this section.

First of all, use your military to keep the enemy under constant pressure by conducting harassing raids that target the enemy economy (citizens, caravans, trading posts) and upset enemy plans. Begin harassing an enemy as soon as you have scouted enough to know the right enemy to harass. This is regardless of whether you're pursuing a program of rapid economic development. In the toughest, most vicious Survival of the Fittest games, a couple of slinger units wandering the countryside can literally change game world events. This is done by wandering into an enemy city, causing plenty of excitement, and subsequently leading a pursuing enemy army right into another enemy army. In Toughest level Survival of the Fittest solo games, make a point of arranging battles between enemy armies that were originally both after your city (see Figure 9.8).

Forming a number of small, fast, cavalry-only corps and letting them roam without a supply wagon is another highly recommended tactic. The only problem lies in the micromanagement necessary: You want to pull your guys back once they dip below 50% hit points. The risk is worth it because cavalry unencumbered by a supply wagon has very high mobility; when led by a general, or better still, two generals, it can conduct incredibly swift marches across half the map to strike at an enemy target and then retreat back, preferably leading excited enemy troops into an ambush. Later on, form armored brigades composed of tanks, scout cars, and mobile AA guns (a dozen all told is a good size). Researching anti-attrition techs and improving your generals through fort research considerably adds to the combat value of these formations.

FIGURE 9.8: *Making sure your enemies beat up on each other is crucial to winning high difficulty games of Diplomacy and Survival of the Fittest.*

Set up plenty of ambushes: They're easy, fun, and profitable. This works beautifully in solo games and against relatively less-experienced human players. The Escalator is a double-ambush tactic that best works as follows:

1. Form three small task groups: two highly mobile (light cavalry, horse archers), one slow (infantry).

2. Use cavalry to attract enemy attention and pursuit by raiding enemy territory or attacking an army in the field.

3. Lead them toward the horse archers, and have the archers attack from the flank.

4. Retreat both cavalry groups toward infantry; move cavalry to sides for flank attacks while infantry attacks from the front.

You may try this tactic with other units too, as long as they fulfill the mobility requirements. Ideally the two mobile groups will lead the pursuing enemy to fight on your territory, and at a chosen site that features nearby unit-healing structures, preferably a fort. The A.I. likes to fight to the death and finds it hard to believe that a small cavalry group has become a full-sized cavalry-and-infantry army; many human players make the same mistake.

Note

Invisible troops under Ambush will not engage the enemy without specific orders. When they do, they become visible.

Remember to keep putting the generals to good use. Once you reach Enlightenment Age, your scouts or explorers will turn into commandos with sabotage skills. A task force of six commandos traveling under the Ambush cloak cast by a general can arrive undetected in the middle of enemy territory and wreak great havoc; follow it up with a standard military unit task force, with another general to finish off the buildings sabotaged by the commandos. Commando sharpshooters positioned behind your lines can be of great help during a battle, too, thanks to their Sniper ability, as long as you can handle the micromanagement.

There are as many ways of waging war as there are players. Nevertheless, in the few years since the appearance of RTS games, gamers have defined a few basic approaches that differ substantially. They are described in the next section.

RUSH, BORDER PUSH, AND OTHER TACTICS

The four most popular RTS strategies are Rush, Boom, Border Push, and Needle-and-Hammer (N&H). The following sections comment on what these terms mean.

Not all approaches work equally well under all circumstances. For this reason, the "strategy reviews" advise when to make a particular choice. Also, note that the game lets you modify rush rules by adjusting pre-game Quick Battle settings. The comments assume that you've been brave and chose No Rush Rules (meaning no limits on aggression).

Rush

Adopting a Rush strategy involves focusing on military unit production, and subsequently overwhelming a competitor with constant attacks that begin almost as soon as the game does. Rushing is an option only with the early discovery of an easily accessible enemy city. If the enemy has progressed to Classical Age and researched Allegiance (attrition tech), definitely reconsider.

Rush is a much more practical option if you choose a starting age other than Ancient Age. If you begin in Industrial Age, for example, you'll quickly have access to powerful units that can easily take a city, however, so will your opponent! A lot depends on respective player skills. In games involving many players, quite a lot also depends on luck.

Tip

Special national bonuses can make a nation particularly suitable for a given strategy. Nations that get free military units with barracks (for example, Aztecs) are particularly well suited for an aggressive strategy (Rush, Needle-and-Hammer). Nations with big economic bonuses are well-suited for a Boom; territorial bonuses enhance the effectiveness of a Border Push approach; and some lucky nations have bonuses that enable them to pursue almost any approach effectively (Germans). Analyze your national bonuses before you settle on a given strategy.

The following table outlines a typical Rush battle plan once you've reached the level of economic development needed to sustain a war (as described earlier in "The War Economy").

ACTION	COMMENTS
Attend to necessary basics: Research Military 1, build barracks, create scout if situation allows, found second city, start caravan route.	
Create a couple of light infantry units.	Bowmen are an option if you have timber and wealth but little food.
Attack enemy lumberjacks.	Cripples enemy effort to build up military; timber is needed for barracks, all early infantry.
Create heavy infantry to attack enemy city.	3–4 units; use in relays, healing units that have been damaged by enemy fire: Withdraw damaged unit substituting a healthy unit in its place, heal damaged unit, use it to replace another unit that's been damaged in the meantime.
Optionally, create bowmen.	Bowmen can attack enemy farmers from beyond city range.
If no other enemy cities are found by the time first enemy city is captured, switch to economic development.	Rush has short legs; continuing to create military units while neglecting the economy spells ultimate defeat.
If other enemy cities are found, attack them but switch half of resources to development or research; develop resources aggressively; change to Needle-and-Hammer tactics.	Watch out for enemies you cannot reach; they might be able to field technologically superior armies.

Rush is especially risky if you're playing against a large number of opponents. It's highly unlikely you'll be able to tackle more than two before the remaining players advance too far for you to dream of catching up. Staying an Age behind means fighting with obsolete units, and taking heavy losses even in victorious battles (see Figure 9.9). In summary, Rush isn't a strategy that can carry you all the way to victory in most games. It offers limited possibilities in strategic terms: to wit, a quick assassination of one, perhaps two, weak empires. It works best on small, land-only maps with just one to three opponents.

Tip

The costs involved in staging a Rush attack may be partially refunded by razing captured enemy buildings.

Warning

Don't try Rushing an enemy by building a single barracks as your first city building, and subsequently turning out only three to four units. You'll damage the development of your economy without achieving anything except on the Easiest difficulty level, or against exceptionally green human players.

FIGURE 9.9: *A few crossbowmen can massacre an opponent who has fallen behind the times.*

Boom

This approach consists of building up the economy before building an army. It is an easy strategy to implement, the assumption being that you'll be able to out-produce your opponent, however, it's a dangerous assumption to make in *RoN*, and it's downright suicidal when playing at the Toughest difficulty level or against an experienced human player. In practice, Boom works best if you haven't been discovered by any of your opponents, who hopefully have discovered each other and are busy fighting. While they spend their resources on war, you can acquire an unbeatable edge in research and create a modern army that will subsequently steamroll over any opposition. Here's a rough template showing how to go about things:

ACTION	COMMENTS
Found a minimum of three cities and build them up so each contains a basic suite of buildings: farms and woodcutter's camp as allowed by Commerce cap, market, temple, plus university after advance to Classical Age.	Two cities might be enough on an Arena map.
Pursue economic development and research aggressively until you advance to the Medieval Age.	At the very least, hit Commerce 2 production cap; Commerce 3 is better.

continued

ACTION	COMMENTS
Build a full suite of military unit-creating buildings (barracks, stable, siege factory) in at least two cities.	At least one set of military buildings should be close to the future battle sites.
While creating an army, build at least one fort not far away from the site of the future battle.	Make sure you have at least one general to lead your forces; build at least two supply wagons even if convinced you'll just need one; protect the workers building the fort.
Conduct extensive reconnaissance while continuing to create offensive military units.	Make sure you create at least one spy; plant informers in enemy buildings and cities.
Select target and launch attack.	Continue attacking until your forces grow too weak or supply lines become overextended; build military unit-producing buildings in newly captured cities.

Boom is easy to implement, but that doesn't mean Boom is best. The opening period of almost total military inactivity is a godsend to the A.I. on Tougher/Toughest difficulty levels; it means it can develop to its plan, and it will always do so faster than you. In multiplayer games, adopting this approach against an experienced player is akin to stating, "Look at all the nice stuff I'm building for you" (see Figure 9.10). The success of a Boom strategy rides on the assumption that your economy is stronger than the enemy's, and that no one will bother you while you go about things. It's often a dangerous assumption to make.

FIGURE 9.10: *Sir, we've captured the Colossus—oh, and we've won the game.*

Border Push

Border Push is especially well-suited to *Rise of Nations* because of the concepts of national borders and attrition. It consists of literally pushing the enemy off the map by slowly yet constantly enlarging your national territory. Naturally this is an approach that works best on small to medium maps, or when used as part of a bigger strategy (for example, you might fight a Border Push war in a small corner of your empire against a weak enemy nation). As noted in the first table entry and earlier in "The War Economy," you should first achieve a level of economic development that lets you support a meaningful war effort. Here's a template:

ACTION	COMMENTS
Pursue economic development and research as described in Age Jump (Chapter 8).	Place special emphasis on temple and tower techs (religion line, attrition line).
Build a couple of forts as near to enemy cities as you can; start creating an army.	Forts must be within your borders; building site turns orange if too close to enemy city.
If no enemy cities nearby, build another city right on the border.	Choose city site that will offer maximum territorial gain; guard builders with army.
Build another fort right on the new border/as close to enemy cities as you can.	Use army to contain enemy attacks; do not engage in pursuit.
Once your border runs right next to enemy city, capture that city.	Do not continue offensive; assume defensive stance and fight off enemy counterattacks while repairing/developing captured city.
Repeat, building new forts and capturing enemy cities one at a time.	Raze old forts to reduce new fort building costs as appropriate.

It is always easier to fight on the defense rather than attack, and the network of forts you've built will allow you to heal damaged units quickly while increasing the garrisoned fort's firepower. Make sure you have a cavalry group that can take out enemy artillery when your opponent attacks your forts. You'll also need a small repair corps (three or so citizens) to work on damaged forts. The Crush or Border Push approach works well in most situations (but extra well with the Russians and the Romans), and it's especially comfortable for players who don't like a lot of micromanagement.

Needle-and-Hammer

This tends to be the best strategy for all high difficulty games (multiplayer and solo games at high difficulty level). It is an adaptation of the Rush approach and consists of dividing your attention and resources between economic development, research, and the deployment of a small number of highly mobile units in raider/intruder role. Those units are combined into two or more small, mobile corps that are used against selected targets with the objective to destroy rather than capture. Sooner or later you'll be presented with an advantage that will call for gathering a couple of the small corps into a small army and taking a weakened enemy city. The one big drawback of this approach is that it calls for plenty of micromanagement; it's just not possible to execute effectively at any game speed above Slow. As usual, you should reach a level of economic development that allows you to launch a military effort, as described earlier in "The War Economy." Here's the template:

ACTION	COMMENTS
Prepare for the Age Jump as described in Chapter 8, but build a couple of scouting units early.	Locate neighboring nations and scout to determine your target (the most dangerous opponent).
Attack enemy lumberjacks with small mobile task groups.	Light infantry with optional ranged infantry support, cavalry work best; heal damaged units and replace them on the front line with fresh units.
Build a fort and create a strong corps to counter any enemy counterattacks/incursions.	Composition of the corps mostly determined by which resources are currently needed for research/economic development.
Keep an eye on battlefield developments; when enemy weakens, combine the harassing units with the defense corps to take enemy city.	Use a spy to locate and scout faraway nations' territories; plant informers to keep an eye on their development.
Repeat the procedure with subsequent enemy cities.	Always harass the strongest opponent first; if you want to attack a weak nation concurrently, build a second harassing corps.

The N&H never fails to have one effect: It always upsets enemy plans, even if you don't take a single city. If you've managed to draw even in terms of losses, you're ahead.

The next chapter discusses Conquer the World: *RoN's* campaign game mode, which offers plenty of opportunities to apply what you've learned here.

CONQUER THE WORLD

10

The campaign game in Rise of Nations isn't just a series of battles linked with a time chain. It actually gives a new dimension to the whole game. The economy gains a new, strategic dimension; Age advances also gain a new, strategic dimension—wherever you turn, there's a new, strategic dimension. This chapter explores these dimensions and tells you what you can expect upon embarking on the ambitious task of conquering the world.

First of all, take a look at the strategic screen. The world map is a scene where your most crucial moves will take place. No amount of tactical brilliance on the battlefield can compensate for a silly move on the strategic screen. In fact, you can kiss your dreams of conquering the world good-bye if you don't learn how to capture multiple territories within a single turn, even though you can attack only once every turn.

After revealing appropriate secrets, this chapter examines the economy on the strategic scale and its influence on the tactical level: the Quick Battle scenarios that take place when a move on the strategic map results in combat. After reviewing research and ways of winning scenarios, this chapter concludes with a look at what you can expect when playing the campaign game on the tactical level.

Note that this chapter assumes that you've read the game manual, completed the Conquer the World tutorial, and that you refer to the in-game text while playing.

LOOKING AT THE WORLD

The world consists of 49 territories; you start with one, and so does every nation. That leaves 31 barbarian territories waiting to be conquered, but you'll be lucky if you can conquer two or three before having to declare war on another nation (or having it declared on you). You're to conquer the 48 territories you do not own within 29 turns. The world progresses in time independently of research done at the tactical (scenario) level: It stays in the Ancient Age for one turn, and for four turns per Age thereafter.

The bright side of things is that the other nations fight each other with a vengeance: Although you need to eliminate everyone else within 29 turns to win, you don't have to capture 17 enemy capitals. In fact, by the time the world advances to Gunpowder Age, there might be only half of the original nations left (see Figure 10.1). Nations are eliminated when their capitals fall to enemy forces no matter how many territories they own; all these territories pass into the hands of the nation that has done the eliminating, that is, captured the capital.

> **Tip**
>
> In most games, you'll have to eliminate personally no more than six to eight rivals. Each time you succeed, you get a bonus card (national Oath of Fealty) that gives you the eliminated nation's special bonuses for one battle.

Owning a territory can bring the following bonuses:

- A bonus card. Bonus cards are discussed later in this chapter. For now, note that a national Oath of Fealty card can be won only once; if you capture the former capital of a nation that has been eliminated, you won't get it.
- Rare resources. These provide a strategic bonus, that is, they count in each and every battle on the tactical level. Owning several rare resources can give you quite an edge in battle.
- Tribute. The amount can vary from 10 to 40 per turn.
- Supply center. This lets you field an extra army.

FIGURE 10.1: *More than half the competing nations are eliminated within the first four Ages of a campaign game.*

Of course owning more territories is better than owning fewer territories; however, their place in the world matters, too. Territories that contain army supply centers and Wonder bonus cards are extra precious, but every territory contributes importantly to the might of your empire. The territory that formerly housed a nation's capital does not contribute anything beyond a national Oath of Fealty bonus card when conquered for the first time; after that its only use is as an army staging area.

Three Quick Ways to Fast Territory Conquest

> **Note**
>
> A territory may offer a maximum of three benefits out of the four possible. Unless the bonus card is particularly useful (Wonder card), it's best to get rare resources, tribute, and a supply center. Remember, however, that a territory's position on the map plays a significant if not decisive role.

You probably already have an inkling how to take multiple territories in a single turn. OK, let's list the basic ways:

- Capturing an enemy nation's capital. This puts all the territories belonging to that nation in your possession.
- Attacking a territory with superior forces. If you have two more armies than the defender, you achieve what's known as an *overrun victory*. An overrun victory that doesn't feature tactical combat (that is, you don't even get to go to the tactical screen) does *not* count as an attack. In other words, you are free to immediately attack another territory within the same turn. If you overrun the enemy again, you may attack for the third time, however, once you've entered the tactical screen for some fighting, your attack counts as an attack, and you have to wait until the next turn to get another chance.

- **Buying territories.** A competing nation may sell one or more of its territories for tribute. You may do the buying and selling both before and after attacking with your army or armies. This is the least attractive way of acquiring more than one territory per turn and generally should be a consideration only when the freshly bought territory enables you to execute a daring strategic maneuver. Don't buy a territory for its bonus card (Wonder cards excepted), resources, or tribute alone. There are better ways of spending precious tribute, which we'll discuss later.

During your campaign, most of your multiple territory gains will be achieved through overrun victories. To get those, you must be well grounded in army management rules.

Army Rules

As you know from the game, armies are governed by strict rules:

- There may be only one army present in any territory.
- An army may move only once from territory to neighboring territory *unless* it's attacking and achieving overrun victories.
- An army is "available for combat" in all the neighboring territories for both defensive and offensive purposes. In case of an attack, it counts toward the territory army total. If a fight takes place, it will take part (appear on the Quick Battle screen), however, it will be controlled by your ally (the A.I. of the particular nation), not by you.

Note

When you move an army, its movement is marked by a green arrow on the world map, and you might see black arrows appear too (see Figure 10.2). These black arrows indicate the movement of armies affected by your attack: allied armies coming in to help out, or extra enemy armies joining in from neighboring provinces. Count them to arrive at opposing army totals; an advantage of two armies grants you an overrun victory.

These three rules make it ultra important you place each army in exactly the right territory. In this respect, the campaign game is similar to a game of checkers: Placing armies just right lets you "jump" an army through several territories. Once you've pondered the world map for a while, you'll start planning your conquests not in the terms of individual territories, but whole chunks of land. Every freshly conquered territory opens fresh possibilities; it's yet another spot to place an army and thus helps to bring down overbearing force (several armies) on an enemy-held territory.

You start each campaign game with just a single army. Naturally, you'll have to acquire more; the next section explains how to set about it.

FIGURE 10.2: *Examine the consequences of a proposed move carefully before clicking Start.*

Gaining New Armies

There are two ways in which you may acquire new armies for the purposes of attacking or defending territories:

> Capture a territory with a supply center. Each supply center gives you one extra army.

> Make alliances. That's right. Although you don't acquire a new army of your own per se, it counts as one in battle. If it's present in a territory neighboring the object of your attack, it will report for combat just like one of your armies, and will count toward the total number of armies attacking the targeted territory. In other words, having allied armies support attacks makes it much easier to achieve overrun victories.

This brings us to the whole issue of alliances. These function differently to what many gamers might expect on the basis of other strategy games: In *Rise of Nations*, they're very, very practical.

Diplomatic Murder

The diplomacy that takes place on the strategic screen is very straightforward. For practical purposes, you and another nation may have one of three relationships:

> Peace. This is self-explanatory. You may not attack the territory of someone with whom you are at peace.

> War. Even more self-explanatory. Allows you to attack enemy territories.

> Alliance. You ally's armies will participate in any of your battles as long as they take place in a neighboring territory. If your ally also happens to be allied with your opponent, they'll abstain from joining in the battle and won't count toward army totals on either side. Naturally this encourages the "bribing" of your enemy's allies into alliances with yourself, so that they don't take part in an upcoming fight.

You may switch from one diplomatic stance to another more than once per turn. This allows some exquisite backstabbing: You may overrun a territory thanks to an ally's help, then enter another alliance with the ally's neighbor, declare war on the poor ally, and overrun one of his territories before you even do any fighting. Of course, all this diplomatic maneuvering doesn't come free of charge: You must have deep pockets, that is, plenty of tribute.

> **Warning**
>
> *Make sure you know who is allied with whom. Read the World Events at the beginning of every new turn, noting the victories, defeats, and diplomatic moves of your opponents.*

Earning and Spending Tribute

Tribute may be earned in several ways:

> Capture and hold territories that pay a specified amount of tribute per turn (see Figure 10.3).

> Abstain from making an attack during a turn. You can capture several provinces with overrun attacks and still get tribute. The amount received grows by increments of 25, so it can add up to a lot.

> Agree to diplomatic deals (alliance, peace) proposed by your opponents. All proposals come with tribute attached. They're mostly one-time offers, so don't turn them down in the hope you'll get offered more tribute later.

Tribute's most important single function is to fuel diplomatic maneuvering that will let you pile up overrun victories and fight off any attacks on your territories with the help of allied armies. There are also other interesting ways to spend it. You may:

FIGURE 10.3: *Captured territories bring tribute every turn.*

◆ Beef up your territories. You may increase a territory's defense rating by one level per turn (if you've got the money). Press the Strength button at the bottom of the Rules panel (obtained by clicking the Rules button in the lower-left corner of the strategic screen).

◆ Purchase new territories. As mentioned earlier, this might open up new and exciting possibilities for expansion.

◆ Purchase bonus cards. Bonus cards are discussed in detail in the following section; suffice to say they can be very valuable.

Most of your tribute will come from owned territories. You'll receive a reassuring trickle every turn (with new conquests, eventually it might turn into a stream), however, if you go to the trouble of arranging a couple of overrun victories, consider abstaining from making yet another attack that would result in a fight, and collect tribute instead. An increment of 25 might not seem as much, but when you forgo attacking three times, the fourth time around, you'll get a 100 tribute in exchange for your forbearance. This, plus income from a few territories, can amount to a pretty bit of cash that might enable you to capture multiple territories on the very next turn.

Obtaining and Playing Bonus Cards

The campaign game features opportunities to acquire and use bonus cards. These cards provide either a strategic advantage (for example, a Wonder that affects all subsequent battles) or a tactical one (the vast, vast majority). You can acquire bonus cards in two ways:

◆ Capture territories that have a bonus card. Note that the card goes to the player that captured the territory first (see Figure 10.4).

◆ Purchase them with tribute on the strategic screen. They begin at 30 tribute a pop; price rises in increments of 40, which means they quickly get very expensive. Compare that with 20-odd tribute commonly paid for an alliance or a declaration of war.

Purchasing bonus cards with the hope of a victorious buy is a little like playing roulette to raise rent money. Once you enter the purchase screen, you'll see the three cards currently on offer. It's not a wise way to spend precious tribute early in the game; it's much better to limit yourself to obtaining cards through conquest of card-carrying territories. A bonus card costs 30 tribute only once; then it costs 70; then it costs so much that it's better to forget about it unless you're absolutely rolling in tribute and there's nothing to be done on the diplomatic/territory upgrade scene.

There are around 40 bonus cards in the game. Of these, three (distinguished by brown back trim) have a strategic dimension, meaning they're played on the strategic map and take immediate effect:

FIGURE 10.4: *Being an assassin of other nations means gaining their lands and Oath of Fealty cards.*

▶ Wonder of the World. This card enables you to build a Wonder from your current age in any owned territory. Two territories contain Wonder cards: South East Asia and Pampas (in South America). Wonder cards do turn up among the trio offered for purchase, which is a powerful incentive to gamble. Note that it is theoretically possible to obtain enough Wonder cards to build all the possible Wonders, but to do so in practice requires incredible skill and a lot of luck. If you're keen on Wonders, you might consider playing the Egyptians: They get the usual Wonder bonuses plus no less than two Wonder cards for free, right at the start of a new campaign.

▶ Treachery. This is a very nice card that transfers any level 4 or lower territory instantly into your possession (enemy capitals excluded), however, you're automatically at war with its owner (as if you cared). It's best to play this card as part of a plan to acquire a series of territories in one turn. It works especially nicely if used in conjunction with Sabotage (see next bullet). The Treachery card may be acquired only through purchase, unfortunately.

▶ Sabotage. This card may be acquired on the map (Mississippi Valley in North America) as well as through purchase. It immediately lowers the level of the territory on which it is played by two levels. If played just before the Treachery card, it lets you painlessly acquire a level 6 territory. This is the weakest of the three strategic bonus cards.

The tactical cards are distinguished by blue back trim. They are played just before the Quick Battle scenario begins and affect that scenario only. You may play as many tactical cards as you like prior to a single Quick Battle scenario. There are three types of tactical cards that together add up to a majority of the total:

- **National Oath of Fealty.** There are 18 of these, of which 17 are obtainable by capturing the capital territory of a rival nation for the first time—a very nice bonus in addition to getting all those new national territories that come with the capital.

- **Eureka.** Playing one of these cards means you'll start a battle with a single extra technology. There are five varieties available: General (random technology), Civic, Commerce, Science, and Military.

- **Economic Boom.** These cards give you a 5% resource bonus in one of the game's resources (including knowledge). Knowledge, wealth, and metal bonuses are the most useful, in that order. These cards aren't worth spending 110 tribute on. They are obtainable on the world map.

All of the other tactical cards are one-of-a-kind and can be obtained both on the map and through purchase. Some comments on specific cards:

- **Cultural Dominance.** Very nice card that deprives the enemy of their national bonuses. It's worth much more than any Economic Boom card.

- **Logistics.** Makes your units immune to attrition damage, and heal 50% faster. It's a very powerful card that can result in a swift scenario victory.

- **Great Thinker.** This is another winner. With all research being 20% cheaper and taking place 20% faster, you're practically guaranteed a technological edge.

- **Merchant Guild.** You receive a 20% bonus on market prices (buy lower, sell higher). It's a very good card provided you know how to trade.

- **Mercenaries.** This grants you extra troops at the start of the battle. Its value is in straight proportion to your skill as a leader.

- **Propaganda.** You gain the enemy's national bonuses. Cutesy but effective, like all propaganda.

- **Partisans.** Enemy units take 50% more attrition damage. Its usefulness is very limited except when playing at the Toughest level; it works only when you're fighting for your miserable life, on the defensive. It's to be shunned by people with a sense of style.

FIGURE 10.5: *You'll receive a Skill Bonus card following a successful field battle.*

Finally, there is one very special tactical bonus card called Skill Bonus (see Figure 10.5). It is issued as a reward for winning a Field Battle Scenario (no cities), and its worth is in proportion to your skill as a general: It's based on the number of troops that have survived the battle and provides you with a number of extra resources in each resource category at the start of a tactical battle. Competent generals playing at the Tough level should expect to get a Skill Bonus of 150–200 units. It's very nice and definitely worth much more than the Economic Boom because the resources are there when it always counts most: right at the start.

Conquer-the-World Economics

Many of the territories on the Conquer the World map feature rare resources. Owning these means a permanent economic bonus in tactical scenarios as long as you retain possession of the territory and its rare resource. For instance, conquering Greenland will not only yield a juicy Cultural Dominance card, but also provide you with furs: +10 food, +10 metal, and a 25% Military research discount in every subsequent fight.

> **Note**
>
> *You have to research Civic level 4 in order to benefit from your Wonder in a tactical scenario.*

A single rare resource might not seem much, but they sure do add up. In real game terms, each rare resource is worth several Economic Boom cards. It's not uncommon to be collecting an extra 100 units in aggregate after a few turns.

Tribute cannot be regarded in ordinary economic terms. It occupies a special politico-economical sphere; players who treat it as an economic resource (buying territories, upgrading owned territories, buying cards) won't be utilizing it to the best of its potential. As a rule of thumb, spend tribute on anything other than diplomacy only if all the diplomatic avenues have already been exhausted and you still have a ton of tribute left. Remember that, given a bit of scheming, tribute can in effect hand you enemy territories on a plate; no other resource can hope to equal this. Finally, although tribute seemingly functions solely on the strategic level, in reality, its expenditure deeply influences the tactical picture: The allied armies and cities that support you in battle will be there thanks to tribute wisely spent.

Research and Age Advancement

In the campaign game, research is conducted solely at the tactical (Quick Battle) level. You begin each battle scenario in the same Age as on the strategic screen. Twelve non-Age advances are needed to advance to the next Age in the *scenario only*; for instance, if the world is currently in the first turn of the Classical Age, you may advance to Medieval Age while fighting a battle, but will revert to Classical Age on the strategic screen and upon commencing the next battle one turn later.

The remaining advances function similarly to the way they do in Quick Battle mode (but playing a Eureka card gives you a free advance). You need to research Civic, Commerce, and Science advances to avail yourself of the usual benefits: ability to build more cities, higher production cap, and so on. Military is different in that better military units are obtainable only after researching Military level 4; advancing an Age isn't enough to perform an upgrade.

BATTLES IN THE CAMPAIGN GAME

During the campaign game, you'll be fighting two types of enemies: barbarians and competing enemy nations (see Figure 10.6). Both types of opponents can be fought in a variety of encounters:

▶ Conquering a barbarian territory might involve a field battle during which you'll be tasked with destroying barbarian armies, destroying barbarian armies plus their encampment (barracks), capturing the barbarian capital (elimination by Sudden Death), or defending a settlement of yours against attacking barbarians. The field battles (no cities involved) with barbarians might have them attacking you, or will direct you to locate and attack them.

▶ Fighting with another nation might be much more complex. You might fight a field battle if the scenario takes place on a territory developed below level 4, and no allies are involved on either side. The various field battle types are similar to those experienced when fighting the barbarians. The plot thickens when the battle takes place on a relatively developed territory with allied armies taking part. These encounters feature numerous cities built by all the participants in the battle (for example, if each of the main combatants is supported by an ally, there are four nations involved).

The formula for determining what you and your ally start with is pretty complex. The difficulty level of your campaign game, level of infrastructure (development) of the territory that's acting as a battlefield, whether you have an army in that territory or not (on the strategic screen), even whether you're attacking or defending—these all play a role. Some hints:

▶ If you're fighting in defense of your territory, you'll start with a city whose size and buildings correspond to the territory infrastructure (development level).

▶ If you're fighting in defense of your capital, you'll always start with a strong army as well.

▶ If there was a reinforcement (black) arrow from an allied army on the strategic map, the allied nation will build cities in that battle.

▶ If there is a reinforcement arrow from one of your armies on the strategic map, you'll receive reinforcements (an extra army) soon after the start of the scenario (possibly more than once, depending on the number of supporting armies/reinforcement arrows).

▶ On the two lowest difficulty levels, you'll have starting armies much more often than on higher difficulty levels.

Finally, note that the topography of the map you'll be fighting on reflects the view on the strategic map. Let's say you're attacking Germany from Scandinavia; the scenario map will consist of two continents separated by a strait. Likewise, the type of terrain will correspond with the territory's geographical whereabouts on the strategic map. Expect snow in the northernmost provinces, sand in the Sahara, and so on.

If there's a single big difference between a campaign game scenario battle and a stand-alone Quick Battle, it is this: In the stand-alone Quick Battle, you get to research as many Age advances as determined by your choice of Starting and Ending Age. You cannot do so in a campaign battle; you may progress only one Age. This means only one new generation of military units per battle, which subtly undermines the importance of research as such while stressing the importance of your administrative and leadership talents.

FIGURE 10.6: *Having lured the Russian army into an ambush, British knights charge enemy artillery on the outskirts of Smolensk in Gunpowder Age.*

CHAPTER 10 CONQUER THE WORLD

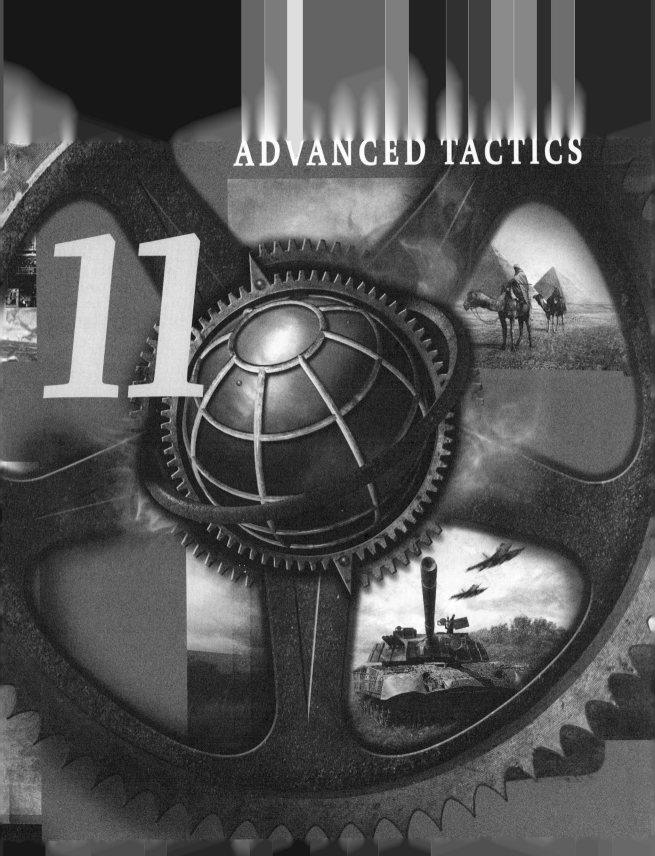

11

This chapter, written by Big Huge Games producer Paul Stephanouk, introduces tactics and strategies that experienced Rise of Nations players use in both multiplayer and single-player games. After a discussion of two major strategic lines of thinking, the chapter covers research; the economy, strengths, and weaknesses of each nation; and combat by land, sea, and air. The skills you learn here will help your nation rise to power.

OFFENSE VS. DEFENSE: BOOMING AND RUSHING

There are many different strategies and styles of play in *Rise of Nations*, but most of them fall under two broad categories: the Boom and the Rush. In a Boom, a player focuses on building up economy. In some cases, a Booming player will all but ignore building military units, but that can be exceptionally risky. More often, the Booming player simply tries to delay and minimize military spending until it's time to attack. At this point, the investments made in creating a powerful economy pay off as a powerful army.

A Rush strategy involves quickly developing military units and attacking in the hopes of catching an enemy unprepared. Early Rushes are more risky for the attacker because key economic development is being put aside to attack. Of course, an early Rusher can sometimes catch a sleeping Boomer totally unprepared. In this case, the Rusher can win the game outright.

FIGURE 11.1: *Scouting your national borders can alert you to planned attacks.*

A key element in succeeding with either strategy is knowing what your enemy is likely doing by understanding your rival nation's tendencies. Some nations by their very nature seem to favor one strategy. Aztecs, for example, need to attack to get the most out of their ability. The chances are high that they will be attacking you sooner rather than later, so be prepared. On the other hand, the Egyptians usually try to get their economy going so they can afford to start building wonders. Attacking them early is a good way to keep them off-balance.

As mentioned elsewhere in this book, always scout your enemies so that you know if a Rush is coming. Always keep the border of your nation well scouted (see Figure 11.1).

Rushing requires that you quickly build a force to overwhelm your enemy. You can Rush anytime; however, the sooner you do so, the greater the risk and the reward. A basic Rush often begins with researching a military tech at the library so that a barracks can be constructed right away. Build several heavy infantry and attack the enemy city. While your heavy infantry are on their way, continue to build troops, including some slingers to counter any enemy archers. If you catch an enemy unprepared, this Rush has the force required to take down a city (except against the Chinese and perhaps the Maya), but it's easily stopped by a tower and a barracks defending the city.

More commonly (and effectively), a player can Rush in the Classical Age by massing two types of complementary units. By the Classical Age, an enemy is likely to have some basic defenses, but by waiting, the Rusher hopes to mass enough force to more than compensate for that. Effective combinations include heavy and light infantry or heavy cavalry with siege equipment.

If you plan to Boom, try to anticipate when you'll be attacked. That way, you'll know when you have to start expending resources for your defense. If an early attack looks likely, quickly building a tower and barracks is usually enough to get you on good defensive footing in the Ancient Age.

Here's a recipe for a Boom start on a land map:

1. Your city starts selected, so rally-point your lumber camp, then queue up two civilians. Keeping new civilians coming is key to the pacing of a good start.

2. Select your library, research the first level of Science, and queue up the first level of Civic; you want the Science to discount the other techs and improve the income from ruins. Most game starts, except for the earliest Rushes, start with Science.

3. Select the scout and shift-click on the mini-map several times to give him a path. On most maps, it's good to send him toward your nearest enemy, at least far enough to find a good city location. Make sure you give him ample waypoints to keep him busy for a while. You can always go back and revise the scout's path later. You just want to get him moving so he'll find you a good spot for your second city and to start generating income from discovered ruins.

4. Use a civilian from your woodcutter to build a farm. If your timing is good, you can even grab a newly created civilian on his way to the lumber camp to do this.

5. Start moving a civilian from timber toward the spot where you think you'll build your second city. Ideally, you'll find a spot that's toward your enemy and that gives you good access to both timber and metal. The timber is the most important element, so if you can't get all three, make sure you at least get that. If your timing is good, you'll be at the spot just as the research for the first Civic technology is complete. Build a city.

6. Build another farm at your first city when you get the timber.

7. When the second city is finished being constructed, have the civilian immediately construct a lumber camp.

8. Continue to populate your lumber camps to capacity, building farms as your wood allows. You'll need to take the first Commerce technology soon to keep this up. You should be able to reach +100 in both Timber and Food this way.

9. Gather food for Classical Age while spending your timber on a market (build it at your first city). If you have a surplus of timber, consider building a temple at your second city. Make sure you keep enough timber so you can build a university immediately when you hit Classical Age.

On a water map, you want to start fishing early, so take Commerce instead of Civic and avoid taking an early farm. You'll need the wood to build a dock, and then a fishing boat. Some water maps keep you isolated from other players so you can go longer without worrying about defending yourself. You'll want to adjust your setup to match the nation you're playing, your enemies (if known), and the map type.

RESEARCH

The order you research things at the library can have a big effect on your nation. Sometimes focusing on one track more than the others can be helpful. Extra Science research makes other research cheaper and improves the bonus from ruins. The Science track, combined with the Age, is also used for the income-enhancing technologies found at the smelter, granary, and woodcutter. Booming players wanting to push their Science ahead should keep careful watch on their gold, as it's easy to buy too many scholars and thus not have enough gold for the next Science upgrade.

FIGURE 11.2: *These woodcutters are wasting their time: The commerce limit has been reached.*

As long as you have resources above your Commerce limit (they are flashing; see Figure 11.2), you should be improving your Commerce technology. A resource not gathered is a resource wasted. Try to anticipate when your next round of upgrades will be available at the smelter, granary, and woodcutter and have your Commerce technology advanced to make room for the increase in production.

Civic technology pushes your borders and enables you to build more cities. Don't buy more levels of Civic than you can build cities for unless you need them to push your borders.

You rarely need to buy Military technology in excess of your Age level unless you are either researching or about to research the next Age. Keep your military tech up with your Age so your unit upgrades will not lag behind.

Age upgrades are of vital importance. If you take some other upgrade when an Age advance is available, you'd better have a very good reason. Being even one Age behind your opponent makes you more vulnerable to attrition when attacking, makes your units less potent versus your opponent, and denies you access to all the new unit types available at the various Ages.

ECONOMY

Your economy is the engine that drives your nation forward. You need a powerful economy to place a large army on the field or quickly research important technologies. Learning how to efficiently grow your economy is an important skill in *Rise of Nations*. Players who fail to continue to expand their economy will find themselves falling further and further behind.

Always pay attention to your Resource Cap and strive to have your resources collect at close to that rate. If the gather rate of a resource is well below the Resource Cap, take steps to increase production in that resource. On the other hand, if the gather rate for a resource is flashing, that means you are actually gathering more than the Resource Cap worth of that resource. You have surplus production that's going to waste. If more than one resource is over the Resource Cap, purchase the next level of Commerce Technology at the library. This will raise your Resource Cap and allow you to realize all of your production. If you think you might be delayed in raising your Resource Cap, reassign some citizens from surplus resources to other, more productive tasks. Simply put, work to make your resources flash, and then upgrade your Commerce when they do. Just don't allow some of the resources to lag too far behind.

FIGURE 11.3: *Farms built near granaries means more food for you.*

There are two basic ways to increase production of a resource: by building more gather buildings (farms for food, woodcutter camps for timber, mines for metal, and so on) or by enhancing the production for existing gather buildings with an enhancer building such as a granary or a lumber mill. These enhancer buildings increase the production for related gather buildings in a given city and contain important upgrades that further improve their effect. Always strive to have gather buildings improved by the related enhancer building and try to place new gather buildings where they can be enhanced. For example, when placing a new farm, try to find a city that already has a granary (see Figure 11.3). This way, the farm will be more productive.

Food

It's usually easy to develop your food income because farms don't require you to find a special map location such as a mountain or forest. Getting the timber to build the farms is usually your only concern for developing food. On a water map, you also have the option of building a dock and making fishing boats. Fishing for food is very productive in the early and mid-game because it also brings in some wealth income. The drawback of fishing is that your fishing boats have to be defended closely to prevent easy raiding by your enemies. Later in the game, as the more powerful granary upgrades become available, fishing isn't quite as productive as farms, so make sure you keep some farms around and continue to enhance your granary.

Timber

Since you need timber to construct buildings, including other gather buildings such as farms, keeping up your timber gather rate is vital for expanding your economy. You'll need lots of timber for most of the game, so pay extra attention to your timber gather rate. This goes double for sea maps, where you're expected to also build a timber-hungry navy.

Metal

Metal arrives in the Classical Age, but some players might not need large amounts of it until later. Early on, you'll need it in large amounts only for certain military units such as heavy infantry, cavalry, and siege. In most games, you'll want to make sure you secure at least a couple of medium-sized mountains to meet your metal needs. Because of their size, mountains are often vulnerable to shifts in national borders. Make an extra effort to place your cities to secure key mountains (see Figure 11.4).

FIGURE 11.4: *Metal becomes precious mid-game, so secure those mountains early!*

Wealth

Most wealth comes from caravans that travel between friendly cities. Instead of being improved by an enhancer building, the value of trade routes is increased by distance and the size of the cities involved. Another key source of wealth is the Taxation series of technologies found at the temple. Since Taxation is based on the amount of territory you control, and caravans improve with distance, it's easy to see that a nation that's spread out has a much-improved ability to generate wealth. Wealth can also be obtained by fishing.

Both caravans and fishing ships are vulnerable to raiding attacks and need to be defended. The light-horse line of units is ideal for protecting caravans due to the line's mobility and advantage over cavalry archers, the most popular raiding unit. Fishing ships are most often raided by light ships, so you'll need either some heavy ships or an equal number of light ships to protect them.

Lastly, markets produce some wealth. Building a couple extra markets to shore up your wealth income often helps.

Knowledge

Knowledge arrives with Metal in the Classical Age and becomes the most important resource for improving your technology at the library. Invest in building up your knowledge early, but be careful because the wealth you use in creating scholars might be needed elsewhere.

Oil

Oil becomes available in the Industrial age. It appears both in the water and in rough terrain on the land. Astute players will notice the rough patches where oil might appear and try to capture that territory in advance of the Industrial age. Oil is very important in the late game, and players often have to shift their attention briefly from combat or other efforts to build oil wells and refineries. Players who arrive early to the Industrial Age should strongly consider buying as much oil as they can from the market. Oil can become very valuable in the late game, so early purchases of oil can be made at bargain prices.

Rare Resources

Rare Resources can give your economy a powerful boost as well as provide useful powers for your nation. Try to place merchants on as many Rare Resources as you can. Remember that you can place merchants on Rare Resources in allied and neutral territory. Consider the abilities of the Rare Resources when selecting which to build on first, but don't overlook the resource income. More modern Rare Resources, such as uranium or coal, can appear later in the game. These late-game Rare Resources are particularly powerful and should not be overlooked. Merchants are subject to being raided, so be sure to make light cavalry to counter enemy raider units. Conversely, raiding enemy merchants is an excellent way to harm an enemy's economy.

Tip

Many buildings provide a resource bonus when built. Careful timing can allow you get resources you lack while adding important buildings. For example, making a farm creates bonus food. This food can then help in creating civilians that can then staff the farm or be sent to a woodcutter to create timber for more farms.

Tip

If you control a large number of Rare Resources, consider building the Porcelain Tower Wonder. It will increase the resource income from Rare Resources in your territory by 200 percent. This power works with the Nubian bonus for Rare Resources, so Nubians can generate an extremely powerful economy this way.

Plunder

The resources you plunder from enemy buildings you destroy or cities you capture can often provide you with the vital resources needed to press an attack, especially in the early game. Capturing an enemy capital is particularly rewarding. In a game with multiple enemies, taking out one enemy early can provide a resource advantage.

NATIONAL TACTICS

Each nation has unique units and abilities. This section covers some of the best ways to use your nation's advantages in its rise to power. Also study the ways of the enemy to better prepare your defenses against his attack.

Aztecs

Aztecs gain additional plunder from buildings and even receive resources from defeating enemy units. The more you fight, the more you're going to gain from this ability, however, this doesn't mean you should attack recklessly. Quickly scout your enemy if you don't already know his nationality. Avoid Rushing in too soon against strongly defensive nations that will crush a premature attack, especially the Chinese or the Maya. Remember that your light infantry won't be able to capture buildings alone, so use them to shield your heavy troops from enemy archers. Attack early in the game and don't stop attacking, relying on the income from defeating your foes to keep your economy up (see Figure 11.5). To get heavy infantry more cheaply, start building some quickly after you build your first barracks.

FIGURE 11.5: *The Aztecs are well suited to early game attacks.*

Bantu

Use your extra city to quickly claim key territory, but don't do it too quickly unless you know you won't be attacked. Many map styles are low in a particular resource type, so try to dominate that resource. Your cities are inexpensive, so you should often be the first to build the next one, giving you a subtle but important advantage when it comes to placing your cities. Try to box your enemy in and continue to increase your border pressure via Civic technology and temple upgrades. Use your extra-quick light infantry to defend your far-flung empire.

British

The British improved Commerce limit allows you to spend more time developing your economic base before having to take the next Commerce technology. Their double income from Taxation provides an excellent source of wealth. The higher Commerce Cap allows the British to delay taking Commerce upgrades, instead using the timber to build archers. Remember to expand your national borders to maximize the effect of Taxation. Their improved ship creation speed allows them to quickly deploy a sizable fishing fleet and combat navy.

Chinese

Large cities are hard for early armies to take down. A Chinese player is almost unassailable in the Ancient Age and therefore can usually spend resources quickly advancing the economy. Instantly created citizens further quickens your early economy. Large cities make for more valuable trade routes and stronger borders, so be sure to capitalize on these facts. Instantly created caravans can quickly take advantage of these improved trade routes; use their cheap Science research to gain discounts on other technology. Defend your nation with gunpowder units that arrive earlier than other nations'.

Egyptians

Build many farms early, making sure to quickly build your capital up to its limit of seven. Build Wonders to gain an advantage over your enemies, but be careful not to cripple your military doing it. Be prepared for an enemy attack whenever you build a Wonder, as the enemy will both feel pressured and realize that you have just spent a large amount of resources that are not going to be used for combat units. In one-on-one matches, don't expect to be able

Tip

Look for Wonder combinations that work well together. One powerful strategy is to build both the Supercollider and the Space Program. This is usually enough to both trigger the Wonder timer and make it very difficult for the enemy to counter-build. Be prepared to be attacked when you do this, but your enemy will be on a short timer.

to build many Wonders. Instead, use your ability to build Wonders and advance Ages early to guarantee that you get exactly the Wonder(s) you want. Consider carefully the Wonders you build, as lots of early Wonders will make the later Wonders very expensive.

French

Once assembled, French armies are very effective at laying siege to enemy forts and cities. Extra siege equipment protected by unique cavalry is a strong combination (see Figure 11.6). Your powerful supply wagons will be an attractive target for your enemy, so guard them well. Be sure to build archers to counter enemy heavy infantry. Further strengthen your armies by making sure to include a general. Healing supply wagons means a large army that can sustain a large amount of momentum in enemy territory.

FIGURE 11.6: *The French cavalry is the perfect complement to siege weapons.*

Germans

Powerful heavy infantry can be used to attack in the early game, and unique tanks can be used in the late game. German air power can be particularly devastating in the late game, so make sure you have ample oil to press your air advantage. Build tanks to eliminate mobile anti-aircraft so that you maintain air superiority. Include commandos in your attacking army to jam enemy radar. Keep building cities to take advantage of the extra resources.

Greeks

Your research powers make you the master of the library. Try to keep ahead of your enemies in technology. Don't forget that your units will receive a combat bonus against lower-aged units. By keeping one step or more ahead at the library, you can keep the pressure on your enemies. Be the first player to key technologies such as gunpowder, airplanes, and nuclear weapons.

Inca

Quickly advance to the Classical Age so you can build mines. Focus on keeping your mines populated and you'll have plenty of wealth and metal. Keep your eye on the market and use your large amount of wealth to supplement other aspects of your economy. Take advantage of the unique siege weapons available mid-game. Focus on building troops that use gold in their cost. Combat losses don't hurt the Inca as much, so attack frequently.

Japanese

Unique heavy infantry allow for very powerful attacks early and for most of the game. Japanese infantry attacks are quite able to capture cities without the help of siege weapons. Build cavalry to protect your heavy infantry from enemy archers. Cheaper ships allow you to build a powerful navy, as well. You're one of the few nations good at attacking in the Ancient Age: Several heavy infantry backed up by slingers or archers can capture the capital of an unprepared opponent. Cheap farms and fisherman give a good early start, but this advantage fades over time.

Koreans

Make sure you take advantage of the free citizens by making city-building a priority. Even in the late game, when building a city might not seem as important, the free citizens make it worth your time, but be sure your population cap is high enough. Your citizens are tough, so you can divert less energy to protecting against a raid and more toward building a strong army. Build cavalry to support your unique archers. Your elite siege equipment makes early-age attacks potent. Temple powers provide tough cities and strong borders.

Maya

You are hard to raid and hard to scout, especially in the early game. Later on, your tougher buildings protect you, but don't rely on that alone. Use your construction bonus to quickly build up your infrastructure. Your building timber bonus helps your economy avoid the early wood crunch that most nations experience. Cheap, quick buildings mean you should build extra defenses. You can often get away with building towers in response to enemy attacks.

> **Note**
>
> The Temple of Tikal's effect on temples makes Mayan cities very tough, indeed.

Mongols

Unique cavalry archers in plentiful supply allow the Mongol player to damage an enemy economy with frequent raids. Discounts at the stable allow you to create large cavalry armies quickly. Enemies will be likely to build heavy infantry, so counter them with archers. Reduced attrition damage decreases reliance on supply wagons; however, they are still desirable in the later game and to supply siege equipment. Work to increase your national borders to take advantage of the food bonus. Use transports on sea maps to sneak raiding forces into the enemy's rear area.

Nubians

Quickly place merchants on Rare Resources to power your economy. Build unique archers to drive off enemy raiders and heavy infantry attacks. Try to expand your borders quickly to include more Rare Resources and to increase the value of your improved caravan routes. Unique camel archers can also be used to guard your merchants and to conduct raids on enemies. Starting with a market gives you additional flexibility in your start.

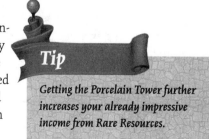

> **Tip**
>
> Getting the Porcelain Tower further increases your already impressive income from Rare Resources.

Romans

Build a barracks early and keep your heavy infantry line upgraded. You lack a strong economic power, so being passive isn't a good idea. Take the battle to your enemy. Save up wood and build several barracks at once when you are ready to attack. Don't just send heavy infantry or you'll suffer at the hands of enemy archers. Instead, build either light infantry or heavy cavalry to complement your heavy infantry. Use your forts to push your borders and threaten a territorial victory. After you build your first barracks, quickly make a few light infantry before building any more barracks, as the price will rise.

Russians

Build a collection of your unique light cavalry and use them to eliminate the supply wagons of invading armies. Archers are also a good build because heavy infantry often guard supply wagons. Use your powerful borders to deny the enemy access to key parts of the map. Your spies are particularly powerful. Station spies near areas you expect to see combat, and bribe enemy units when they show up.

Tip

Consider building Wonders that further enhance your border-pushing ability. Don't forget that the Temple of Tikal's temple bonus has a big effect on borders in the mid and late game.

Spanish

Consider getting one or even two early levels of Science to increase the value of ruins. If you scout well, this will result in a healthy income of bonus resources at the start of the game. If the game goes long, don't forget about your free scouts because they become useful commandos. Use your free ships to dominate fishing on maps with oceans. Be sure to signal your allies and tell them where Rare Resources and ideal building spots are.

Turks

Powerful siege makes for powerful offense. Start attacking your enemy early on and keep up the pressure. Be sure to keep your siege guarded by heavy infantry and in steady supply. Scout the enemy well and try to lay siege to new cities just being set up. Your siege will take them down quickly, and your fast assimilation will make it harder for your enemy to reclaim them. On sea maps, your bombard ships also enjoy the increased range of your siege equipment.

LAND COMBAT

Combat in *Rise of Nations* usually falls into three categories: field battle, attacking a city (or group of buildings), or defending a city (or group of buildings). Understanding how to use your units in these situations is vital to the success of your nation. Let's talk about how to handle field battles first (see Figure 11.7).

A field battle is any battle in which two armies (groups of units) meet each other without buildings playing a major role. Often armies will come to blows at the edge of a nation's borders or encounter each other en route to other planned engagements. When your army encounters another, quickly assess the

FIGURE 11.7: *Quickly size up an opponent's army when you meet in the countryside.*

strength of the opposition by evaluating how much ability the enemy army has to counter yours and vice versa. Battles that involve high proportions of counter-units are going to be over quickly and very decisively. Learning which units counter each other is the key to success. This graphic shows how units created at the stable and barracks counter each other.

After unit relationships, evaluate what Age the enemy units are from. Often you are ahead of or behind your enemy in unit upgrades. It's rare to fight units that are several Ages apart, but a one or even two Age difference can occur with some frequency. Be sure to upgrade your assessment of units that overage their enemy. For example, an enemy hoplite would be good against your unit of slingers, but a phalanx (the upgrade of the hoplite) would be even more powerful. Higher-aged units get a combat bonus when fighting earlier-aged units, and they usually having better combat stats.

If your force clearly counters the enemy, you probably should stay on the battlefield even if you're outnumbered. Units attacking strongly countered targets will inflict a great deal of damage, making the fight worthwhile even if superior numbers allows the enemy to keep the field. You'll have lost the battle but be winning the war. Of course, you'll want to do this only to a point. Units that are grossly outnumbered will be eliminated so fast they might not have time to even deal fatal damage to an enemy unit, so avoid sending small numbers of units against large armies even if the unit you are sending is a counter-unit.

If your enemy army clearly counters your own, immediately retreat from the battlefield. In this situation, having your units stay and inflict as much damage as they can before they die usually results in a total loss of your army for little return. A full retreat that costs your army half its force is better than losing the entire force with only slight damage to the enemy. In this situation, your enemy is now free to attack you knowing that your army is fully defeated.

If you think both armies are closely matched, then attack. Try to meet the enemy army head-on with the bulk of your army head-on. This will pin the enemy army to that spot. If they try to retreat or

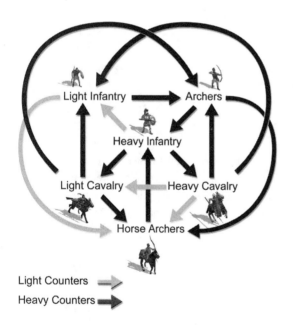

Light Counters ➡
Heavy Counters ➡

maneuver, they will suffer heavy damage. Use more mobile elements of your army, such as cavalry or light infantry, to attack the flank of the enemy. If the battle is going on in your territory, a flank attack is vital to reaching enemy supply wagons. With the enemy supply wagons eliminated, attrition will be a powerful advantage for your side.

In fact, the flanking attack on an enemy army is so powerful, to make it easier, always try to keep some units apart from your main force (see Figure 11.8). Trying to split off units from your army for a flank attack is much harder than having a second force of units come in from another angle. For best results, keep a group of cavalry nearby to be used as a flanking force for your main army.

FIGURE 11.8: *Flanking an enemy's forces will win you many battles.*

If the battle is large and looks as if it could take some time, reinforcements are a good idea. Try to send units that counter the type most used by the enemy army. Reinforcements can turn the tide of battle, but be careful! Once you've clearly lost a battle, do not continue to trickle in units one at a time. These units will be defeated in turn without the opportunity to do much damage.

Attrition can be a powerful factor in combat, so pay extra attention to supply wagons. If you are fighting in enemy territory, make sure you have ample defense for your wagons. If you lose your wagons and begin taking heavy attrition damage, consider retreat. Ideally you should have more than one supply wagon when moving an army in enemy territory. Cavalry is the most likely enemy unit to attack your supply wagons, so try to guard your wagons with heavy infantry. Lacking heavy infantry, use your own cavalry. In cases in which attrition is extreme, eliminating an army's supply wagons is often enough to force its retreat.

When your army encounters an enemy, your units will try their best to select the most efficient target on their own. This means that all other things being equal, your archers will try to shoot an enemy phalanx instead of an enemy slinger, and so on. Your units will also try to distribute their shots against multiple targets. This will produce the most efficient damage to the enemy but it might not always be exactly what you want. Occasionally, there might be a key enemy unit such as a general or a light cavalry unit that's headed for your supply wagon. In those cases, you can opt to manually target some or all of your units on that enemy. This does more damage (obviously), but be aware that when multiple ranged units attack an enemy unit, the damage it takes from each additional attacker is reduced slightly. So be careful to have a mass of units attack a single unit only when it's very important.

After reaching Industrial Age, strongly consider either keeping anti-air units with your army or flying air-cover over your army. Without protection against enemy fighters, your siege and supply wagons are particularly vulnerable to being quickly eliminated.

It's also a good idea to keep a scout mixed into your army. Scouts act as detectors for things such as enemy spies, decoys, and armies that might be protected by a general's ambush ability. Later on they'll also jam the radar of any enemy anti-air units or buildings that are nearby. Keeping a scout on hand makes your army much less vulnerable to dirty tricks.

Attacking enemy cities or groups of buildings is best accomplished by siege, although heavy infantry can also be effective. Make sure that your siege equipment is well protected and in supply. Remember that even if the enemy doesn't have attrition researched yet, your siege equipment will fire faster when

FIGURE 11.9: *The best way to survive a siege is to immediately counterattack.*

it's either inside your national borders or in the radius of a supply wagon. The best way to lay siege to a city is to have a powerful army accompany a few siege weapons. Avoid attacking the city directly with the army. Instead, counterattack on your siege with your units (see Figure 11.9). A good siege army will have units to counter both enemy cavalry and enemy archers. When laying siege to enemy buildings near your border, consider building a strongpoint using a castle or some towers. Having your siege fire from the protective cover of a strongpoint forces the enemy into deciding to either take a beating at the hands of your siege or send troops into range of your buildings to attack the siege weapons directly.

Defending your city against a determined siege can be tough. The best defense is not to let the situation develop in the first place.

Don't allow the enemy to build a strongpoint on your border that's within siege range of your buildings. The only successful way to break a siege is to counterattack, either by striking the besieging army or by laying siege to some vital part of the enemy's nation. When a city falls under siege, continue to reinforce that city, but also begin forming a second group of units on the attacker's flank, outside the line of sight of enemy units, if possible. A good idea is to keep a stable or two located far outside your big city. Cavalry can rally from these stables and more easily attack enemy siege and supply wagons. If you have units garrisoned inside the city, have them attack just before you attempt to flank the besieging army. This will add to the strength of your attack and hopefully pull units away from defending vulnerable siege and supply wagons.

AIR COMBAT

If you're the first person to the Industrial Age, you might enjoy a brief period when your biplanes can attack nearby enemies unopposed, but that advantage will be short-lived. Don't forget that special-forces units can jam radar. Jam an enemy anti-aircraft building and then attack it with bombers or fighters while it's unable to return fire.

Bombers are great for taking down cities, and universities also make great targets (see Figure 11.10). Setting back an enemy's research can bring a decisive shift to the end-game. If an enemy has only one or two libraries, simultaneously strike both. If the enemy is researching something, you'll set him back time and resources. Destroying a missile silo that's attempting to research nuclear weapons is also a key mission for bombers. Remember that stealth bombers can't be targeted by ground-based anti-aircraft. If you reach stealth bombers, quickly use them to eliminate all of the enemy's airbases so that they can work unopposed.

FIGURE 11.10: *Universities are good targets for bombing runs.*

SEA COMBAT

Sea combat is fairly straightforward, as it has a much smaller unit mix. Pay close attention to the size of your navy. Too many ships can be wasted resources. Too few can result in all of your fishing ships being sunk and your shores bombarded. Remember to garrison damaged ships to heal them.

Docks have a lot of hit points. This means that a dock that comes under fire usually has plenty of time to heal ships inside it and build new ones to repel the attack. Make sure that your navy has a good mix of ships. You'll need light ships to screen the heavy ships from fireships and subs. Keep your heavy ships to the rear and spread out so that a fireship that does make it past the light ships doesn't damage more than one heavy ship.

MISSILES

Missiles are expensive, but when used properly can shift the balance of power. Conventional missiles are best used for damaging important buildings. Taking out a missile silo that's researching nuclear weapons is an excellent job for them. Damaging or destroying a Wonder that's under construction can be devastating to an enemy. When using nuclear weapons, use extra care and planning to make sure the effects of the embargo don't cripple your ability to research key technologies or buy needed units. It's also important to note the progress of your enemies toward gaining the Missile Shield. Nuclear weapons are a costly investment that can be rendered worthless against a shielded opponent. If you're going to use nuclear weapons, be sure you can deploy them before an enemy is able to get the Missile Shield. One powerful tactic is to nuke a city, then have a nearby army immediately roll up and capture it.

ADVANCED TIPS

Here are some additional tips and tricks to help you win at *Rise of Nations*. Focus on incorporating a new one into your strategy each time you play and you'll be a pro in no time.

- Learn to use hotkeys. Start by using the Tab key to cycle between buildings that have available technologies and upgrades to research. Learning to how to quickly build buildings can also be a big advantage.
- Having unspent resources is missed opportunity. Good players always keep investing their resources in units and upgrades.
- Build your military buildings behind your city. This will protect them and allow the fight to continue even if the city falls.
- Force your opponent to react to you. Even if you don't intend to launch a full attack, use raiding, spies, and special forces to keep him busy and distracted.
- Scout your opponent throughout the game. Finding weaknesses and knowing when an attack is coming are key. Ruins are a valuable source of income. A player who scouts well will enjoy a significant advantage.
- A strong army is one that's made up of multiple types of units (see Figure 11.11). Make sure you select units that complement each other by countering enemy units that could be a problem. For example: If you have a lot of heavy infantry, you are particularly vulnerable to enemy archers. Give your infantry some heavy cavalry to cut down any enemy archers you might encounter before they can ravage your infantry.
- When an enemy makes a large resource investment, such as taking an Age upgrade or building a Wonder, they might be low on some resources, which could hamper their ability to defend. Consider attacking at these times.
- If you're sending an army a long distance, try to take unit upgrades after the army is en route instead of before it departs. This will save you time and allow you to build more units for the army.

- Pay attention to all of the victory conditions. Territory and Wonder wins can creep up on you.
- Protect your capital. If you can't keep an army nearby to protect it, at least build a castle. Having your capital fall into enemy hands, even briefly, can seriously hurt your chances of winning.
- Place lookout towers at your forward cities early on. They will spot enemy armies massing for the attack over the border, act as detectors for enemy spies and hidden units, and later on become important air defenses.
- Always build an extra library or two in the early game. This will allow you to research two technologies at once and protect you from being crippled if one is destroyed. In the later game, build several to prevent your opponent from easily disrupting critical research. This is also true with missile silos. Since your opponent knows you're researching nuclear weapons, having a single silo that can be located and destroyed can be costly. Always have several scattered about your nation.
- In a team game, once you reach your third level of Commerce, you will be able to trade with allied cities. Take a moment to select each caravan and right-click on a nearby city. This will cause the caravan to recalculate its best route. Be careful when you do this to make sure you're not sending your caravans into danger, especially on water maps. Trade with distant allied cities can help your wealth income considerably.

FIGURE 11.11: *Create armies of complementary units so you can always counter your enemy.*

12

If you're good in single play, you're on your way to winning multiplayer games. You'll be playing the same game with identical rules, but these rules are applied differently in multiplay. This chapter focuses on these differences. It reviews the main aspects of leading a nation against other human-controlled nations, highlighting areas where good solo play and multiplay diverge.

If there's a threshold of sorts, an exam to pass on the way to playing good multiplayer, it's winning tough solo games (land-only or single land-mass map, seven opponents, Survival of the Fittest) on the Tough difficulty level. If you can do that, there's definitely no shame in showing your face in multiplayer. Once you start playing against other people, you'll quickly discover extreme flexibility as your biggest asset. Good players play a different game every time; they do so even given the same map. If you play in a predictable way, a smart enemy will know what your plans are even before you fully do yourself. Your solo games likely have told you by now that predictable play is the computer opponent's greatest single weakness.

With that in mind, let's look at what needs to be done to win multiplayer games.

WHAT TO DO WITH PEOPLE

First of all, a word about something that is a common problem in multiplayer: When you're trying to defeat other people—wipe the floor with their lovingly nurtured little empires, in fact—it pays to be nice. Be nice when attempting to set up a game in the multiplayer lobby, nice when you're winning, and especially nice when you're losing. As you'll see yourself, few things are as irritating as poor losers who quit a carefully balanced multiplayer game just because they lost a single battle or were asked to pay tribute. If you stay nice, you'll have no difficulty in finding good games: People will be glad to let you in on theirs, and you'll enjoy more success as a host. If you don't stay nice, people might let you join a game solely for the purpose of uniting against you. Even very good players won't win often under these circumstances.

The sections that follow advise you on what must be done to destroy those evil people who dare to threaten your empire. Bear in mind that they begin with the earliest point possible in the game: with Nomad citizens and an unexplored game world. If you start the game at a higher level of development (Town Center, Small City, Large City) some initial comments might not apply; skip through to the point where a player has a city and some buildings. Similarly, players who start the game with a very generous amount of resources will find some hints irrelevant.

> **Tip**
>
> It's often a good move to stop beating up on an already defeated foe and offer a temporary peace or even alliance instead. It makes you shine as an honorable, merciful warrior, and also lets you deal with the other, stronger players more effectively.

Getting Off to a Good Start

Chapter 8 reviews in detail how to get your nation going, and a lot of the comments made there apply in multiplayer, too. Now, let's have a look at the national development differences in multiplayer:

When founding your first city, your starting resources determine your choice between two very different policies:

➤ The first policy (resources Normal or better) envisages banging down the capital plus library as quickly as you can. This reveals your national territory and lets you instantly set off to found a second city. If your capital turns out to be poor in timber, you simply build your second city where it will let you gather plenty. This policy is the right one to follow in most multiplayer games. Staking out as much territory as you can as quickly as you can tends to be much more important than in solo games (see Figure 12.1).

➤ The second policy applies when you start with Low resources, and particularly so if you've also selected high Technology research costs in the pre-game options. It allows for the fact that humans can never gather resources as rapidly as the computer at the Tougher or Toughest difficulty level. You can spend a little extra time above the guidelines set out in Chapter 8 looking around *if* you have grounds to believe that might result in finding a perfect city site. This might be risky if another player is engaged in the same activity and in the same general area of the map (if that occurs, use the civilian intruder tactic described in Chapter 8).

Once you've built your capital city, the stress is on grabbing as much territory as fast as you can while expanding your economy concurrently. Players who opt to wait for Classical Age with a single city will be punished swiftly. Reaching level 2 in Commerce in Ancient Age is obligatory, while reaching level 3 is preferred; the same rule applies to Civic research. Also,

FIGURE 12.1: *Swift territorial and economic expansion is a must in all multiplayer games.*

you must research Military level 1 earlier than in any solo games but those played at the highest difficulty level. Start building a barracks the moment your second city is finished. As with the criteria that determine how quickly you should start building your capital city, there are policy differences that correspond to the amount of your starting resources:

➤ If you began playing with Normal or double resources, research Science 1, Civic 1 (for second city), Commerce 1, then Military 1.

➤ If you started with Low resources, research Civic 1, Military 1, then Commerce 1 and Science 1. Research Science earlier if you can, that is, you are absolutely sure you're safe for the time being.

You can afford to research Science 1 first only if you've started the game with very generous resources, or with a complete city plus normal resources. It's necessary to hurry because playing other people requires you to start building military units the moment it's possible without ruining economic progress. The payoff for a little economic slowdown is twofold:

- Improved national security. As remarked in Chapter 8, a unit of bowmen per city is enough initially; the point is they must be created early. If you can see an enemy border adjoining yours, create bowmen even before you create a scout. In multiplayer games, owning a city or two without owning a single military unit is a disaster waiting to happen. Citizens are very easy to kill, and once you've got no farmers left, you'll quickly run out of food to create new citizens.

- The possibility of destroying someone else's national security. In Ancient Age, even a couple of slinger units can cause great havoc, especially if the targeted enemy has only a single city (see citizen comments in previous bullet). You don't even have to kill anyone; all you have to do is prevent enemy citizens from working.

Roughly speaking, by the time you have three to four cities, you

> **Note**
>
> *Mainstream military research acquires extra importance in multiplayer games (see Figure 12.2). Good players don't mismanage units the way the A.I. sometimes does, making every unit count and increasing the pressure on raising the Population Cap. Remember also that staying ahead in Military research decreases unit costs.*

FIGURE 12.2: *Multiplayer games emphasize the importance of mainstream Military research. Note the city layout, offering freedom of movement and ease of defense.*

should have a corresponding number of bowmen and slinger units: three to four of each. This ensures protection against a strong raid, and gives you modest but effective offensive options, which grow more feasible the moment you build your first stable. Unless committed to a Rush attack (which requires creating at least four units of expensive heavy infantry), you should refrain from creating more units until you build a stable. Then you should create at least four units of light cavalry, and send half of these out on a raid.

> **Note**
>
> *Remember that every Science advance not only reduces research costs and speed, but also lets you explore more efficiently (longer line of sight, increased value of goody boxes found in ruins). The downside is that early Science advances cost a lot of timber and wealth, which seriously slows down economic and military development.*

Exploration in Multiplayer

In multiplayer, swift exploration of the game world is even more important than in solo games on the highest difficulty level. If your game allows diplomacy, getting the best alliance deal is possible only if you know what all the other deals have to offer. This means you have to have a good idea of every nation's worth in military and real estate terms.

Warning

The scout is immune to attrition; slingers and other military combat units are not. You need to monitor their health if using them to explore within enemy territory.

You should preferably explore with an efficient scout, but if you absolutely can't afford both the scout and the slingers, explore with slingers. Just don't expect to find many goody boxes that way. If you keep your slingers exploring not too far from one of your cities, you may delay garrisoning bowmen in that particular city, and quickly use the timber and wealth you've saved to create a scout.

Don't stop exploring until you've located *all* the players, and obtained a clear idea of their potential. It's a popular mistake to expend all your force against a couple of enemies, then discover that your official or accidental ally that has been nibbling away at them from the other side is much bigger than yourself, and poised to win the game. All other comments made elsewhere in this guide about using spies, setting up informer observation networks, military patrols, and so on also apply in multiplayer; if anything, they're even more important.

Naturally, you should do your utmost to prevent competitors from exploring the world in general and your territory in particular. This necessity rises to a high pitch if the winning conditions are Sudden Death or even Capture Capital. Military patrols (light cavalry) set up along your border should be helpful in intercepting enemy scouts. Later on, you'll be forced to build at least a few lookouts and more scouts to detect enemy spies and remove planted informers. In fact, the lookout as a structure becomes fully useful only in multiplayer games; its primary value is as a spy detector, and spies become much more dangerous in human hands.

The Age Jump in Multiplayer

In multiplayer games, the Age Jump described in Chapters 4 and 8 is no longer a highly recommended option; it's a necessity. Fortunately, it's a necessity that can be taken care of easily, because the frenzied pace of early growth results in an economy that is gushing resources at the maximum permissible rate (Commerce level 2 in ancient Age, level 3 in Classical Age are your targets). Start creating military units that don't require food even as you're executing the Age Jump; keep on making as many as you can without meaningfully affecting the pace of your continuing economic effort (building universities, mines, and production-enhancing buildings during Classical Age).

Also conduct other research that doesn't require food: notably, catch up with Science if the pressures of a multiplayer game against aggressive opponents have moved Science research to the back burner. Shoot for advancing to Science level 3 soon after arriving in the Medieval Age at the very latest. Remember that Science improves your unit and building line of sight, which is very useful in the forthcoming intense fighting. Also, Science advances are needed to build a smelter and research the smelter-based special military techs. And as mentioned earlier, strive to keep ahead with military research (both mainstream and specialized). Being able to perform military upgrades quickly is essential (see Figure 12.3).

FIGURE 12.3: *Rapid upgrading of all military units to new Age standards gains even more importance in multiplayer.*

Don't neglect military activity while executing the Age Jump. You don't need to upgrade your military units to Classical Age standards for them to perform well in the raider/intruder role (but do switch from slingers to cavalry once you've built a stable). As long as you've got a minimum of three cities, you don't really need to capture any cities right away; it always takes time to build up your own cities to full potential. If you do need to attack right away—possibly because you got caught between two opponents whose borders limited your empire to a couple of cities—then attack early, using all the units you've got (even bowmen garrisoning cities). Your objective is to break enemy resistance quickly, and to deprive the enemy of the means of creating new military units (by shutting down enemy timber production, for example). Once that's done, you can continue laying siege to the enemy city while units committed to city and border defense return to their posts.

MULTIPLAYER WAR

Unless special circumstances force you to capture a city early on, the warfare conducted in the early stages of the game (Ancient Age, beginning of Classical Age) is best directed against the following targets:

- Enemy scouts/scouting military and civilian units. Clobbering these before they get anywhere near your territory is best, but as with all ideals, it's hard to achieve. The less your enemies get to see, the better for you.

- Resource-gathering enemy citizens and civilian units with economic significance. Focus on destroying enemy citizens, merchants, and caravans before thinking about destroying a building (the trading post is an exception).

Once you've advanced to Medieval Age, built a couple of forts, and generally followed the advice set out in earlier chapters, begin an offensive aimed at capturing enemy cities. Naturally, in more than one game you'll be forced to defend your territory even as you continue to chase enemy lumberjacks. You'll find that keeping a highly mobile defense force of light cavalry (four to six units) will help you deal with all but extremely serious threats (such as a full-sized siege army complete with several catapults).

> **Note**
>
> Remember that an enemy nation cannot grow if it hasn't got citizens working on its farms and in its woodcutter's camps and mines. A woodcutter camp without a single lumberjack is as useful as no woodcutter's camp. What's more, all the civilian units are "soft" targets, without any armor (prior to Militia upgrade, anyway) and with relatively few hit points.

If you've taken the trouble to explore the game world and to put your border under watch, you'll be apprised in advance of any serious threats headed your way. Use this time and light cavalry/ranged-attack units to delay the enemy advance, and to direct this advance onto a battlefield of your choice (preferably where both terrain and your defensive structures can assist you, and where reinforcements can be funneled quickly; see Figure 12.4).

FIGURE 12.4: *Knowing where to fight lets you win easily. Note the cavalry corps covering the flank of the main army body.*

> **Note**
>
> Try to keep the size of your forces proportionate to the situation; avoid overkill. The computer tends to throw forces at the same spot; people who know how to play don't. It's disconcerting to find raiders beginning to rampage through your territory while your whole army is busy wiping out a couple of enemy units, much too far away to intervene.

When it's time to go fully offensive, conduct a thorough reconnaissance before ordering your army to march. An army ambushed while on the march can easily suffer horrific losses even when attacked by a much weaker but skillfully handled enemy; you might be forced to turn back and lick your wounds before setting out anywhere again. Of course, take this as yet another hint to lay ambushes yourself, as recommended earlier in this book.

Finally, fight all engagements in a decisive manner; a battle won quickly is always a bigger victory than a battle won slowly.

FIGURE 12.5: *The final stage of the battle shown in Figure 12.4: an assault with all forces on the enemy city.*

Continuously strive to maintain only as big an army as you can afford; letting most of this army stay tied down in prolonged battles (especially sieges—see Figure 12.5) isn't in your interest. A quick resolution frees up forces to continue your offensive.

Special Moves

Many of these moves aren't really special. They are relatively simple and require little effort, yet they are effective. For one reason or another, however, they are overlooked by a lot of players.

The first and simplest of these is to always launch an attack from more than one direction. Execute a minimum of one diversionary attack in addition to your primary attack; two extra attacks (one with potential to do real damage, one purely diversionary) are ideal. This does involve considerable micromanagement, because the extra attacks should take place well away from your main attack; after all, their aim is to weaken enemy defense of your main attack objective.

For example, let's say your main objective consists of capturing a city. Don't limit activity to the forming and sending out of a single siege army. If that's all you've got, at least detach a couple of units for a raid in another spot. In intense Survival of the Fittest games where you might be fronting three or four enemies simultaneously, this translates into engaging one enemy with a diversionary tactic while assaulting a city belonging to a different enemy with your main forces.

Employ air power extensively as soon as you advance to Industrial Age, even though the early fighters inflict meaningful damage only on artillery and tanks. It's a

> **Tip**
>
> *Cavalry-only armies are ideal for diversionary attacks, perhaps even a little too ideal. Experienced players will recognize their activity for what it is: a diversion without follow-up in the form of artillery with infantry. Of course you can trump that by actually having a backup artillery/supply wagon combo ready to join your cavalry (see Figure 12.6).*

FIGURE 12.6: *A bombard joins a squadron of dragoons in a small local operation.*

good move to order planes from a given airbase to patrol an area where there is significant enemy troop movement (assembly point) or commercial activity (every crossroads is a meeting place for caravans). Your planes will be patrolling on automatic, leaving you free to arrange other surprises for your foe, who will be busy in the meantime pulling units out of harm's way.

On sea maps, you'll be also building a navy. This is an area that merits special interest, for solo games do not lead to full appreciation of the importance of creating a strong naval force. In multiplayer games, your opponents will do their utmost to sink your troop transports (the computer doesn't), and exposure to naval bombardment becomes a major factor when placing buildings near a seashore. In the late game, your navy will become even more important: Its roles will now include defending any oil platforms you might have. It all adds up to making a much bigger naval effort than in solo games; what's more, such effort should be undertaken very early to prevent enemy ships and scouts from discovering new lands. Light ships are very affordable, and building a dock to create half a dozen or so is a very high priority.

Dirty Tricks

The human capacity for treachery and underhanded methods is starkly on display in multiplayer games. Multiplayer games abound in spies, sabotage, and special operations. All these activities begin with Classical Age (which lets you build forts and create generals), intensify in Medieval Age (which lets you create spies), then again in Enlightenment Age (which turns your explorers into commandos with combat abilities). On sea, Classical Age ushers in the fire raft, which is the first of a line of increasingly destructive fire ships. These one-use, expensive vessels are a poor investment if you cannot use them competently. Deploy them always as a part of a larger operation—for instance, in a grand sea battle in which splitting up the enemy ship formation brings tangible benefits.

> ### Note
>
> Most battles (and most wars) are won by players who have mastered the art of combining forces for several simultaneous attacks. Using hotkeys effectively is a must; you cannot hope to get things done quickly enough with the mouse only.

Chapter 9 discusses special operations in some detail, so let's just recap the main points. Point number one is that you cannot have enough generals; this is even more true in multiplayer than in solo games. You absolutely must have a well-developed information network; placing informers in enemy cities and buildings is an ultra-high priority. Once air power appears on the scene, sabotage missions gain a new lethality: You no longer need a second land force to finish off structures damaged by your saboteurs, because your airplanes can do the job instead.

Using spies to bribe enemy units becomes a truly valuable tactic in multiplayer. Be on the lookout for enemy units posted to protect civilians from your raids, bribe those units, and subsequently conduct swift massacres of enemy workers, inflicting painful damage on the enemy economy. You can also time such an action to coincide with an attack made elsewhere; it's a very good diversionary tactic.

Warning

The enemy can do everything you can, sometimes more. Create a network of spy detectors to maintain national security at an acceptable level (it's never perfect). Use scouts and spies of your own for this as well as lookouts.

Please note that, as mentioned earlier, the tactics and strategies described in chapters 6, 7, 8, and 9 also work well in multiplayer. For reasons of space, this chapter fills out the blanks without repeating all the points made earlier.

Final Multi Thought

If you want to be able to admire the game's beautiful graphics while you play, play a solo game. Multiplayer games are very busy games. The guiding principle is that if you're doing nothing, something's seriously wrong: An empire that's not a busy empire is about to become a losing empire. Most importantly, you'll be fighting from the moment you create your first military units. Being able to micromanage more than one ongoing battle is a priceless asset. Make a point of acquiring that ability while playing solo.

Warning

Don't accumulate resources unless saving them up for a specific goal. A small strategic reserve is fine; thousands of units accumulating for no purpose is not, unless there's no need to spend them because you've won the game anyway.

BUILDINGS

This appendix contains the stats for the buildings and structures in Rise of Nations. Many of the values contained in the following tables are also available in game; all the same, the sections that follow should be helpful in gaining a further understanding of the game.

HOW TO READ THE TABLES

You'll notice that the tables vary: for example, some contain Garrison values, and others do not. This is simply because some buildings can garrison units, and others cannot; the same rule applies to all other values that appear intermittently. All in all, the values represented belong to the following categories:

- Building name. Sometimes, a name change doesn't mean a significant change in buildings stats; these instances are highlighted in the Comments column.

- Prerequisites. Only the "new" prerequisites are included; for example, if a building requires Military 1, it will require it regardless of Age.

- Cost. This may vary depending on the Age you build in, regardless of prerequisites. For instance, you may opt to build a tower in Ancient Age (62 timber, 30 wealth) instead of Classical Age (50 metal, 30 wealth)—a good move that saves metal toward researching Allegiance quickly upon reaching Classical Age.

- Base hit points. These can be increased in various ways (through lumber mill research, building temples, etc.).

- Attack strength (the higher the value, the better) and reload time (the lower the value, the better). Remember that actual damage inflicted is modified by other factors such as enemy unit's armor, movement, etc. Only a few buildings have this ability, so this value will be absent from many tables.

- Armor. If all the buildings in a class have none, this value will be missing from the relevant table.

- Range. This is applicable only to buildings that can fire on the enemy.

- Garrison. This applies only to buildings that can have units garrisoned inside for defensive and/or healing purposes. In many cases, there are restrictions on the type of unit that is allowed to garrison inside; these are noted in the Comments column.

- LOS. This is the building's line of sight or spotting range.

- Plunder. This lets you know what to expect in return for destroying an enemy building. Note that city plunder is not a set value, but is calculated for each city you capture on the basis of many game variables.

- Comments. This column contains extra info explaining and/or complementing the info in all the other columns.

    If you want to find out everything there is to know about any building, follow these steps:

1. Locate the buildings.xml file within the *RoN* folder.
2. Make a backup copy of the file.
3. Open the file and look around as much as you want (use the Edit menu's Find command to locate buildings by name).

THE BUILDINGS

Cities

Cities are more than just "buildings": They are the pillars supporting your whole nation. Reducing them to a row of stats is almost sacrilegious, and city data are available in game; nevertheless it would have been equally sacrilegious to leave cities out. Note that national bonuses may modify city stats (the Chinese can build Large cities from the start, Mayan cities have more hit points, Roman cities generate wealth, etc.). Also, remember that a city has to be garrisoned to attack enemies (Mayan cities excepted), and that garrison strength influences its attack.

BUILDING	PREREQUISITES	COST	BASE HIT POINTS	ATTACK/ RELOAD	ARMOR	RANGE	GARRISON	LOS	COMMENTS
small city	none	10 food, 10 timber/ 50 food, 50 timber	1200	8/30	3	10	10	12	can garrison foot and cavalry (not vehicle) units only; produces 10 food and 10 timber
large city	Medieval Age	20 food, 20 timber/ 50 food, 50 timber	2500	9/30	5	10	15	14	as above
major city	Industrial Age	50 food, 50 timber/ 50 food, 50 timber	5000	11/30	7	10	20	16	as above

City Buildings

This class includes buildings that must be built within city radius, and of which there cannot be more than one per city. Buildings in this class have enormous importance: You'll make very little progress without a library, and sometimes the need for an extra university is the main factor behind the founding of a new city.

BUILDING	PREREQUISITES	COST	BASE HIT POINTS	ARMOR	GARRISON	LOS	PLUNDER	COMMENTS
library	none	30 timber/ 10 timber	1200	2	0	6	30 timber	the most important single building in the game; multiple libraries let you research mainstream advances concurrently
market	Commerce 1	80 timber/ 30 timber	1200	2	10	6	30 wealth	produces +10 wealth; lets you build and garrison (for healing) merchants and caravans

continued

BUILDING	PREREQUISITES	COST	BASE HIT POINTS	ARMOR	GARRISON	LOS	PLUNDER	COMMENTS
temple	Science 1	80 timber/ 30 timber	1200	2	0	6	30 wealth	plays a major role in strengthening your state; the effectiveness of your government is determined by temple research
university	Classical Age	60 timber, 30 gold/ 20 timber, 20 gold	1200	0	7	6	30 wealth	produces +10 knowledge; can accommodate up to 7 scholars; no other units allowed

Resource-Gathering Buildings

The buildings in this class all exist solely for the purpose of gathering resources. All of them require citizen workers in order to function, and all except the farm can be built anywhere within your national boundaries.

BUILDING	PREREQUISITES	COST	BASE HIT POINTS	ARMOR	LOS	PLUNDER	COMMENTS
farm	none	40 timber/4 timber	400	0	6	20 food	can be built within city radius only; 5 per city (Egyptians 7)
woodcutter's camp	none	50 food/20 food	800	0	6	25 timber	needs protection for its workers; a primary raid target
mine	Classical Age	50 timber/20 timber	800	0	6	30 metal	
oil well	Industrial Age	100 timber, 50 metal/15 timber, 15 metal	800	0	6	75 oil	needs one citizen worker
oil platform	Industrial Age	100 timber, 50 metal/20 timber, 20 metal	800	3	6	75 oil	needs one citizen worker; can be built outside national territory and still enjoy refinery production boost

Production-Enhancing Buildings

This group includes buildings that boost production of selected resources. With the exception of the refinery, all allow specialized research with far-reaching effects. You cannot have more than one type of building per city. Remember that granaries, lumber mills, and smelters only affect corresponding resource-gathering buildings within the city radius, but refineries affect all oil wells and platforms owned by your nation.

BUILDING	PREREQUISITES	COST	BASE HIT POINTS	ARMOR	LOS	PLUNDER	COMMENTS
granary	Classical Age, Science 2	60 timber, 10 gold/40 timber	1000	3	6	30 food	food production and unit-enhancing lines of techs
lumber mill	Classical Age, Science 2	50 food, 20 metal/40 metal	1000	3	6	35 timber	timber production and building-improving lines of techs
smelter	Classical Age, Science 3	70 timber, 50 gold/40 timber	1000	3	6	60 metal	metal production and anti-attrition lines of techs
refinery	Industrial Age, Science 6	200 timber, 100 metal/30 timber, 30 metal	1000	3	6	150 oil	each refinery affects all national oil wells and platforms

Military Unit-Creating Buildings

This class consists of buildings whose main purpose is to allow creation of military units and unit upgrades. The dock is an exception, playing several important roles: In addition to creation of military naval units, it enables your units to cross bodies of water, and also lets you create fishermen (waterborne merchants). Note that the buildings in this group cannot attack the enemy even when full of troops.

BUILDING	PREREQUISITES	COST	BASE HIT POINTS	GARRISON	ARMOR	LOS	PLUNDER	COMMENTS
barracks	Military 1	120 timber/ 25 timber	1200	10	3	8	40 food	allows garrisoning of infantry
stable	Classical Age, Military 1	120 timber/ 25 timber	1200	10	3	8	50 food	changes into auto plant with Industrial Age (same stats except for plunder, which is 50 metal); allows garrisoning of cavalry and vehicles
siege factory	Classical Age, Military 2	60 timber, 60 metal/ 25 timber	1200	20	3	8	60 metal	changes into factory in Industrial Age (same stats); allows garrisoning of artillery units (including AAA guns) and supply wagons
dock	Commerce 1	70 timber/ 30 timber	2400	20	3	8	30 timber	changes into anchorage with Gunpowder Age, shipyard with Industrial Age (same stats as dock in both cases); allows garrisoning of naval units

continued

BUILDING	PREREQUISITES	COST	BASE HIT POINTS	GARRISON	ARMOR	LOS	PLUNDER	COMMENTS
airbase	Industrial Age, Military 2	70 oil, 80 wealth/ 25 oil, 25 wealth	1200	10	2	12	50 oil	cannot accommodate fighter-bombers
missile silo	Modern Age, Military 2	70 oil, 80 wealth/ 25 oil, 25 wealth	1200	1	2	12	50 oil	allows research and creation of rocket and missile units; only one unit allowed per silo

The Tower Line

The tower is an extremely important building not because of its lackluster battle potential, but because of the specialized research it allows: the militia and, most importantly, attrition lines of techs. All the tower models allow garrisoning of foot and cavalry (not vehicle) units only.

BUILDING	PREREQUISITES	COST	BASE HIT POINTS	ATTACK/ RELOAD	ARMOR	RANGE	GARRISON	LOS	PLUNDER
tower	Military 1	50 metal, 30 wealth/ 25 metal, 10 wealth	750	12/30	4	10	5	10	40 metal
	COMMENTS: Ancient Age cost is 62 wood, 30 timber								
keep	Medieval Age	50 metal, 30 wealth/ 25 metal, 10 wealth	1000	12/30	4	10	5	10	50 metal
stockade	Enlightenment Age, Military 4	50 metal, 30 wealth/ 25 metal, 10 wealth	1300	12/30	4	11	5	14	60 metal
bunker	Modern Age, Military 6	50 metal, 30 wealth/ 25 metal, 10 wealth	1700	12/30	4	12	5	16	70 metal

The Fort Line

Forts are even more important than towers: They let you create spies and generals, expand your national borders, and can garrison all types of land units. They also allow specialized research that further increases their benefits and improves on the abilities and cost of generals and spies. Fort-based research also allows you to garrison more units inside forts and towers.

BUILDING	PREREQUISITES	COST	BASE HIT POINTS	ATTACK/ RELOAD	ARMOR	RANGE	GARRISON	LOS	PLUNDER
fort	Classical Age, Military 2	300 metal, 100 wealth/ 75 metal, 25 wealth	2000	18/30	5	10	10	10	160 metal
	COMMENTS: building a fort as early as possible is mandatory in all games, including those that don't allow war								
castle	Medieval Age	300 metal	2800	18/30	6	10	10	12	180 metal
fortress	Enlightenment Age, Military 4	300 metal	3700	18/30	7	11	10	14	200 metal
redoubt	Modern Age, Military 6	300 metal	4600	18/30	8	12	10	16	220 metal

The Lookout Line

The units in this line assume extra importance the moment any player in the game reaches Industrial Age. In addition to spotting spies and allowing observation of the area defined by LOS, these buildings have an anti-aircraft capability that includes the rare ability to hit passing aircraft.

BUILDING	PREREQUISITES	COST	BASE HIT POINTS	ATTACK/ RELOAD	RANGE	LOS	PLUNDER	COMMENTS
lookout	none	60 timber/ 6.5 timber or 4 timber, 2 metal	170	6/20	5	9	10 timber	building cost changes with Classical Age; all values rounded down in game (6.5 to 6); 75% chance to hit attacking aircraft, 33% chance to hit passing aircraft
observation post	Gunpowder Age	80 timber, 60 metal/ 15 timber, 15 metal	210	13/20	5	9	10 metal	75% chance to hit attacking aircraft, 33% chance to hit passing aircraft
air defense gun	Industrial Age	120 timber, 120 metal/ 25 timber, 25 metal	260	26/20	8	9	40 metal	as above
radar air defense	Modern Age	120 timber, 120 metal/ 25 timber, 5 metal	275	29/20	10	9	70 metal	as above
SAM installation	Information Age	120 timber, 120 metal/ 25 timber, 25 metal	280	31/20	12	9	80 metal	as above

APPENDIX A Buildings

STANDARD UNITS

B

This appendix compiles, for reference and planning purposes, the most important standard RoN unit data. Most stats given here are available in-game, though not before you have the option to upgrade to a particular type of unit. Some of the numbers are real eye-openers (did you know a trebuchet takes longer to reload than a catapult?), and above all, they'll be very helpful in letting you calculate unit upgrade cost.

The anti-aircraft (AA) capability of units is also included. Note that the chances of hitting an aircraft by an AA weapon are determined by two separate rolls. First, the AA unit rolls to see whether it actually can hit the aircraft; then the aircraft unit rolls to see if it got hit. A hit is scored only if both independent rolls say so. You'll find all the probabilities involved in the relevant tables that follow.

UNIT UPGRADE COSTS

The costs involved are influenced by two factors: the base cost of the old unit and the base cost of the new unit. If old and new unit base costs are the same, the cost of the upgrade is expressed in this formula:

unit upgrade cost = unit base cost × 2

There are four exceptions to this rule: advanced fighters, stealth bombers, nuclear missiles, and nuclear ICBMS. In their case, the unit base cost is multiplied by three.

If the old and new unit base costs are different (the new unit always being more expensive), you'll also have to pay that difference for every owned unit of the upgraded type. This can lead to a nasty shock at times, as when you upgrade elite javelineers into arquebusiers: Owning many elite javelineer units means you have to spend a small fortune in food and timber. The changed unit costs will hit you particularly heavy on transition from Enlightenment to Industrial Age, however, some unit types or classes undergo base cost changes in other Ages, and some more frequently than twice. This is exactly where the tables in this Appendix come in handy: All feature unit cost.

There is one important thing to remember when reading the damage stats. The damage inflicted by a particular unit can be many times greater if the unit is attacking the kind of target it specializes in. For instance, a trebuchet reducing the defenses of a city reduces city hit points by roughly 85 in each attack, not 23 (exact amount varies depending on circumstances such as city size). It's a powerful inducement to follow the recommendations on the in-game unit panel, which always state the selected unit's preferred targets.

Land Units

Land units are the most numerous unit class in *Rise of Nations*. The following tables group units by type and are accompanied by brief comments where appropriate. Keep in mind that how you actually use the unit is as important as its stats.

The stats given include

- Prerequisite. Only the latest prerequisite is listed, to avoid repetition.
- Cost. This includes the base unit cost and cost increase for each extra unit.
- Hit points. This is an area of particularly interesting comparisons.
- Attack and reload time. A unit's attack strength is the number of hit points it will destroy in an unmodified attack. Opponents' armor and suitability as a target can affect this value drastically, in accordance with the in-game tips. Reload is a value indicating how much time will pass until the unit can attack again; a lower value is better. Note that many "light" units with relatively weak attacks compensate with higher attack frequency.
- Armor is a good indication of a unit's resistance to damage. The value given is subtracted from the attack value of an attacking unit.
- Range. This refers to a unit's combat or firing range (for your passing interest, it's measured in coordinate tiles—not that it helps calculate distances in-game). Note that some units require minimum range, that is, they cannot fire at targets that are too close.
- Speed. This value determines how fast a unit moves; the higher it is, the better.
- LOS (line of sight). The unit's spotting range.

If you'd really like to know every tiny detail about every unit, follow these steps:

1. Locate the unitrules.xml file in the *Rise of Nations* directory.
2. Make a backup copy of the file.
3. Open the copy and browse to your heart's content.

If you want to stay abreast of all the latest developments in *RoN* unit tactics, make sure to periodically visit game fan sites on the Internet. You'll be sure to find many by typing **"Rise of Nations"** into your preferred search engine.

Light Infantry

Light infantry is likely to be one of the most numerous unit types in your games, at least until you reach Industrial Age. The new weapons that appear on the scene then reduce its importance slightly, but it's still the best unit to capture cities with thanks to its speed.

UNIT	PREREQUISITES	COST	HIT POINTS	ATTACK/ RELOAD	ARMOR	RANGE	SPEED	LOS	COMMENTS
slingers	Military 1	40 food, 40 timber/ 1 food, 1 timber	85	10/33	1	6	28	8	ideal for armed reconnaissance very early in the game
javelineers	Classical Age	40 food, 40 timber/ 1 food, 1 timber	95	11/33	1	6	29	8	
elite javelineers	Medieval Age	40 food, 40 timber/ 1 food, 1 timber	110	13/33	1	6	30	8	excellent for capturing cities with reduced defenses
arquebusiers	Gunpowder Age	70 food, 60 timber/ 1 food, 1 timber	132	18/44	2	10	24	11	much more expensive; slower but more deadly
musketeers	Enlightenment Age	70 food, 60 timber/ 1 food, 1 timber	142	20/44	2	10	24	11	25% chance to hit attacking aircraft
riflemen	Industrial Age	80 food, 70 timber/ 1 food, 1 timber	156	22/32	3	12	27	13	30% chance to hit attacking aircraft
infantry	Modern Age	80 food, 70 timber/ 1 food, 1 timber	161	24/32	4	13	32	14	33% chance to hit attacking aircraft
assault infantry	Information Age	80 food, 70 timber/ 1 food, 1 timber	180	25/32	4	14	34	15	33% chance to hit attacking aircraft

Heavy Infantry

In the very early game, heavy infantry is the unit of choice for destroying enemy buildings (and for reducing city defenses in Ancient Age). Later, it mainly escorts artillery and ranged infantry, and provides the killing punch in special operations until the advent of aircraft. In the late game, heavy infantry provides protection from enemy vehicles, some protection from enemy aircraft, and valuable assistance when destroying enemy buildings.

UNIT	PREREQUISITES	COST	HIT POINTS	ATTACK/ RELOAD	ARMOR	RANGE	SPEED	LOS	COMMENTS
hoplites	Military 1	50 food, 30 metal/ 1 food, 1 metal	120	13/32	4	N/A	25	6	hoplites created in Ancient Age cost timber instead of metal (5:4 ratio)
phalanx	Classical Age	50 food, 30 metal/ 1 food, 1 metal	145	15/32	4	N/A	25	7	
pikemen	Medieval Age	50 food, 30 metal/ 1 food, 1 metal	170	17/32	4	N/A	25	8	
elite pikemen	Gunpowder Age	60 food, 50 metal/ 1 food, 1 metal	195	19/32	4	N/A	25	9	
fusiliers	Enlightenment Age	60 food, 50 metal/ 1 food, 1 metal	200	20/32	4	6	25	10	heavy infantry receives firearms; 20% chance to hit attacking aircraft
anti-tank rifle	Industrial Age	80 food, 60 metal/ 1 food, 1 metal	215	22/32	4	8	25	11	20% chance to hit attacking aircraft
bazooka	Modern Age	80 food, 60 metal/ 1 food, 1 metal	247	23/32	5	9	25	13	20% chance to hit attacking aircraft
anti-tank missile	Information Age	80 food, 60 metal/ 1 food, 1 metal	265	24/32	5	10	25	15	20% chance to hit attacking aircraft

Ranged Attack Infantry

This category exists separately only up to Enlightenment Age; once you reach Enlightenment and firearms become widespread, all infantry acquires ranged attack capability. Prior to that, ranged attack infantry is mainly used for defense, garrisoned in cities, towers, and forts as well as in the field, where it's most often deployed as part of a siege army. It can also be used independently, especially when there's a building nearby it can hide in.

UNIT	PREREQUISITES	COST	HIT POINTS	ATTACK/ RELOAD	ARMOR	RANGE	SPEED	LOS	COMMENTS
bowmen	Military 1	50 timber, 40 wealth/ 1 timber, 1 wealth	70	12/30	0	10	26	11	
archers	Classical Age	50 timber, 40 wealth/ 1 timber, 1 wealth	80	14/30	0	10	26	11	
crossbowmen	Medieval Age	50 timber, 40 wealth/ 1 timber, 1 wealth	90	16/30	0	10	26	11	upgrade to musketeers (light infantry)

Modern Infantry

The advent of Industrial Age brings about big changes in your armed forces, and infantry's no exception. A couple of new and lethal unit types (flamethrower, machine gun) make their first appearance. Note that the following table does not contain modern light infantry, which has been included earlier. All the units in this group excel at fighting enemy infantry; the flamethrower, in spite of its low range and speed, is a very versatile and powerful unit that can do pretty much everything except shoot down airplanes. Combine flamethrowers with anti-tank (heavy) infantry for optimum infantry anti-armor defense.

UNIT	PREREQUISITES	COST	HIT POINTS	ATTACK/ RELOAD	ARMOR	RANGE	SPEED	LOS	COMMENTS
flamethrower	Industrial Age	80 food, 60 metal/ 1 food, 1 metal	125	20/30	0	6	24	7	powerful unit that ejects units garrisoned in attacked buildings
machine gun	Industrial Age	80 food, 70 metal/ 1 food, 1 metal	140	33/50	2	14	20	15	33% chance to hit attacking aircraft
heavy machine gun	Modern Age	80 food, 70 metal/ 1 food, 1 metal	155	36/50	2	15	21	16	33% chance to hit attacking aircraft
advanced machine gun	Information Age	80 food, 70 metal/ 1 food, 1 metal	170	39/50	2	17	22	18	33% chance to hit attacking aircraft

Light Cavalry

This group comprises light cavalry units from Classical through Enlightenment Age. With Industrial Age, light cavalry upgrades into armored cars, but it's a very versatile and useful unit long before that. Its high mobility makes it excel both in offense and mobile defense. Use it to raid the enemy; as an advance guard for your siege armies; to take out enemy raiders, artillery, supply wagons; and to patrol your border if appropriate. It also works well as part of an independent cavalry corps, particularly if the corps includes few ranged attack cavalry (see following table). It's an excellent unit for pursuit.

UNIT	PREREQUISITES	COST	HIT POINTS	ATTACK/ RELOAD	ARMOR	RANGE	SPEED	LOS	COMMENTS
light horse	Classical Age, Military 1	60 food, 40 timber/ 1 food, 1 timber	73	12/25	2	N/A	41	6	
light cavalry	Medieval Age	60 food, 40 timber/ 1 food, 1 timber	91	13/25	2	N/A	41	7	
elite light cavalry	Gunpowder Age	60 food, 40 timber/ 1 food, 1 timber	109	14/25	3	N/A	41	8	
hussar	Enlightenment Age	60 food, 40 timber/ 1 food, 1 timber	131	16/25	3	N/A	41	9	upgrades to armored car

Heavy Cavalry

Just like light cavalry, this group includes units from Classical through Enlightenment Age. With Industrial Age, mounted units of this type upgrade into tanks (see following table). Heavy cavalry comprises your shock troops, combining toughness (armor, hit points) with a strong attack. It can be used independently in mobile defense or in support of siege armies; it's also the preferred unit for escorting ranged attack cavalry. Combine these two types under the command of a general to create a dangerous cavalry corps that can be subsequently used for raids, reconnaissance in force, as army avant-garde, for pursuit, and of course for mobile defense.

UNIT	PREREQUISITES	COST	HIT POINTS	ATTACK/ RELOAD	ARMOR	RANGE	SPEED	LOS	COMMENTS
cataphract	Classical Age, Military 2	60 metal, 50 wealth/ 1 metal, 1 wealth	85	15/35	4	N/A	30	6	
knight	Medieval Age	60 metal, 50 wealth/ 1 metal, 1 wealth	110	16/30	4	N/A	31	7	
heavy knight	Gunpowder Age	70 metal, 60 wealth/ 1 metal, 1 wealth	135	17/30	5	N/A	32	8	
cuirassier	Enlightenment Age	70 metal, 60 wealth/ 1 metal, 1 wealth	160	18/30	5	N/A	33	9	upgrades into light tank

Ranged Attack Cavalry

Like all other cavalry, the units in this group stretch from Classical to Enlightenment Age. Upon the advent of Industrial Age, they upgrade into armored cars. In the meantime, ranged attack cavalry is at its best when used offensively. It excels in the raider role; and when protected by a screen of other cavalry, it can inflict massive economic damage upon the enemy until forced to confront a full-size army. It's also a good unit to use in ambushes, and works brilliantly as part of an independent cavalry corps. Its qualities are somewhat wasted in the defensive role, although it can be particularly helpful in engaging enemy heavy infantry and targeting artillery and supply vehicles. Keeping a small independent task force of ranged attack cavalry in support of an army can pay off well; its superior line of sight lets you detect any threats quickly. For this reason, if not required for other duties, it may be used to augment your border patrols.

UNIT	PREREQUISITES	COST	HIT POINTS	ATTACK/ RELOAD	ARMOR	RANGE	SPEED	LOS	COMMENTS
horse archer	Classical Age, Military 2	60 timber, 40 wealth/ 1 timber, 1 wealth	65	13/25	0	8	30	9	
heavy horse archer	Medieval Age	60 timber, 40 wealth/ 1 timber, 1 wealth	82	15/25	1	8	30	9	
dragoon	Gunpowder Age	60 timber, 40 wealth/ 1 timber, 1 wealth	97	17/30	1	9	30	10	20% chance to hit attacking aircraft
carabineer	Enlightenment Age	60 timber, 40 wealth/ 1 timber, 1 wealth	114	19/30	2	10	30	11	20% chance to hit attacking aircraft; upgrades to armored car

Combat Vehicles

This group includes two types of units: tanks and armored cars (mobile AA units belong to a group of their own because of their very weak ground combat capability). Both types of units are made at the new auto plant (formerly stable). As mentioned earlier, light cavalry and ranged cavalry upgrade into armored cars, and heavy cavalry into tanks; both upgrades tend to be very expensive. Don't use tanks on their own; they have no AA defenses at all, and don't perform well against anti-tank infantry and flamethrowers. It's best to combine them into with armored cars into an armored corps, adding mobile AA guns if available.

UNIT	PREREQUISITES	COST	HIT POINTS	ATTACK/ RELOAD	ARMOR	RANGE	SPEED	LOS	COMMENTS
light tank	Industrial Age	80 metal, 60 oil/ 1 metal, 1 oil	187	19/40	6	12	36	13	
tank	Modern Age	80 metal, 60 oil/ 1 metal, 1 oil	210	20/40	6	13	48	13	
main battle tank	Information Age	80 metal, 60 oil/ 1 metal, 1 oil	245	22/40	7	14	40	15	
armored car	Industrial Age	90 food, 40 oil/ 1 food, 1 oil	150	20/30	4	11	42	12	33% chance to hit attacking aircraft
armored scout car	Information Age	90 food, 40 oil/ 1 food, 1 oil	168	21/30	4	12	45	13	33% chance to hit attacking aircraft
armored cavalry	Information Age	90 food, 40 oil/ 1 food, 1 oil	186	22/30	4	13	47	14	33% chance to hit attacking aircraft

Artillery and Supply Wagons

Artillery and supply wagons go together for two reasons: Both are created at the siege factory/factory, and artillery units need a supply wagon to maintain their optimum firing rate (as given in table reload times). Both types of units are slow, relatively easy to destroy, and a high priority target for your enemies. Letting them travel without escort is very unwise, and they should always be deployed with other units. Artillery is principally used to reduce city defenses, and also to provide anti-infantry support in field battles. Both artillery and supply wagons are very vulnerable to air attacks. Note that the LOS given all apply to unpacked artillery; all packed artillery has a LOS of 4 that's not modified by Science advances.

UNIT	PREREQUISITES	COST	HIT POINTS	ATTACK/ RELOAD	ARMOR	RANGE	SPEED	LOS	COMMENTS
catapult	Classical Age, Military 1	70 timber, 70 metal/ 20 timber, 20 metal	75	17/55	0	3-15	19	10	minimum range requirement; cannot hit units alongside
trebuchet	Medieval Age, Military 2	70 timber, 70 metal/ 20 timber, 20 metal	92	23/65	0	3-16	21	12	minimum range requirement; cannot hit units alongside
bombard	Gunpowder Age, Military 3	80 timber, 80 metal/ 20 timber, 20 metal	120	26/60	0	1-17	23	14	minimum range requirement; cannot hit units alongside; damages units neighboring target
cannon	Enlightenment Age, Military 4	80 timber, 80 metal/ 20 timber, 20 metal	143	32/60	0	1-18	25	16	minimum range requirement; cannot hit units alongside; damages units neighboring target
artillery	Industrial Age, Military 5	100 timber, 100 metal/ 20 timber, 20 metal	172	36/55	0	1-20	28	16	minimum range requirement; cannot hit units alongside; damages units neighboring target
howitzer	Modern Age, Military 6	100 metal, 100 oil/ 20 metal, 20 oil	200	42/55	0	1-21	32	16	minimum range requirement; cannot hit units alongside; damages units neighboring target
rocket artillery	Information Age, Military 7	100 metal, 100 oil/ 20 metal, 20 oil	230	48/55	0	1-25	35	16	minimum range requirement; cannot hit units alongside; damages units neighboring target
supply wagon	Medieval Age	80 food, 80 timber/ 40 food, 40 timber	90	N/A	0	N/A	25	4	destroying supply wagons brings plunder (50 wealth)

Anti-Aircraft Weapons

You gain the option to create mobile AA weapons once Industrial Age has transformed the siege factory into a modern factory. These units can also target other enemy units beside aircraft, however, the damage they cause then is negligible. Use them in two roles: to augment static AA defenses, and to provide AA protection to other unit types. Group them together with armies and armored corps, and remember they're practically defenseless against enemy vehicles. The term "passing aircraft" refers to aircraft flying over while on their way to the target or airbase.

UNIT	PREREQUISITES	COST	HIT POINTS	ATTACK/ RELOAD	ARMOR	RANGE	SPEED	LOS	COMMENTS
AA gun	Industrial Age	80 food, 80 wealth/ 20 food, 20 wealth	110	36/25	2	10	27	10	90% chance to hit attacking aircraft, 50% chance to hit passing aircraft
AA battery	Modern Age	80 food, 80 wealth/ 20 food, 20 wealth	150	37/25	2	13	35	13	90% chance to hit attacking aircraft, 50% chance to hit passing aircraft
AA missile	Information Age	80 food, 80 wealth/ 20 food, 20 wealth	155	39/35	2	14	43	14	90% chance to hit attacking aircraft, 50% chance to hit passing aircraft

Special Land Units

This category includes the scout line of units (created at the barracks) as well as the general and the spy (created at the fort). All these units function through use of special abilities that subsequently take some time to recover. Note that both the spy and the general can be improved through appropriate fort-based research.

UNIT	PREREQUISITES	COST	HIT POINTS	ATTACK/ RELOAD	ARMOR	RANGE	SPEED	LOS	COMMENTS
general	Classical Age, Science 2, Military 2	100 metal, 100 wealth/ 20 metal, 20 wealth	109	N/A	0	N/A	42	8	non-combat unit with special abilities and armor bonus to military units within action radius; destroying generals brings plunder (100 wealth)
spy	Medieval Age, Science 2, Military 2	50 metal, 50 gold/ 10 metal, 10 gold	40	N/A	0	N/A	21	8	non-combat unit with a variety of special abilities; cannot be detected except by detector units and structures (scout line of units, spies, lookouts)
scout	Military 1	40 metal, 40 wealth/ 10 metal, 10 wealth	50	N/A	0	N/A	34	4	immune to attrition; can detect spies and remove informers (at ranges up to 3)
explorer	Medieval Age	40 metal, 40 wealth/ 10 metal, 10 wealth	70	N/A	0	N/A	35	6	as above; detection range up to 4; instant death for targeted foot/cavalry unit (Sniper special ability)
commando	Enlightenment Age	40 metal, 40 wealth/ 10 metal, 10 wealth	90	N/A	0	6	37	8	as above (detection range 6); can use Sniper ability on selected types of units; Saboteur ability on buildings (damage equals 50% or 200 building hit points, whichever is greater)
special forces	Modern Age	40 metal, 40 wealth/ 10 metal, 10 wealth	110	N/A	0	7	39	10	as above (detection range 7; damage equals 50% or 400 hit points, whichever is greater)
elite special forces	Information Age	as above	130	N/A	0	9	42	12	as above (detection range 12; damage equals 50% or 800 hit points, whichever is greater)

Citizens and Militia

Your citizens can play a military role too. This tends to happen most often in the very early stages of the game, when something as simple as delaying the construction of a new barracks by the enemy might be all you need for victory. Don't count on citizens to actually destroy anything or anyone, though. Later on, once you've researched appropriate techs at the tower, your citizens may be transformed into paramilitary units, and back into civilians, by clicking the appropriate button on the citizen orders panel; however, this transformation doesn't improve their combat abilities enough to make the paramilitary unit (militia, minuteman, partisan) really useful. Its usefulness stays confined to special situations, such as attacking unprotected artillery or badly damaged infantry units. In solo games, the A.I. likes to turn all the citizens of a certain city into paramilitaries the moment city defenses are reduced. If all the infantry you've got available consists of a couple units with red health bars, you might not get to take that city after all!

> **Tip**
>
> Citizens receive permanently the hit point and armor upgrade bonuses resulting from research. This is major incentive to complete it even if you don't intend to form a single paramilitary unit.

UNIT	PREREQUISITES	COST	HIT POINTS	ATTACK/ RELOAD	ARMOR	RANGE	SPEED	LOS	COMMENTS
citizen	none	20 food/ 1 food	40	4/30	0	N/A	25	2	might be useful in the intruder/ explorer role in the very early game
militia	Classical Age, Military 1, Militia	N/A	50	10/35	1	N/A	24	6	
minutemen	Enlightenment Age, Military 4, Minutemen	N/A	65	19/35	2	8	24	8	
partisans	Modern Age, Military 6, Partisans	N/A	85	24/35	3	10	24	10	

Miscellaneous Civilian Units

This group includes scholars, merchants, and caravans. Scholars are interesting in that they actually have combat abilities (all those heavy books, plus rulers, rolled-up maps—hey, you can poke someone's eye out with a pencil). Note that you have to destroy a university or torch it with a flamethrower to force the scholars out into the open. Targeting caravans and merchants, or rather their trading posts, with your raiders and special operations teams (later air strikes) is a mandatory activity in all games.

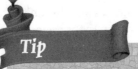

Tip

Damaged caravans can be healed inside a market, however, this terminates their current trade route; a new route has to be established when the caravan is fully healed.

UNIT	PREREQUISITES	COST	HIT POINTS	ATTACK/ RELOAD	ARMOR	RANGE	SPEED	LOS	COMMENTS
caravan	Commerce 1	10 food, 30 timber/ 10 food, 5 timber	90	N/A	0	N/A	26	3	destroying caravans brings plunder (50 wealth)
merchant	Commerce 1	30 timber, 10 gold/ 10 timber, 10 gold	90	N/A	0	N/A	23	3	sets up trading post (90 hit points)
scholar	Classical Age	30 wealth/ 2 wealth* *(increases by 1 wealth per 7 scholars)	50	3/30	0	N/A	24	2	destroying scholars brings plunder (30 wealth)

Naval Units

Naval units play a role only in games that take place on maps featuring bodies of water (rivers don't count, but inland lakes do). Combat naval units are essential to ensure freedom of the waterways, so to speak, so that your land troops can invade and conquer other islands and continents. This and other uses of naval units are commented on as appropriate in the following sections. One thing worth noting is that all later combat naval units, especially light ships, have good AA capability. The civilian naval units consist of transport vessels that are created when a unit has to cross a body of water. Note that the toughest land unit becomes defenseless and easy to destroy during a crossing.

Light Ships

These are very versatile units, and you'll likely create more light ships than all other naval combat units put together. In the beginning of the game, they're great for exploring the map (and the fact that they're reasonably priced doesn't hurt). They're also perfect for coast guard duties, armed reconnaissance, and escorting other naval units: Light ships work well against fireships, and are the only naval unit capable of spotting and attacking submarines.

UNIT	PREREQUISITES	COST	HIT POINTS	ATTACK/ RELOAD	ARMOR	RANGE	SPEED	LOS	COMMENTS
bark	Ancient	30 food, 30 timber/ 1 food, 1 timber	140	11/25	1	5	47	10	excellent for reconnaissance very early in the game
dromon	Classical Age	30 food, 30 timber/ 1 food, 1 timber	145	12/25	1	6	50	11	
caravel	Medieval Age	30 food, 30 timber/ 1 food, 1 timber	160	13/25	1	7	53	12	
corvette	Gunpowder Age	30 food, 30 timber/ 1 food, 1 timber	175	14/25	1	8	54	13	
sloop	Enlightenment Age	30 food, 30 timber/ 1 food, 1 timber	200	17/25	2	9	57	14	45% chance to hit attacking aircra
destroyer	Industrial Age	70 metal, 70 oil/ 2 oil	205	18/25	2	11	63	15	66% chance to hit attacking aircraft, 25% chance to hit passing aircraft
cruiser	Modern Age	70 metal, 70 oil/ 2 oil	210	19/25	2	13	67	16	66% chance to hit attacking aircraft, 25% chance to hit passing aircraft
missile cruiser	Information	70 metal, 70 oil/ 2 oil	215	20/25	2	14	69	17	66% chance to hit attacking aircraft, 25% chance to hit passing aircraft

Heavy Ships

The main role of heavy ships is to provide you with an appropriately heavy punch during combat between fleets. They can also assist in destroying enemy transports, and can lend valuable support during invasions of foreign continents or islands. Their presence on these occasions is important to the safety of your troop transports, and they can also provide fire support once your land units engage the enemy. Form a main battle fleet composed of at least around half a dozen heavy ships in almost every game played on a sea map.

UNIT	PREREQUISITES	COST	HIT POINTS	ATTACK/ RELOAD	ARMOR	RANGE	SPEED	LOS	COMMENTS
trireme	Military 1	40 timber, 40 metal/ 2 timber, 2 metal*	180	20/40	3	9	35	9	
galley	Classical Age	40 timber, 40 metal/ 2 timber, 2 metal*	210	22/40	3	9	37	11	
carrack	Medieval Age	40 timber, 40 metal/ 2 timber, 2 metal*	250	24/40	4	9	39	12	
frigate	Gunpowder Age	40 timber, 40 metal/ 2 timber, 2 metal*	270	26/40	4	10	41	13	
man of war	Enlightenment Age	60 timber, 60 metal/ 2 timber, 2 metal	300	29/40	5	11	43	14	
dreadnought	Industrial Age	140 metal, 90 oil/ 5 metal, 5 oil	325	35/50	5	22	44	19	30% chance to hit attacking aircraft
battleship	Modern Age	140 metal, 90 oil/ 5 metal, 5 oil	335	36/40	5	24	47	20	50% chance to hit attacking aircraft
advanced battleship	Information	140 metal, 90 oil/ 5 metal, 5 oil	375	41/40	6	26	49	21	70% chance to hit attacking aircraft

*Ancient Age triremes cost 90 timber initially, +4.5 timber cost increase (rounded down)

Fireships and Submarines

This class includes "special" naval units: It begins with the fire raft in Classical Age and ends with the attack submarine in the Information Age. Up to Enlightenment Age, the units in this class consist of progressively more powerful variants of the original fire raft; eventually, Industrial Age sees their transformation into submarines. This is a welcome development, since units of the fireship family can be used only once. Submarines remain invisible to all enemy units, with the exception of light ships and helicopters.

UNIT	PREREQUISITES	COST	HIT POINTS	ATTACK/ RELOAD	ARMOR	RANGE	SPEED	LOS	COMMENTS
fire raft	Classical Age	20 timber, 40 wealth/ 1 timber, 1 wealth	120	53 once only	1	1 for max. damage; up to 2	38	8	damages all enemy units within a radius of 2
heavy fire raft	Medieval Age	20 timber, 40 wealth/ 1 timber, 1 wealth	140	62 once only	1	as above	40	8	as above
fireship	Gunpowder Age	40 timber, 60 wealth/ 1 timber, 1 wealth	170	71 once only	1	as above	42	9	as above
heavy fireship	Enlightenment Age	40 timber, 60 wealth/ 1 timber, 1 wealth	210	80 once only	1	as above	44	9	as above; upgrade into submarines
submarine	Industrial Age	60 oil, 80 wealth/ 2 oil	250	98/50	1	9	46	11	unit is invisible to all other units except light ships, helicopters
attack submarine	Information Age	60 oil, 80 wealth/ 2 oil	290	106/50	1	12	50	14	as above

Special Combat Ships

This class consists of two types: shore bombardment vessels and aircraft carriers. Shore bombardment vessels are rather short-lived: They appear in Gunpowder Age, but change into dreadnoughts soon after (Industrial Age). Shore bombardment ships are the first ship type that can be used effectively against enemy buildings, so in spite of their brief service life, you're likely to use them quite often. The aircraft carrier is a very special unit: It comes with a set of seven fighter-bombers, with the option to create replacements on board. Note that fighter-bombers cannot be transferred to a standard airbase; if the carrier is sunk, they're lost.

UNIT	PREREQUISITES	COST	HIT POINTS	ATTACK/ RELOAD	ARMOR	RANGE	SPEED	LOS	COMMENTS
bomb vessel	Gunpowder Age and Military 3	80 timber, 80 metal/ 1 timber, 1 metal	200	29/55	3	4–19	29	17	minimum range requirement, cannot fire at targets alongside; damage inflicted on buildings/units next to target
bomb ketch	Enlightenment Age and Military 4	80 timber, 80 metal/ 1 timber, 1 metal	220	34/55	3	4–20	32	18	as above; upgrades to dreadnought
aircraft carrier	Modern Age	650 wealth, 650 oil/ 100 wealth, 100 oil	600	60/50	none	9	42	16	90% chance to hit aircraft, 33% chance to hit missile; a floating, mobile airbase for up to 7 fighter-bomber aircraft

The Civilian Navy

Non-combat naval units consist entirely of transports and merchant ships; they are "temporary" units and do not incur any costs. Note that you need a dock first to send units across the water, and that colonization of new continents requires Commerce level 2. As noted often in this guide, all civilian ships are terribly vulnerable.

UNIT	PREREQUISITES	COST	HIT POINTS	ARMOR	SPEED	LOS	COMMENTS
fishermen	Commerce 1 (dock)	40 timber/5 timber	170	0	38	6	the seagoing merchant
merchant fleet	Classical Age	N/A	172	1	22	6	caravans turn into merchant fleets to cross seas
modern merchant fleet	Industrial Age	N/A	230	1	22	6	as above
transport barge	Classical Age	N/A	50	0	25	6	land units turn into transport barges to cross seas
transport galleon	Gunpowder Age	N/A	90	0	25	6	upgraded transport barge
transport freighter	Industrial Age	N/A	130	0	25	6	upgraded transport galleon

Aerial Units

This group includes several types of airplanes as well as missiles. Aerial units are very useful on all kinds of maps, but they do assume extra significance on sea maps. Unfortunately, they appear rather late in the game; if you like playing with airplanes, you might want to consider starting a game later than Ancient Age.

Airplanes

Airplanes make their first appearance in Industrial Age. The first biplanes tend to be more of an irritant than a serious combat unit, however, they too can be quite effective when used in groups. The split into fighters, bombers, and fighter-bombers appears in Modern Age. Fighters are useful for both strafing runs (principally against enemy foot units) and attacking enemy planes; they're essential for tackling such advanced aircraft as the advanced fighter and the stealth bomber, which cannot be hit by ground fire. Bombers are best deployed against enemy buildings and troop concentrations; they're more effective against infantry than against vehicles. Fighter-bombers operate solely from carriers, and can be deployed against both enemy aircraft and ground units/structures, but don't perform either task as efficiently as dedicated fighter and bomber aircraft.

UNIT	PREREQUISITES	COST	HIT POINTS	ATTACK/ RELOAD	ARMOR	RANGE	SPEED	LOS	COMMENTS
biplane	Industrial Age	90 wealth, 90 oil/ 2 wealth, 2 oil	118	39/30	3	2–7	55	16	50% chance of getting hit
fighter	Modern Age	90 wealth, 90 oil/ 2 wealth, 2 oil	138	45/30	3	2–7	75	16	25% chance of getting hit by ground fire; improved combat radius
jet fighter	Information Age	90 wealth, 90 oil/ 2 wealth, 2 oil	140	46/20	3	2–10	90	16	10% chance of getting hit; improved combat radius
advanced fighter	Information Age, Global Prosperity	90 wealth, 90 oil/ 2 wealth, 2 oil	155	50/20	3	2–12	115	16	cannot be hit by ground fire; improved combat radius
bomber	Modern Age	110 wealth, 110 oil/ 5 wealth, 5 oil	300	43/30	1	1–3	60	16	10% chance of getting hit; damage to units/buildings next to target; greater combat radius than any fighter
strategic bomber	Information Age	110 wealth, 110 oil/ 5 wealth, 5 oil	340	52/40	1	1–3	80	16	5% chance of getting hit; increased damage to units/buildings next to target; increased combat radius
stealth bomber	Information Age, Global Prosperity	110 wealth, 110 oil/ 5 wealth, 5 oil	380	60/40	1	1–4	100	16	cannot be hit by ground fire; increased damage to units/ buildings next to target; increased combat radius
fighter-bomber	Modern Age, aircraft carrier	90 wealth, 90 oil/ 2 wealth, 2 oil	200	43/30	3	1–7	75	16	can be created aboard aircraft carriers only; 25% chance of getting hit
jet fighter-bomber	Information Age	90 wealth, 90 oil/ 2 wealth, 2 oil	240	47/20	3	1–10	90	16	as above; 5% chance of getting hit

continued

UNIT	PREREQUISITES	COST	HIT POINTS	ATTACK/ RELOAD	ARMOR	RANGE	SPEED	LOS	COMMENTS
helicopter	Modern Age	90 wealth, 90 oil/ 1 oil	95	14/40	1	1–7	75	12	20% chance of getting hit while attacking, 10% chance of getting hit while on way to target/base
attack helicopter	Information Age	90 wealth, 90 oil/1 oil	130	20/40	1	1–7	75	12	as above

Rockets and Missiles

This group consists of four units; two of these have nuclear warheads. The V2 rocket and cruise missile work best against structures and naval units. The nuclear missile and ICBM work well on pretty much everything; however, use of nuclear weapons brings a market trading embargo and starts the Armageddon clock, which shows the allowable number of nuclear detonations before the game world collapses, leaving no winners. The actual number is determined by considerations such as the size of the map, number of players, and type of game being played. Make sure that if anybody uses nukes, it's you and not the other guys; remember also that researching future military tech (Missile Shield) will protect your territory from all missile attacks.

UNIT	PREREQUISITES	COST	ATTACK	RANGE	SPEED	COMMENTS
V2 rocket	Modern Age, Military 6	100 oil, 100 knowledge/ 20 oil, 20 knowledge	150	40	115	created in missile silo; damages units/buildings next to target
cruise missile	Information Age, Military 7	100 oil, 100 knowledge/ 20 oil, 20 knowledge	300	40	115	damages units/buildings within a small radius
nuclear missile	Modern Age, Military 7	600 oil, 500 knowledge/ 50 oil, 50 knowledge	1,200	infinite	115	researched and created in missile silo; damages units/buildings within a large radius
nuclear ICBM	Information Age, Military 7	900 oil, 750 knowledge/ 75 oil, 75 knowledge	4,000	infinite	115	damages units/buildings within a very large radius

UNIQUE
NATIONAL UNITS

This appendix contains the most important stats of all of the unique national units in Rise of Nations. As with the standard units listed in Appendix B, the stats given are, for the most part, available in game; however, reviewing and comparing the numerical values can often be very revealing. Each national unit group is preceded by short comments, which complement the unique units overview in Chapter 6.

The unique units' data is contained in the game's unitrules.xml file (together with the standard units). If you wish to examine all the details, follow the procedure laid out in Appendices A and B to browse through the file.

Aztec Units

The Aztec unique unit lineup is consistent with other Aztec national bonuses, and encourages very aggressive offensive play right from the start of the game. Remember also that you get free units of the unique Aztec light infantry every time you build a new barracks.

UNIT/ UNIT TYPE	PREREQUISITES	COST	HIT POINTS	ATTACK/ RELOAD	ARMOR	RANGE	SPEED	LOS	COMMENTS
Atl-Atls/ light infantry	Military 1	40 food, 40 timber/ 1 food, 1 timber	95	10/33	1	6	31	8	
Royal Atl-Atls/ light infantry	Classical Age	40 food, 40 timber/ 1 food, 1 timber	105	11/33	1	6	32	8	
Xopilli Atl-Atls/ light infantry	Medieval Age	40 food, 40 timber/ 1 food, 1 timber	120	13/33	1	6	33	8	
Jaguar Infantry/ light infantry	Modern Age	80 food, 70 timber/ 1 food, 1 timber	171	25/32	5	13	45	14	33% chance to hit attacking aircraft
Jaguar Assault Infantry	Information Age	80 food, 70 timber/ 1 food, 1 timber	181	27/32	5	15	37	16	33% chance to hit attacking aircraft

Bantu Units

The Bantu are unique in that two types of fighter aircraft are part of their unique unit lineup. However, on balance the three light infantry types are much more valuable; they're helpful in executing early expansion plans, and early expansion is the correct strategy when playing the Bantu.

UNIT/ UNIT TYPE	PREREQUISITES	COST	HIT POINTS	ATTACK/ RELOAD	ARMOR	RANGE	SPEED	LOS	COMMENTS
Umpakati/ light infantry	Military 1	40 food, 40 timber/ 1 food, 1 timber	85	11/33	1	6	28	8	
Yangombi Umpakati/ light infantry	Classical Age	40 food, 40 timber/ 1 food, 1 timber	95	12/33	1	6	29	8	
Impi/ light infantry	Medieval Age	40 food, 40 timber/ 1 food, 1 timber	110	14/33	1	6	30	8	
Hawk Fighter/ fighter aircraft	Modern Age	90 oil, 90 wealth/ 20 oil, 20 wealth	138	45/30	3	2-7	75	16	25% chance of getting hit by ground fire
Eagle Fighter/ fighter aircraft	Information Age	90 oil, 90 wealth/ 20 oil, 20 wealth	140	45/20	3	2-10	90	16	10% chance of getting hit by ground fire

British Units

British longbowmen have a special place in history books, so it's not surprising that British unique units include three types of ranged attack infantry. These are complemented by two very good unique light infantry units, which are effective against all types of enemy infantry.

UNIT/ UNIT TYPE	PREREQUISITES	COST	HIT POINTS	ATTACK/ RELOAD	ARMOR	RANGE	SPEED	LOS	COMMENTS
Longbowmen/ ranged attack infantry	Classical Age	40 timber, 50 wealth/ 1 timber, 1 wealth	80	14/30	0	10	26	11	upgraded from bowmen free of charge
King's Longbowmen/ ranged attack infantry	Medieval Age	40 timber, 50 wealth/ 1 timber, 1 wealth	90	16/30	0	10	26	11	upgraded from longbowmen free of charge
King's Yeomanry/ ranged attack infantry	Gunpowder Age	40 timber, 50 wealth/ 1 timber, 1 wealth	110	18/30	0	11	26	12	upgraded from king's longbow- men free of charge
Highlanders/ light infantry	Enlightenment Age	70 food, 60 timber/ 1 food, 1 timber	142	20/44	2	10	24	11	25% chance to hit attacking aircraft
Black Watch/ light infantry	Industrial Age	70 food, 60 timber/ 1 food, 1 timber	152	22/32	3	12	28	13	33% chance to hit attacking aircraft

Chinese Units

The Chinese acquire firearms earlier than any other nations. This doesn't give them an overwhelming advantage, but can be helpful in early-to-middle game expansion efforts. Note that the Chinese research bonuses might enable you to give your armed forces a technological edge over your opponents.

UNIT/ UNIT TYPE	PREREQUISITES	COST	HIT POINTS	ATTACK/ RELOAD	ARMOR	RANGE	SPEED	LOS	COMMENTS
Fire Lances/ light infantry	Medieval Age	40 food, 40 timber/ 1 food, 1 timber	110	14/37	1	10	30	11	25% chance to hit attacking aircraft
Heavy Fire Lances/light infantry	Gunpowder Age	70 food, 60 timber/ 1 food, 1 timber	132	18/37	2	12	24	13	25% chance to hit attacking aircraft
Manchu Musketeers/ light infantry	Enlightenment Age	70 food, 50 timber/ 1 food, 1 timber	142	20/44	2	12	24	13	25% chance to hit attacking aircraft
Manchu Riflemen/ light infantry	Industrial Age	80 food, 60 timber/ 1 food, 1 timber	156	22/32	3	13	27	14	30% chance to hit attacking aircraft
Manchu Infantry/light infantry	Modern Age	80 food, 60 timber/ 1 food, 1 timber	161	24/32	4	14	32	15	33% chance to hit attacking aircraft

Egyptian Units

The Egyptians have one of the nicer unique unit lineups in the game. It's tailor-made for offensive war-fare, and coupled with the strong Egyptian economic bonuses it gives you a good shot at victory.

UNIT/ UNIT TYPE	PREREQUISITES	COST	HIT POINTS	ATTACK/ RELOAD	ARMOR	RANGE	SPEED	LOS	COMMENTS
Chariot/ranged attack cavalry	Classical Age, Military 2	60 timber, 40 wealth/ 1 timber, 1 wealth	65	13/25	0	8	30	9	
Heavy Chariot/ ranged attack cavalry	Medieval Age	60 timber, 40 wealth/ 1 timber, 1 wealth	82	15/25	0	8	30	9	
Mameluke/ ranged attack cavalry	Gunpowder Age	60 timber, 40 wealth/ 1 timber, 1 wealth	97	17/30	1	9	30	10	20% chance to hit attacking aircraft
Royal Mameluke/ ranged attack cavalry	Enlightenment Age	60 timber, 40 wealth/ 1 timber, 1 wealth	114	19/30	2	10	30	11	20% chance to hit attacking aircraft
Light Camel/ light cavalry	Classical Age	60 food, 40 timber/ 1 food, 1 timber	73	12/25	2	N/A	41	6	
Camel Warrior/ light cavalry	Medieval Age	60 food, 40 timber/ 1 food, 1 timber	91	13/25	2	N/A	41	7	
Elite Camel Warrior/ light cavalry	Gunpowder Age	60 food, 40 timber/ 1 food, 1 timber	109	14/25	3	N/A	41	8	

French Units

The most important French military bonus is not a unique unit, but rather the free general you get with every fort and the supply wagons that heal your troops. However, the four types of unique heavy cavalry featured in the following table don't hurt either.

UNIT/ UNIT TYPE	PREREQUISITES	COST	HIT POINTS	ATTACK/ RELOAD	ARMOR	RANGE	SPEED	LOS	COMMENTS
Chevalier/ heavy cavalry	Classical Age, Military 2	60 metal, 50 wealth/ 1 metal, 1 wealth	90	16/33	4	N/A	31	6	faster and tougher than standard heavy cavalry
Heavy Chevalier/ heavy cavalry	Medieval Age	60 metal, 50 wealth/ 1 metal, 1 wealth	115	17/30	4	N/A	32	7	
Horse Grenadier/ heavy cavalry	Gunpowder Age	70 metal, 60 wealth/ 1 metal, 1 wealth	140	18/30	5	N/A	33	8	
Horse Guard Grenadier/ heavy cavalry	Enlightenment Age	70 metal, 60 wealth/ 1 metal, 1 wealth	165	19/27	5	N/A	34	9	

German Units

Germans are arguably the most blessed single nation in the game. In addition to a terrific economic bonus, they receive a unique heavy infantry series that are helpful in early conquest and a second wave of unique units in the late game (together with another meaningful military bonus consisting of free fighter aircraft with every airbase).

UNIT/ UNIT TYPE	PREREQUISITES	COST	HIT POINTS	ATTACK/ RELOAD	ARMOR	RANGE	SPEED	LOS	COMMENTS
Solduri/ heavy infantry	Military 1	50 food, 30 metal/ 1 food, 1 metal	130	13/32	5	N/A	25	6	costs 50 food, 37 timber in Ancient Age
Barbarians/ heavy infantry	Classical Age	50 food, 30 metal/ 1 food, 1 metal	155	15/32	5	N/A	25	7	
Vandals/heavy infantry	Medieval Age	50 food, 30 metal/ 1 food, 1 metal	180	17/32	5	N/A	25	8	
Landsknechts/ heavy infantry	Gunpowder Age	60 food, 50 metal/ 1 food, 1 metal	205	19/32	5	N/A	25	9	
Tiger/tank	Modern Age	80 metal, 60 oil/ 1 metal, 1 oil	220	21/40	6	13	39	14	
Leopard/tank	Information Age	80 metal, 60 oil/ 1 metal, 1 oil	255	23/40	7	14	42	15	
Volksgrenadiers/ light infantry	Modern Age	80 food, 70 timber/ 1 food, 1 timber	171	24/32	4	13	35	14	33% chance to hit attacking aircraft
MG 42/heavy machine gun	Modern Age	70 metal, 80 wealth/ 1 metal, 1 wealth	155	36/50	2	15	21	16	33% chance to hit attacking aircraft

APPENDIX C Unique National Units

Greek Units

The main thing about Greek military units is that given the Greek research advantage, they tend to be more modern than those of competing nations. The Greek unique unit lineup is very similar to the French: It consists of four types of ultra-fast heavy cavalry.

UNIT/ UNIT TYPE	PREREQUISITES	COST	HIT POINTS	ATTACK/ RELOAD	ARMOR	RANGE	SPEED	LOS	COMMENTS
Companion/ heavy cavalry	Classical Age, Military 2	60 metal, 50 wealth/ 1 metal, 1 wealth	85	15/35	4	N/A	36	6	the fastest heavy cavalry in the game
Royal Companion/ heavy cavalry	Medieval Age	60 metal, 50 wealth/ 1 metal, 1 wealth	110	16/30	4	N/A	36	7	
Stratiotai/heavy cavalry	Gunpowder Age	60 metal, 50 wealth/ 1 metal, 1 wealth	135	17/30	5	N/A	36	8	
Royal Stratiotai/ heavy cavalry	Enlightenment Age	60 metal, 50 wealth/ 1 metal, 1 wealth	160	18/30	5	N/A	36	9	

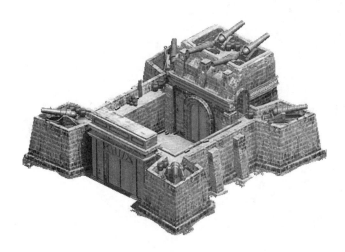

Inca Units

Inca unique units include two types of light infantry with a melee attack instead of the traditional (for light infantry) ranged attack. Don't forget that when leading them in combat! The national artillery units received later are nice, but much less important that the Inca wealth bonus (each miner produces 10 wealth), which among other advantages lets you modernize your armed forces very quickly once you reach Industrial Age.

UNIT/ UNIT TYPE	PREREQUISITES	COST	HIT POINTS	ATTACK/ RELOAD	ARMOR	RANGE	SPEED	LOS	COMMENTS
Inti Clubmen/ light infantry	Classical Age	40 food, 40 timber/ 1 food, 1 timber	104	14/33	2	N/A	29	8	melee attack
Inti Macemen/ light infantry	Medieval Age	40 food, 40 timber/ 1 food, 1 timber	118	16/33	2	N/A	30	8	melee attack
Mortar/artillery	Enlightenment Age, Military 4	80 timber, 80 metal/ 20 timber, 20 metal	143	32/60	0	218	25	16	
Siege Mortar/ artillery	Industrial Age, Military 5	100 timber, 100 metal/ 20 timber, 20 metal	172	36/55	0	2-20	28	16	

Japanese Units

The Japanese lineup ideally complements this nation's other military bonuses: All five unique units are heavy infantry, which fits in neatly with cheaper barracks units and extra infantry damage to buildings. It's the perfect setup for aggressive offensive play right from the start of the game.

UNIT/ UNIT TYPE	PREREQUISITES	COST	HIT POINTS	ATTACK/ RELOAD	ARMOR	RANGE	SPEED	LOS	COMMENTS
Ashigaru spearmen/ heavy infantry	Military 1	50 food, 30 metal/ 1 food, 1 metal	125	14/30	5	N/A	25	6	costs 50 food, 37 timber in, Ancient Age
Bushi/ heavy infantry	Classical Age	50 food, 30 metal/ 1 food, 1 metal	150	16/30	5	25	7	7	
Elite Bushi/ heavy infantry	Medieval Age	50 food, 30 metal/ 1 food, 1 metal	175	18/30	5	N/A	25	8	
Samurai/ heavy infantry	Gunpowder Age	60 food, 50 metal/ 1 food, 1 metal	200	20/15	5	N/A	25	9	
Gun Samurai/ heavy infantry	Enlightenment Age	60 food, 50 metal/ 1 food, 1 metal	205	21/30	5	6	25	10	20% chance to hit attacking aircraft

Korean Units

No other nation in the game has armored foot archers. These, and the two types of artillery that deal out extra damage to buildings, favor the creation of foot armies to siege enemy cities the moment you reach Classical Age.

UNIT/ UNIT TYPE	PREREQUISITES	COST	HIT POINTS	ATTACK/ RELOAD	ARMOR	RANGE	SPEED	LOS	COMMENTS
Hwarang/ ranged attack infantry	Military 1	40 timber, 50 wealth/ 1 timber, 1 wealth	77	13/30	1	10	26	11	armored archers
Elite Hwarang/ ranged attack infantry	Classical Age	40 timber, 50 wealth/ 1 timber, 1 wealth	87	15/30	1	10	26	11	armored archers
Royal Hwarang/ ranged attack infantry	Medieval Age	40 timber, 50 wealth/ 1 timber, 1 wealth11	97	17/30	1	10	26	11	armored archers
Elite Royal Hwarang/ranged attack infantry	Gunpowder Age	40 timber, 50 wealth/ 1 timber, 1 wealth	117	19/30	1	10	26	11	armored archers
Flaming Arrow/ artillery	Classical Age	70 timber, 70 metal/ 20 timber, 20 metal	75	17/60	0	2–15	19	10	extra damage to buildings
Heavy Flaming Arrow/artillery	Medieval Age, Military 2	70 timber, 70 metal/ 20 timber, 20 metal	92	23/60	0	2–16	21	12	extra damage to buildings

Maya Units

The Maya unique light infantry is more versatile than other nations': It can be deployed with equal success against enemy ranged attack and light infantry. The late-game heavy infantry units add to the Maya city defensive bonus (50% more building hit points); don't let this make you favor defensive play, which is always a bad move.

UNIT/ UNIT TYPE	PREREQUISITES	COST	HIT POINTS	ATTACK/ RELOAD	ARMOR	RANGE	SPEED	LOS	COMMENTS
Balamob Slingers/light infantry	Military 1	40 food, 40 timber/ 1 food, 1 timber	85	10/33	1	6	28	8	
Royal Balamob Slingers/ light infantry	Classical Age	40 food, 40 timber/ 1 food, 1 timber	95	11/33	1	6	29	8	
Eagle Balamob Slingers/ light infantry	Medieval Age	40 food, 40 timber/ 1 food, 1 timber	110	13/33	1	6	30	8	
Recoilless Gun/ heavy infantry	Modern Age	80 food, 60 metal/ 1 food, 1 metal	247	23/32	5	9	25	14	20% chance to hit attacking aircraft
Dragon AT Missile/ heavy infantry	Information Age	80 food, 60 metal/ 1 food, 1 metal	265	24/32	5	10	25	15	20% chance to hit attacking aircraft

Mongol Units

Mongol unique units reinforce this nation's other special bonuses, making it the ideal choice for fast-paced offensive play. Note that the Mongols receive free ranged attack cavalry with every new stable.

UNIT/ UNIT TYPE	PREREQUISITES	COST	HIT POINTS	ATTACK/ RELOAD	ARMOR	RANGE	SPEED	LOS	COMMENTS
Nomad/ranged attack cavalry	Classical Age, Military 2	60 timber, 40 wealth/ 1 timber, 1 wealth	65	13/25	0	8	30	9	
Steppe Nomad/ranged attack cavalry	Medieval Age	60 timber, 40 wealth/ 1 timber, 1 wealth	85	15/25	1	8	30	9	
Horde/ranged attack cavalry	Gunpowder Age	60 timber, 40 wealth/ 1 timber, 1 wealth	97	17/25	1	9	30	10	20% chance to hit attacking aircraft
Golden Horde/ ranged attack cavalry	Enlightenment Age	60 timber, 40 wealth/ 1 timber, 1 wealth	114	19/25	2	10	30	11	20% chance to hit attacking aircraft

Nubian Units

The Nubians are among the game's most heavily favored nations. Their economic bonuses are reinforced with a unique unit lineup that's helpful both in offense and in defense.

UNIT/ UNIT TYPE	PREREQUISITES	COST	HIT POINTS	ATTACK/ RELOAD	ARMOR	RANGE	SPEED	LOS	COMMENTS
Kushite Archers/ ranged attack infantry	Classical Age	40 timber, 50 wealth/ 1 timber, 1 wealth	80	14/30	0	10	26	11	
Royal Kushite Archers/ranged attack infantry	Medieval Age	40 timber, 50 wealth/ 1 timber, 1 wealth	90	16/30	0	10	26	11	
Apedemak Archers/ranged attack infantry	Gunpowder Age	40 timber, 50 wealth/ 1 timber, 1 wealth	110	18/30	0	10	26	11	
Camel Archer/ ranged attack cavalry	Classical Age, Military 2	60 timber, 40 wealth/ 1 timber, 1 wealth	65	13/25	0	8	30	9	
Heavy Camel Archer/ranged attack cavalry	Medieval Age	60 timber, 40 wealth/ 1 timber, 1 wealth	82	15/25	1	8	30	9	
Camel Raider/ ranged attack cavalry	Gunpowder Age	60 timber, 40 wealth/ 1 timber, 1 wealth	97	17/30	1	9	30	10	20% chance to hit attacking aircraft
Camel Corps/ ranged attack cavalry	Enlightenment Age	60 timber, 40 wealth/ 1 timber, 1 wealth	114	19/30	2	10	30	11	20% chance to hit attacking aircraft

Roman Units

Romans have only three unique units: All are national versions of the heavy infantry class. However, Romans also receive free heavy infantry with every new barracks; this puts them in an excellent offensive position early in the game.

UNIT/ UNIT TYPE	PREREQUISITES	COST	HIT POINTS	ATTACK/ RELOAD	ARMOR	RANGE	SPEED	LOS	COMMENTS
Legions/ heavy infantry	Classical Age	50 food, 30 metal/ 1 food, 1 metal	145	15/32	4	N/A	27	7	versatile heavy infantry
Caesar's Legions/ heavy infantry	Medieval Age	50 food, 30 metal/ 1 food, 1 metal	170	17/32	4	N/A	27	8	versatile heavy infantry
Praetorian Guards/ heavy infantry	Gunpowder Age	60 food, 50 metal/ 1 food, 1 metal	195	19/32	4	N/A	27	9	versatile heavy infantry

Russian Units

It's nice to be Russian: The national bonuses include many unique units. The light cavalry are outstanding at emasculating siege armies by destroying their supply wagons, at which point the deadly national attrition bonus takes over.

UNIT/ UNIT TYPE	PREREQUISITES	COST	HIT POINTS	ATTACK/ RELOAD	ARMOR	RANGE	SPEED	LOS	COMMENTS
Rusiny Lancer/ light cavalry	Medieval Age	60 food, 30 timber/ 1 food, 1 timber	91	13/22	2	N/A	41	7	
Cossack/ light cavalry	Gunpowder Age	60 food, 30 timber/ 1 food, 1 timber	109	14/22	3	N/A	41	8	
Don Cossack/ light cavalry	Enlightenment Age	60 food, 30 timber/ 1 food, 1 timber	131	16/22	3	N/A	41	9	
Red Guards/ light infantry	Modern Age	80 food, 60 timber/ 1 food, 1 timber	161	24/32	4	13	32	14	33% chance to hit attacking aircraft
Shock Infantry/ light infantry	Information Age	80 food, 60 timber/ 1 food, 1 timber	180	26/32	4	14	34	15	33% chance to hit attacking aircraft
Katyusha Rocket/artillery	Modern Age, Military 6	100 metal, 100 oil/ 20 metal, 20 oil	200	42/55	0	1-21	32	16	damages units and buildings near the target
T 80/tank	Information Age	70 metal, 50 oil/ 1 metal, 1 oil	245	22/40	7	14	40	15	

Spanish Units

The Spanish are unique in having heavy infantry equipped with firearms in the Gunpowder Age. However, all in all the four types of unique heavy infantry aren't as meaningful as the national exploration bonus, which is worth any number of unique unit types.

UNIT/ UNIT TYPE	PREREQUISITES	COST	HIT POINTS	ATTACK/ RELOAD	ARMOR	RANGE	SPEED	LOS	COMMENTS
Scutari/ heavy infantry	Classical Age	50 food, 30 timber/ 1 food, 1 timber	145	15/32	4	N/A	25	7	
Royal Scutari/ heavy infantry	Medieval Age	50 food, 30 timber/ 1 food, 1 timber	170	17/32	4	N/A	25	8	
Tercios/ heavy infantry	Gunpowder Age	60 food, 50 metal/ 1 food, 1 metal	195	19/44	4	5	25	9	equipped with firearms; strong ranged attack
Royal Tercios/ heavy infantry	Enlightenment Age	60 food, 50 metal/ 1 food, 1 metal	200	20/44	4	6	25	10	

Turkish Units

The Turkish unique units are ideal for building strong siege armies in the middle game. They work extremely well with related Turkish national bonuses: fast assimilation of conquered cities, and the many special advantages that come with Turkish artillery (extra range and LOS, free upgrades, and free units with new siege factories/factories).

UNIT/ UNIT TYPE	PREREQUISITES	COST	HIT POINTS	ATTACK/ RELOAD	ARMOR	RANGE	SPEED	LOS	COMMENTS
Janissaries/ light infantry	Gunpowder Age	70 food, 60 timber/ 1 food, 1 timber	132	19/45	2	10	27	11	25% chance to hit attacking aircraft
Royal Janissaries/ light infantry	Enlightenment Age	70 food, 60 timber/ 1 food, 1 timber	142	21/40	2	10	27	11	25% chance to hit attacking aircraft
Basilica Bombard/ artillery	Gunpowder Age, Military 3	80 timber, 80 metal/ 20 timber, 20 metal	120	26/57	0	1-17	23	14	
Basilica Cannon/ artillery	Enlightenment Age, Military 4	80 timber, 80 metal/ 20 timber, 20 metal	143	32/60	0	1-18	25	16	

SYBEX

OFFICIAL
strategies & secrets™

Master Your Favorite Microsoft Games!

Each official, exclusive Sybex guide is created with the full support of the games' developers, and contains:

- Hardcore tactics and analysis
- Comprehensive, detailed statistics
- Battle-tested multiplayer strategies
- Thorough maps
- Step-by-step walkthroughs
- And more!

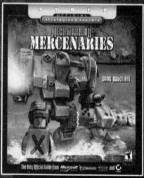

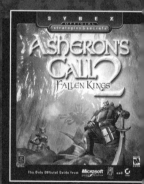

Combat Flight Simulator 3: Sybex Official Strategies & Secrets™
by Michael Rymaszewski
ISBN 0-7821-4165-X • US $19.99
Free Poster Inside

Age of Mythology™: Sybex Official Strategies & Secrets™
by Doug Radcliffe
ISBN 0-7821-4166-8 • US $19.99
Free Poster Inside

MechWarrior® 4: Mercenaries: Official Strategies & Secrets™
by Doug Radcliffe
ISBN 0-7821-4163-3
US $19.99

Asheron's Call® 2: Sybex Official Strategies & Secrets™
ISBN 0-7821-4164-1
US $19.99
Free Poster Inside

Dungeon Siege: Sybex Official Strategies & Secrets™
by Doug Radcliffe
ISBN 0-7821-2944-7
US $19.99

SYBEX
www.sybex.com